MICROFINANCE METAVERSE

INTERVENTION IN CHANGING CONTEXT

Dr. M. Sanjoy Singh
Prof. S. K. Baral

TRUE SIGN
PUBLISHING HOUSE

Published by True Sign Publishing House
Address: SY. No. 21/2 & 21/3, Sonnenahalli,
Krishnarajapura, Bengaluru,
Karnataka - 560049 India
E-mail: truesignbooks@gmail.com
Website: www.truesign.in

Microfinance Metaverse
Intervention in Changing Context

Editors: Dr. M. Sanjoy Singh, Prof. S. K. Baral

ISBN: 978-93-5904-739-3

First Edition: 2023

Preface

Due to the growing demand for microloans from the MSME sector, the Indian microfinance business is expected to expand at a rapid compound annual growth rate (CAGR) of more than 40% by 2025. There are a few features of the domain that are critical. A crucial enabler of rural job growth is microfinance. Additionally, it has developed a strong stance in favor of Atmanirbhar Bharat and Women's Empowerment. By enabling participants to experience the procedure as part of their training, the metaverse will have an impact on practical learning and change education into a more all-encompassing endeavour. Similar to how the internet changed the world at the turn of the century, the emergence of the metaverse signifies a paradigm shift in digital interaction. The metaverse is essentially a large, dynamic virtual world where users can explore, develop, and take part in a wide range of activities. The goal is to develop an all-encompassing digital environment that melds naturally with the real world so that users can exist and perform well in both.

India is regarded as one of the world's largest economies and is growing steadily. In recent years, there has been a noticeable recovery in the Indian economy. The deficits in the trade and budget have decreased, while inflation has calmed. The Indian government has also started implementing policies and reforms to boost productivity, promote investment, and guarantee fiscal sustainability. Even now, around 25% of Indians are considered to be below the poverty level. In India, microfinance has emerged as an effective tool for the economically disadvantaged to avoid the debt problems of unorganised and arbitrary lenders. There will be a change from the primary intent of microloans, which was to only earn money. Indian women in rural areas are gradually adjusting to the changing dynamics. There will be challenges, but with more information on the makeup and incomes of households, the use of data analytics, and the substitution of technology for manual labour, operational costs will eventually drop significantly.

Digital technologies are now being studied and used in a variety of disciplines, including business, banking, and government regulations as well as education, healthcare, and social communication. Many academics have looked at the connections between modern technology and society in the context of what is known as the "digital divide" between wealthy and developing nations. As technology has become more affordable and accessible, it has been hypothesized repeatedly that country factors have a moderating influence on its productivity effects. This edited book aims to compile all of the developments that the Indian economic environment and society have undergone in the 21st century in one place. There are many emerging issues have been undertaken in context to Self-help Group in India, Microfinance in India, Grameen Bank, Non-Performing Assets (NPA) of Public and Private Sector Banks, Microfinance and Women Empowerment, Microfinance and Poverty Eradication, Banking and Fintech Industry, Microfinance Metaverse Technology, Metaverse in Financial Market and Application of Metaverse for New Microfinance Business Models, etc. by the authors.

Keeping in view the change is going to involve more than just investing in technology. It is necessarily going to involve a long hard look in the mirror. And that kind of change management is hard to do. Given this understand customer needs. clear strategy, commitment and focus, and skills are those challenges that play a critical role in the countries. As ways and means for solving unemployment problems, generating income, a business plan, and the technology changes, understanding what customers need and are willing and able to pay for, IT skills, and digital transformation towards microfinance, the authors have undertaken this development. We are very happy to bring this volume. The present book attempts to provide various related **'Microfinance Metaverse: Intervention in Changing Contexts'** with nineteen high-quality chapters.

We are thankful to True Sign publishing house, for taking pain in the conversion of manuscripts to the present book volume in a short time. Last but not least, we would like to express our sincere gratitude to the chapter contributors, family members, colleagues, and well-wishers for their unwavering support and inspiration in finalising this wonderful book.

Finally, the almighty God, whose benevolence and blessings shower to us in making completing this effort within the stipulated time.

Dr. M. Sanjoy Singh
Prof. S. K. Baral

Contents

List of Contributing Authors

1

Technologies of Metaverse and its Applications for Business Model: A Birds Eye Approach

Raj Maurya[1] *& Dr. Kh. Tomba Singh*[2]

Abstract

The awareness of virtual enterprises is addressed as a crucial component of business models that make use of the metaverse. Users explore, interact with, and make purchases within virtual surroundings. The Metaverse technology provides a diversity of revolutionary opportunities for enterprises as an integrated shared environment based on virtual reality. This study approaches a birds-eye perspective of metaverse technologies and investigates their uses in creating cutting-edge business strategies. The study examines the underlying technologies supporting the metaverse, such as haptic feedback devices, artificial intelligence algorithms, and virtual reality headsets. It shows how companies could employ the metaverse to improve client interactions, encourage immersive brand involvement, and generate new income. Similarly recognizes the challenges and factors involved in using metaverse technology in the context of business. The necessity for ethical and inclusive metaverse growth is highlighted by the discussion of issues such as data privacy, security, and equal access. The finding shows that businesses need the transformative potential of metaverse technologies. Technologies such as Blockchain, Interaction technology, IoT, Network and computing technology, AI Technology and computer game technology offer an immersive learning experience for businesses. There is a need for organizations to actively explore and hold these technologies to stay competitive and thrive in an increasingly digital and interconnected world.

Keywords: *Metaverse, technology, business models, customer experience, productivity, and virtual meetings*

Introduction

The development of metaverse technology has inspired considerable excitement and curiosity, as corporations and individuals predict a future in which virtual reality-based shared spaces will revolutionize all parts of our lives (Bibri, 2022). The metaverse, which is usually described as a collaborative virtual reality experience, has the potential to reshape how we connect, conduct business, and explore new frontiers (Allam et al., 2022). Dwivedi et al., (2023) provided an overview of metaverse technologies and their applications in the development of creative business models, based on existing research and insights. Neal Stephenson, a science fiction novelist, developed the word "metaverse" in his 1992 novel "Snow Crash," which depicted a futuristic virtual reality environment where humans could depart from their physical realities. Recent advances in

[1] Research Scholar, Department of Commerce Indira Gandhi National Tribal University, Amarkantak, Madhya Pradesh

[2] Professor, Department of Commerce Manipur University, Canchipur, Imphal, Manipur

virtual reality (VR), augmented reality (AR), and other immersive technologies have drawn the metaverse concept closer to reality (Kozinets, 2022; Mystakidis, 2022; Bale et al., 2022). The metaverse is being controlled by powerful VR headsets, haptic feedback devices, and advanced artificial intelligence algorithms to provide a physical platform for transformational experiences (Lee et al., 2021). According to Kraus et al. (2022), businesses across industries are recognizing the metaverse's immense potential for rethinking their operations, consumer engagement strategies, and sources of income. The capacity to build immersive and engaging brand experiences within virtual worlds offers new possibilities for increasing customer engagement and brand loyalty (Hoyer et al., 2020; Biaklova, 2022; Wongkitrungrueng & Suprawan, 2023). According to Rathore (2017), virtual commerce is a key application of the metaverse, allowing users to browse, interact with products, and make purchases within virtual spaces, blurring the boundaries between physical and digital retail. The metaverse offers promising opportunities for fostering organizational collaboration and productivity (Graf et al., 2023). Virtual meetings, workspaces, and simulations enable remote teams to collaborate seamlessly, transcend geographical barriers, and unlock new possibilities for innovation and problem-solving (Dwivedi et al., 2023b; Groff, 2013; Kumar, 2009). Aguayo & Eames (2023) suggested in the study that the training and development initiatives are enhanced through immersive simulations, providing realistic and immersive learning experiences. While the metaverse holds tremendous potential, it presents challenges and considerations that must be addressed. Issues related to data privacy, security, and equitable access need to be carefully navigated to ensure responsible and inclusive metaverse development. For companies to function legally, they must be aware of the changing legal and regulatory environment around metaverse technology. With a birds-eye perspective, the article provides an extensive examination of metaverse technologies and their applicability to business models. Businesses are provided with the information and knowledge required to strategically and efficiently utilize the metaverse by studying existing research, industry insights, and developing trends.

Conceptual Framework of Metaverse Technology

Metaverse technology is an immense and interconnected digital universe that suggests to users an immersive and shared experience where they interact with each other and virtual environments in real time. According to Davis et al. (2009), the Metaverse includes virtual worlds and environments that act as digital places where users can communicate, explore, and engage with one another and diverse items. Kohler et al. (2009) said that these virtual worlds can range from realistic simulations of real-world locations to imaginative and entirely fictional landscapes, offering a diverse and engaging experience. Avatars are digital personalities that represent users in the Metaverse. Individuals can employ avatars to customize their look and identity, allowing for self-expression and creativity (Nagy & Koles, 2014). According to Balkin (2004), users can build and operate their avatars to navigate and interact within virtual environments, blurring the barriers between their physical characters and their digital appearance.

As it develops a sense of community and unites people from all over the world, social interaction is an essential aspect of the Metaverse (Oh et al., 2023). Real-time user interaction, collaboration, and sharing of experiences allow for the growth of substantial relationships and cross-cultural cooperation. Ford et al., (2023) found in the study that immersive technologies, such as virtual reality (VR), augmented reality (AR), mixed reality (MR), and haptic feedback, play a significant role in shaping the Metaverse's realistic and engaging experience. These technologies provide a sensory-rich environment that further blurs the distinction between the physical and virtual worlds, enhancing the overall user experience. User-generated content is a defining feature of the Metaverse. De Roure (2009) designed and realized that users create, upload, and share their digital assets, including virtual objects, experiences, and environments. According to Tromp in 2022 this dynamic and constantly evolving ecosystem fosters creativity and innovation, allowing users to shape the virtual landscape and contribute to the collective experience. Cheng (2023) mentioned that virtual economies and virtual currencies are integral to the Metaverse technologies, providing users with opportunities to buy, sell, and trade digital assets, virtual goods, and services. Park & Kim (2022) said that the Metaverse is not confined to a single platform or device but spans multiple platforms, applications, and hardware, where users access and interact with it from various devices, such as PCs, consoles, smartphones, and VR headsets, enabling widespread participation and accessibility. Data privacy and security are critical considerations within the Metaverse. With a vast amount of user data being generated and shared, implementing robust measures to protect user information and ensure a safe virtual environment is vital to fostering trust among users (Atlam & Wills, 2020). The Metaverse's conceptual framework presents a complex and interconnected ecosystem that revolves around virtual worlds, social interactions, user-generated content, immersive technologies, virtual economies, and the need for data privacy and governance. By understanding and addressing these key components, businesses, creators, and users can harness the full potential of the Metaverse and contribute to its continued growth and evolution.

Statement of the Problem

The existing literature often focuses on theoretical concepts and potential applications but lacks in-depth empirical studies and practical guidelines for businesses to navigate the metaverse landscape. Limited attention has been given to the ethical and societal implications of metaverse technologies within a business context. Issues related to data privacy, security, inclusivity, and equitable access are crucial considerations that need further exploration. Understanding how businesses can address these challenges and promote responsible metaverse development is essential for ensuring the metaverse-enabled business model's long-term viability and acceptance.

Objectives of the Study

1. To study the technologies and applications that businesses use to fully utilize metaverse technology.
2. To study the valuable insights for businesses that embrace metaverse technologies by enabling them to make knowledgeable decisions, develop robust strategies, and unlock the full potential of the metaverse.

Research Methodology

To accomplish the objective of providing an in-depth study of metaverse technologies and their business model applications, it extensively reviewed the body of knowledge, research papers, industry reports, and other publications on metaverse technologies and their effects on business models. This is intended as the starting point for understanding the level of knowledge at the moment, recognizing significant ideas, and obtaining awareness of the possibilities and challenges connected to the metaverse. Different studies of effective implementations and applications of metaverse technology were selected from various papers. These techniques have improved knowledge of how companies might use the metaverse efficiently by offering useful insights into real-world applications, experiences, and best practices.

Business Model Overview

Metaverse Technologies is a cutting-edge corporation focused on creating and delivering innovative metaverse technologies (Mozumder et al., 2023). According to Wider et al. (2023), the business model relies on developing a comprehensive and immersive metaverse platform and providing a diverse set of applications and services to businesses in a variety of industries. Rathore (2023) stated that the goal is to revolutionize the way people connect, cooperate, and conduct business in the digital environment by integrating virtual reality, augmented reality, blockchain, and artificial intelligence.

Important Components of the Business Model

1. **Metaverse Platform Development:**
   According to Chen (2022), metaverse technologies have invested in the research, development, and maintenance of a powerful metaverse platform. According to Scavarelli et al. (2021), the metaverse platform will serve as the foundation for establishing a shared virtual area where users may interact, explore, and engage with one another.
2. **Virtual Reality (VR) and Augmented Reality (AR) Solutions:**
   In 2022, Kozinets investigated immersive VR and AR experiences that allow users to access the metaverse through wearable devices such as headsets, offering a seamless blend of the real and virtual worlds.
3. **Blockchain Integration:**
   To guarantee security, transparency, and decentralized ownership of digital assets, Metaverse technologies have integrated blockchain technology into the Metaverse platform (Mourtzis et al., 2023). According to Longshak et al. (2023), businesses may build relationships with customers, facilitate safe transactions, and safeguard intellectual property by utilizing blockchain.
4. **Artificial Intelligence:**
   Develop apps and tools that are driven by artificial intelligence (AI) to improve user experiences in the metaverse. According to Davenport & Ronanki (2018), AI algorithms have made it possible for organizations to get useful insights and effective processes, enabling personalized suggestions, intelligent avatars, natural language processing, and smart automation.
5. **Solutions Tailored to Specific Businesses**
   Metaverse Technologies has made its products specifically for real estate, retail, entertainment, education, healthcare, and other businesses (Damar, 2022). Allam et al. (2022) said that metaverse platforms and apps can be modified to satisfy the particular requirements of companies within each industry, producing custom virtual worlds and experiences.
6. **Collaborative Spaces and Social Features:**
   Zhu et al. (2023) pointed out in their studies about collaborative spaces and social features that the metaverse platform offers collaborative spaces so that teams and individuals may cooperate, have meetings, and encourage innovation.

Table1.1: Various Technologies of Metaverse used in Different Business	
	Technological base of the metaverse
Blockchain Integration	Technology for hasting and timestamping Mechanism for data transmission and transaction verification Mechanism of consensus Storage that is dispersed Smart contracts and distributed ledgers
Interaction technology	AR technology (virtual reality) MR imaging technology The use of holographic displays Somatosensory environment sensing technology
IoT	loT management system Sensors loT network communication support
Network and computing technology	Cloud Computing 5G/6G network Edge computing
AI Technology	Vision in Computers Learning by machine Natural language understanding Intelligent speech
Computer Game Technology	3D modelling Real-time rendering Game Engine

Applications of Metaverse for Business Models

Metaverse, a virtual environment parallel to reality, employs digital twin technology, which is also a key way of constructing a smart city, virtual showrooms, events and conferences, training and education real estate, collaborations and remote work, advertising and sponsorships (Aloqaily et al., 2022). According to Popa et al. (2021) digital twin technology creates a visible, controllable, and manageable digital transformation by digitally mapping the real environment, completely capturing urban data such as people, cars, objects, and space, and forming a visible, controllable, and manageable digital transformation.

1. **Virtual Showrooms:**
   According to Abdelmaged in 2021 businesses like healthcare, entertainment, tourism, education and retail create interactive virtual showrooms to showcase their products and services, allowing customers to explore and make purchases in a visually stunning and immersive environment.
2. **Virtual Events and Conferences:**
   George et al. (2021) have explained that the metaverse is the next stage of human beings where companies host virtual events, conferences, and trade shows within the metaverse, providing a scalable and cost-effective alternative to physical gatherings. Attendees can participate remotely, network with industry professionals, and engage in interactive sessions.
3. **Virtual Training and Education:**
   In 2022 Chen has explored virtual training and education where metaverse technologies are utilized to develop virtual training programs

and educational simulations. Virtual reality applications allow businesses to offer immersive learning experiences, conduct virtual workshops, and train employees in a safe and engaging environment.

4. **Virtual Real Estate:**
   Radhakrishna (2022) suggested that real estate companies leverage the metaverse to showcase properties virtually, allowing potential buyers to explore homes, apartments, or commercial spaces remotely. This eliminates the need for physical visits and enables global reach.
5. **Virtual Collaboration and Remote Work:**
   Hakonen & Bosch-Sijtsema (2014) mentioned about the virtual worlds where metaverse technologies provide collaborative spaces where remote teams can work together, brainstorm ideas, and foster creativity. Businesses can create virtual offices, enabling employees to connect and collaborate regardless of their physical location.
6. **Virtual Advertising and Sponsorships:**
   Ahn et al. (2023) reported that companies can utilize the metaverse platform to advertise their products and services, sponsor virtual events, and engage with users through immersive and interactive ad experiences.

Mckinsey reported in 2022 about the metaverse platform, some various tools and platforms that help make the economy thrive. These include advertising and asset stores that allow people to buy, sell, and showcase their virtual items or creations. Mozumder et al. (2022) have shown a roadmap of metaverse platforms and pointed out that platforms are managing digital identity, avatars, and social connections, helping users create and maintain their online personas. The below points from the McKinsey report discussed the distribution of metaverse technologies platforms and defined their characteristics.

Figure 1.1: Distribution of Metaverse Technologies Platforms

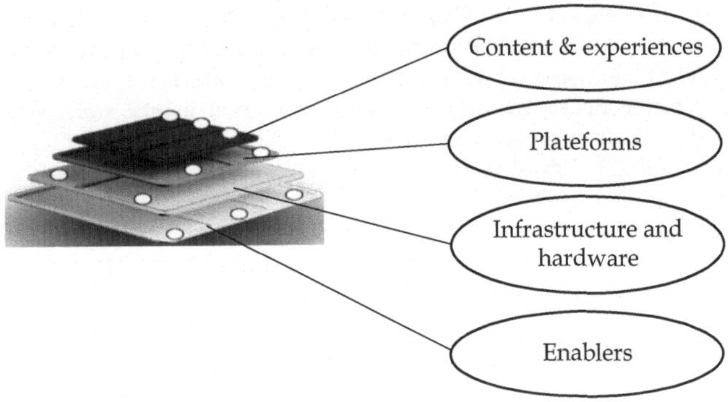

Source: McKinsey & Company Senior Executive Survey, April 2022

Enablers

Payments and Monetization:

Platforms and tools (advertising, asset stores) to enable the metaverse economy

Identity:

Platforms that manage digital identity, avatars, and social graphs

Security, Privacy, and Governance:

Security, privacy, and governance are essential aspects of the metaverse. Some platforms ensure data security, identity protection, and content moderation to maintain a safe and trustworthy environment. These measures are put in place to protect users' privacy and prevent harmful content from spreading.

Infrastructure and Hardware

Infrastructure:

The infrastructure powering the metaverse includes various components like cloud services, semiconductors, and networks.

Devices, OS and Accessories:

Devices, operating systems, and accessories all play important roles in the human-metaverse interaction. People connect and engage with the virtual environment using these tools, which range from VR headsets and controllers to mobile devices with specific operating systems.

Platforms

Access and Discovery:

Platforms for access and identification help people in finding and accessing metaverse information, experiences, and apps. Browsers, search engines, app stores, and in-app marketplaces are examples of tools that help individuals explore the virtual world.

Creators/3D development platforms:

Creators and developers have specialized platforms to build 3D experiences, including design tools, game engines, and artificial intelligence services. These platforms enable individuals to unleash their creativity and bring innovative virtual content to life.

Virtual Worlds:

Virtual worlds are places where large numbers of users can gather, interact, create, and move between various experiences. These environments offer diverse possibilities for socializing, learning, collaborating, and exploring together.

Applications:

The metaverse also caters to specific use cases through various applications. These can range from educational experiences, collaborative workspaces, and virtual events, to industry-specific applications, all enriching the metaverse with unique and immersive functionalities.

Challenges Associated with Adopting Metaverse Technologies in a Business Context

In 2021 Di Pietro & Cresci pointed out that the adoption of metaverse technologies raises several critical challenges that businesses must address behaviors of technologies for successful implementation and user acceptance. Periyasami & Periyasami (2022) mentioned in their study that users were facing different challenges in their businesses in securing virtual assets, transactions, and digital identities within the metaverse presents unique cybersecurity challenges that demand attention.

Data Privacy and Security:

Warin & Reinhardt (2022) said about data privacy and security that the adoption of metaverse technologies raises concerns regarding the collection, storage, and security of user data. To preserve consumer trust and comply with regulatory obligations, businesses must traverse complicated privacy legislation and implement comprehensive data protection procedures (Takabi et al., 2010; Koohang et al., 2023). Safeguarding virtual assets, transactions, and digital identities within the metaverse presents new cybersecurity concerns that have to be addressed.

Inclusivity and Digital Divide:

The metaverse has the potential to create a digital divide, where certain segments like education, health and businesses of the population may have limited access to the necessary technologies or skills required to participate fully (Kaddoura & Husseiny 2023). Meena et al. (2023) noted ensuring equitable access to the metaverse and addressing barriers related to connectivity, affordability, and digital literacy are crucial challenges that businesses need to consider to avoid growing societal inequalities.

Ethical Considerations:

Metaverse technologies present ethical challenges, including issues of virtual property rights, consent, and the potential for addiction or overreliance on virtual experiences (Koohang et al., 2023). Businesses must establish ethical guidelines and frameworks to address these concerns and promote responsible use of the metaverse within their operations and interactions with customers.

Integration with Existing Business Models:

Integrating virtual reality, augmented reality, and other metaverse components may require significant investments in infrastructure, hardware, software, and talent (Mancuso et al., 2023). Organizations need to assess the compatibility of their current systems, develop appropriate integration strategies, and potentially redesign their workflows and processes to fully leverage the benefits of the metaverse.

Businesses must focus on these critical areas for effective metaverse integration and expansion: recognizing and accommodating user preferences, safeguarding their intellectual property, and continuing to change regulatory and legal requirements. Businesses could position themselves for success in this transformational era of technology by successfully addressing these challenges.

Ethical and Societal Implications of Metaverse Technologies within a Business Context

Businesses leveraging metaverse technologies are proactively addressing ethical and societal implications to foster responsible development (Chaudhari & Anand, 2023). Kaur et al. (2023) emphasised that data privacy and security are paramount, with businesses investing in robust measures like encryption, secure authentication, and data anonymization to safeguard user information from unauthorized access or breaches. Wang et al. (2022) mentioned that to ensure inclusivity and accessibility, efforts are being made to bridge the digital divide by making metaverse experiences accessible to individuals with disabilities and diverse user groups, investing in connectivity and digital literacy initiatives. Trauthig & Woolley (2023) addressed that responsible content creation and moderation are prioritized to mitigate harmful content, supported by content moderation policies and AI algorithms to identify and remove problematic content. Banerji (2023) reported that digital well-being and potential addiction are concerns, leading to the incorporation of features promoting healthy usage habits, tools for screen time management, and resources to support users' mental health. Businesses explore fair and sustainable monetization models that respect user privacy and preferences while striving to create a fair virtual economy by implementing mechanisms against fraud and unfair practices (Al-Ghaili et al., 2022). Businesses recognize their broader social impact, engaging in corporate social responsibility initiatives to support causes, promote diversity and inclusivity, and drive positive change in virtual communities. By addressing these implications, businesses establish a commitment to creating a safe, inclusive, and socially responsible metaverse ecosystem. Businesses are signifying a commitment to responsible metaverse development by addressing these ethical and societal implications.

Results and Discussions

The findings of the study highlight the transformative potential of metaverse technology for organizations, providing immersive virtual reality-based shared spaces that may revolutionize consumer interaction, stimulate innovation, and establishment for new income. Metaverse is used in diverse sectors including virtual showrooms, events, training, real estate, collaboration, and advertising, allowing organizations to engage with consumers, workers, and partners in creative and efficient ways. Businesses must address data protection, security, inclusiveness, ethical issues, integration with current models, user uptake, and regulatory compliance to achieve responsible development. The metaverse business model combines VR, AR, blockchain, and AI technology, including collaborative spaces with social elements, payments, identity management, and bespoke solutions for various sectors. Enabling technologies like blockchain, VR, AR, IoT, and AI play a vital role in building the metaverse ecosystem. Businesses are actively addressing ethical and societal implications, such as data privacy, inclusivity, content moderation, digital well-being, fair virtual economy, and social impact to create a safe and inclusive metaverse environment. Practical guidelines and insights are essential for businesses to navigate the metaverse effectively, considering user preferences, addressing challenges, and complying with regulations. The digital twin technology, used in constructing smart cities, contributes to the metaverse's potential and offers opportunities for smart urban planning and management. By responsibly adopting metaverse technologies, businesses can revolutionize their operations, engage customers more effectively, and thrive in an interconnected digital age.

Recommendations

The study provided comprehensive insights into metaverse technology and business model applications. The present study has given organizations the information and knowledge needed to strategically and efficiently use the metaverse by adopting a bird's eye view and reviewing existing research, industry insights, and developing trends. We have emphasized the metaverse's ability to change businesses throughout the research. The metaverse offers a variety of options for businesses to innovate, engage customers, and promote expansion, from virtual commerce and improved customer experiences to virtual collaboration and remote work capabilities. We have given businesses an overview for understanding the technical aspects and potential of the metaverse by examining the underlying technologies that operate within that, including virtual reality, augmented reality, and artificial intelligence. The study has also emphasized how crucial it is to think about societal and ethical consequences before using metaverse technology. Businesses must take privacy, security, inclusiveness, and responsible creation of content considerations to make the metaverse a secure, equitable platform for all users. Organizations must actively investigate and use these technologies as the metaverse develops and shapes the future of business.

References

1. Abdelmaged, M. A. M. (2021). Implementation of virtual reality in healthcare, entertainment, tourism, education, and retail sectors. Retrieved from https://mpra.ub.uni-muenchen.de/id/eprint/110491
2. Aguayo, C., & Eames, C. (2023). Using mixed reality (XR) immersive learning to enhance environmental education. *The Journal of Environmental Education*, *54*(1), 58-71. Retrieved from https://doi.org/10.1080/00958964.2022.2152410

3. Ahn, S. J., Kim, J., & Kim, J. (2023). The future of advertising research in virtual, augmented, and extended realities. *International Journal of Advertising, 42*(1), 162-170. Retrieved from https://doi.org/10.1080/02650487.2022.2137316
4. Al-Ghaili, A. M., Kasim, H., Al-Hada, N. M., Hassan, Z., Othman, M., Hussain, T. J., & Shayea, I. (2022). A review of metaverse's definitions, architecture, applications, challenges, issues, solutions, and future trends. *IEEE Access* 125835 -125866. Retrieved from https://doi.org/10.1109/ACCESS.2022.3225638
5. Allam, Z., Sharifi, A., Bibri, S. E., Jones, D. S., & Krogstie, J. (2022). The metaverse as a virtual form of smart cities: Opportunities and challenges for environmental, economic, and social sustainability in urban futures. *Smart Cities, 5*(3), 771-801. Retrieved from https://doi.org/10.3390/smartcities5030040
6. Atlam, H. F., & Wills, G. B. (2020). IoT security, privacy, safety and ethics. *Digital twin Technologies and Smart Cities*, 123-149. Retrieved from https://doi.org/10.1007/978-3-030-18732-3_8
7. Bale, A. S., Ghorpade, N., Hashim, M. F., Vaishnav, J., & Almaspoor, Z. (2022). A comprehensive study on Metaverse and its impacts on humans. *Advances in Human-Computer Interaction*, 1-11. Retrieved from https://doi.org/10.1155/2022/3247060
8. Balkin, J. M. (2004). Virtual liberty: Freedom to design and freedom to play in virtual worlds. *Virginia Law Review, 90*(8), 2043-2098. Retrieved from https://doi.org/10.2307/1515641
9. Banerji, S. (2023). Future of Well-being-The Metaverse Era. *OCAD University Open Research Repository*. Retrieved from https://openresearch.ocadu.ca/id/eprint/4103
10. Bialkova, S. (2022). From attention to action: Key drivers to augment VR experience for everyday consumer applications. *IEEE Conference on Virtual Reality and 3D user Interfaces Abstracts and Workshops (VRW)*, 247-252. https://doi.org/10.1109/VRW55335.2022.00058
11. Bibri, S. E. (2022). The social shaping of the metaverse as an alternative to the imaginaries of data-driven smart Cities: A study in science, technology, and society. *Smart Cities, 5*(3), 832-874. Retrieved from https://doi.org/10.3390/smartcities5030043
12. Chaudhuri, A., & Anand, A. (2023). Enable the metaverse and smart society with trustworthy and sustainable 'things'. *Journal of Data Protection & Privacy, 5*(4), 363-373.
13. Chen, Z. (2022). Exploring the application scenarios and issues facing Metaverse technology in education. *Interactive Learning Environments*, 1-13. Retrieved from https://doi.org/10.1080/10494820.2022.2133148
14. Cheng, S. (2023). Metaverse and Digital Asset. In *Metaverse: Concept, Content and Context, Springer Nature, Cham* 123-144. Retrieved from https://doi.org/10.1007/978-3-031-24359-2_6
15. Damar, M. (2022). What the literature on medicine, nursing, public health, midwifery, and dentistry reveals: An overview of the rapidly approaching metaverse. *Journal of Metaverse, 2*(2), 62-70. Retrieved from https://doi.org/10.57019/jmv.1132962
16. Davenport, T. H., & Ronanki, R. (2018). Artificial intelligence for the real world. *Harvard Business Review, 96*(1), 108-116.
17. Davis, A., Murphy, J., Owens, D., Khazanchi, D., & Zigurs, I. (2009). Avatars, people, and virtual worlds: Foundations for research in metaverses. *Journal of the Association for Information Systems, 10*(2), 91-117. Retrieved from https://doi.org/10.17705/1jais.00183
18. Dwivedi, Y. K., Hughes, L., Baabdullah, A. M., Ribeiro-Navarrete, S., Giannakis, M., Al-Debei, M. M., & Wamba, S. F. (2022). Metaverse beyond the hype: Multidisciplinary perspectives on emerging challenges, opportunities, and agenda for research, practice and policy. *International Journal of Information Management, 66*, 102542. Retrieved from https://doi.org/10.1016/j.ijinfomgt.2022.102542.

19. Dwivedi, Y. K., Hughes, L., Wang, Y., Alalwan, A. A., Ahn, S. J., Balakrishnan, J., & Wirtz, J. (2023). Metaverse marketing: How the metaverse will shape the future of consumer research and practice. *Psychology & Marketing, 40*(4), 750-776. Retrieved from https://doi.org/10.1002/mar.21767
20. George, A. H., Fernando, M., George, A. S., Baskar, T., & Pandey, D. (2021). Metaverse: The next stage of human culture and the internet. *International Journal of Advanced Research Trends in Engineering and Technology (IJARTET), 8*(12), 1-10. Retrieved from http://www.ijartet.com/
21. Graf, M., Zoll, A., Wahl, N., Ellenrieder, S., Hager, F., Sturm, T., & Vetter, O. A. (2023). Designing the Organizational Metaverse for Effective Socialization, *Pacific Asia Conference on Information System Nanchang (PACIS) Proceedings*. Retrieved from https://aisel.aisnet.org/pacis2023/46
22. Groff, J. (2013). Technology-rich innovative learning environments. *OCED CERI Innovative Learning Environment Project*, 1-30.
23. Hakonen, M., & Bosch-Sijtsema, P. M. (2014). Virtual worlds enabling distributed collaboration. *Journal For Virtual Worlds Research, 7*(3), 1-19. Retrieved from https://doi.org/10.4101/jvwr.v7i3.6158
24. Hoyer, W. D., Kroschke, M., Schmitt, B., Kraume, K., & Shankar, V. (2020). Transforming the customer experience through new technologies. *Journal of Interactive Marketing, 51*(1), 57-71. Retrieved from https://doi.org/10.1016/j.intmar.2020.04.001
25. Kaddoura, S., & Al Husseiny, F. (2023). The rising trend of Metaverse in education: challenges, opportunities, and ethical considerations. *PeerJ Computer Science, 9*. Retrieved from https://doi.org/10.7717/peerj-cs.1252
26. Kaur, D., Singh, B., & Rani, S. (2023). Cyber Security in the Metaverse. In Handbook of Research on AI-Based Technologies and Applications in the Era of the Metaverse, *IGI Global*, 418-435. Retrieved from https://doi.org/10.4018/978-1-6684-8851-5.ch023
27. Kim, J. (2021). Advertising in the metaverse: Research agenda. *Journal of Interactive Advertising, 21*(3), 141-144. Retrieved from https://doi.org/10.1080/15252019.2021.2001273
28. Kohler, T., Matzler, K., & Füller, J. (2009). Avatar-based innovation: Using virtual worlds for real-world innovation. *Technovation, 29*(6-7), 395-407. Retrieved from https://doi.org/10.1016/j.technovation.2008.11.004
29. Koohang, A., Nord, J. H., Ooi, K. B., Tan, G. W. H., Al-Emran, M., Aw, E. C. X., & Wong, L. W. (2023). Shaping the metaverse into reality: a holistic multidisciplinary understanding of opportunities, challenges, and avenues for future investigation. *Journal of Computer Information Systems, 63*(3), 735-765. Retrieved from https://doi.org/10.1080/08874417.2023.2165197
30. Kozinets, R. V. (2022). Immersive netnography: a novel method for service experience research in virtual reality, augmented reality and metaverse contexts. *Journal of Service Management, 34*(1), 100-125. Retrieved from https://doi.org/10.1108/JOSM-12-2021-0481
31. Kraus, S., Kanbach, D. K., Krysta, P. M., Steinhoff, M. M., & Tomini, N. (2022). Facebook and the creation of the metaverse: radical business model innovation or incremental transformation?. *International Journal of Entrepreneurial Behavior & Research, 28*(9), 52-77. Retrieved from https://doi.org/10.1108/IJEBR-12-2021-0984
32. Kumar, S. (2009). Virtual architectural workspaces digitally mediated collaboration in the architectural design process.
33. Lee, L. H., Braud, T., Zhou, P., Wang, L., Xu, D., Lin, Z., ... & Hui, P. (2021). All one needs to know about metaverse: A complete survey on technological singularity, virtual ecosystem, and research agenda. *ArXiv Preprint arXiv:2110.05352*. Retrieved from https://doi.org/10.48550/arXiv.2110.05352
34. Longshak, J. E., Oyeboade, S. A., Abdullahi, M. S., & Chanai, K. M. (2023). Intellectual Property Rights (IPR) in the Blockchain Era. *In Global Perspectives on Sustainable Library*

Practices, 263-296. Retrieved from https://doi.org/10.4018/978-1-6684-5964-5.ch020

35. Mancuso, I., Petruzzelli, A. M., & Panniello, U. (2023). Digital business model innovation in metaverse: How to approach virtual economy opportunities. *Information Processing & Management, 60*(5). Retrieved from https://doi.org/10.1016/j.ipm.2023.103457
36. McKinsey. (2022). Value creation in the metaverse. Retrieved from https://www.mckinsey.com/capabilities/growth-marketing-and-sales/our-insights/value-creation-in-the-metaverse
37. Meena, S. D., Mithesh, G. S. S., Panyam, R., Chowdary, M. S., Sadhu, V. S., & Sheela, J. (2023). Advancing Education through Metaverse: Components, Applications, Challenges, Case Studies and Open Issues. *International Conference on Sustainable Computing and Smart Systems (ICSCSS)* 880-889. Retrieved from https://doi.org/10.1109/ICSCSS57650.2023.10169535
38. Mourtzis, D., Angelopoulos, J., & Panopoulos, N. (2023). Blockchain integration in the era of industrial metaverse. *Applied Sciences, 13*(3). Rertreived from https://doi.org/10.3390/app13031353
39. Mozumder, M. A. I., Sheeraz, M. M., Athar, A., Aich, S., & Kim, H. C. (2022). Overview: Technology roadmap of the future trend of metaverse based on IoT, blockchain, AI technique, and medical domain metaverse activity. *International Conference on Advanced Communication Technology (ICACT)* 256-261. Retrieved from https://doi.org/10.23919/ICACT53585.2022.9728808
40. Mozumder, M. A. I., Theodore, A. T. P., Athar, A., & Kim, H. C. (2023). The metaverse applications for the finance industry, its challenges, and an approach for the metaverse finance industry. *International Conference on Advanced Communication Technology (ICACT)* 407-410. Retrieved from https://doi.org/10.23919/ICACT56868.2023.10079695
41. Mystakidis, S. (2022). Metaverse. *Encyclopedia,* 2(1), 486-497. Retrieved from https://doi.org/10.3390/encyclopedia2010031
42. Nagy, P., & Koles, B. (2014). My avatar and her beloved possession: Characteristics of attachment to virtual objects. *Psychology & Marketing, 31*(12), 1122-1135. Retrieved from https://doi.org/10.1002/mar.20759
43. Oh, H. J., Kim, J., Chang, J. J., Park, N., & Lee, S. (2023). Social benefits of living in the metaverse: The relationships among social presence, supportive interaction, social self-efficacy, and feelings of loneliness. *Computers in Human Behavior, 139*. Retrieved from https://doi.org/10.1016/j.chb.2022.107498
44. Owens, D., Mitchell, A., Khazanchi, D., & Zigurs, I. (2011). An empirical investigation of virtual world projects and metaverse technology capabilities. *ACM SIGMIS Database: the DATABASE for Advances in Information Systems,* 42(1), 74-101. Retrieved from https://doi.org/10.1145/1952712.1952717
45. Park, S. M., & Kim, Y. G. (2022). A metaverse: Taxonomy, components, applications, and open challenges. *IEEE Access, 10,* 4209-4251. Retrieved from https://doi.org/10.1109/ACCESS.2021.3140175
46. Popa, E. O., van Hilten, M., Oosterkamp, E., & Bogaardt, M. J. (2021). The use of digital twins in healthcare: socio-ethical benefits and socio-ethical risks. *Life Sciences, Society and Policy, 17*(1), 1-25. Retrieved from https://doi.org/10.1186/s40504-021-00113-x
47. Radhakrishna, G. (2022). Legal Issues with Real Estate in the Metaverse. In *International Conference on Law and Digitalization (ICLD 2022),* 74-82. Retrieved from https://doi.org/10.2991/978-2-494069-59-6_7
48. Rathore, B. (2017). Virtual Consumerism an Exploration of E-Commerce in the Metaverse. *International Journal of New Media Studies: International Peer Reviewed Scholarly Indexed Journal,* 4(2), 61-69. Retrieved from https://www.ijnms.com/index.php/ijnms/article/view/109

49. Rathore, B. (2023). Digital Transformation 4.0: Integration of Artificial Intelligence & Metaverse in Marketing. *Eduzone: International Peer Reviewed/Refereed Multidisciplinary Journal, 12*(1), 42-48. Retrieved from https://www.eduzonejournal.com/index.php/eiprmj/article/view/248
50. Scavarelli, A., Arya, A., & Teather, R. J. (2021). Virtual reality and augmented reality in social learning spaces: a literature review. *Virtual Reality, 25,* 257-277. Retrieved from https://doi.org/10.1007/s10055-020-00444-8
51. Stephenson, N. (1992). Snow Crash, *Bantam Books, New York* 1– 440.
52. Takabi, H., Joshi, J. B., & Ahn, G. J. (2010). Security and privacy challenges in cloud computing environments. *IEEE Security & Privacy, 8*(6), 24-31. Retrieved from https://doi.org/10.1109/MSP.2010.186
53. Trauthig, I., & Woolley, S. (2023). Addressing Hateful and Misleading Content in the Metaverse. *Journal of Online Trust and Safety, 1*(5). Retrieved from https://doi.org/10.54501/jots.v1i5.109
54. Wang, M., Yu, H., Bell, Z., & Chu, X. (2022). Constructing an Edu-Metaverse ecosystem: A new and innovative framework. *IEEE Transactions on Learning Technologies, 15*(6), 685-696. Retrieved from https://doi.org/10.1109/TLT.2022.3210828
55. Warin, C., & Reinhardt, D. (2022). Vision: Usable Privacy for XR in the Era of the Metaverse. In *Proceedings of the 2022 European Symposium on Usable Security,* 111-116. Retrieved from https://doi.org/10.1145/3549015.3554212
56. Wider, W., Jiang, L., Lin, J., Fauzi, M. A., Li, J., & Chan, C. K. (2023). Metaverse Chronicles: A Bibliometric Analysis of Its Evolving Landscape. *International Journal of Human-Computer Interaction,* 1-14. Retrieved from https://doi.org/10.1080/10447318.2023.2227825
57. Wongkitrungrueng, A., & Suprawan, L. (2023). Metaverse Meets Branding: Examining Consumer Responses to Immersive Brand Experiences. *International Journal of Human–Computer Interaction,* 1-20. Retrieved from https://doi.org/10.1080/10447318.2023.2175162
58. Zhu, S., Vennemeyer, S., Xu, C., & Wu, D. T. (2023). Adopting a metaverse-based workspace to support research team collaboration: a pilot study from an academic health informatics laboratory. *JAMIA Open, 6*(1). Retrieved from https://doi.org/10.1093/jamiaopen/ooad010

2

An Initiative Towards Banking Industry Transformation through Metaverse: A Systematic Review

Pushpam Singh[1] & Dr. Sukanta Kumar Baral[2]

Abstract

There is a growing trend among banking institutions to enhance their digital exposure. The banking industry is actively tapping into newly emerging technologies, including the metaverse, to shift to an augmented workspace. This study reviews the existing research on metaverse banking by adopting the SLR process on Google Scholar to identify the trends of metaverse banking studies through the publication year and methodology adopted. After a thorough study, 14 related research articles were identified for review to comply with the objectives once the selection criteria were met. The second objective of this study is to examine the role of the metaverse in the banking sector. The potentiality of the metaverse, used to merge social networks with augmented reality (AR) technology, will revolutionize the banking industry by delivering pleasant experiences to customers. There is a need for government institutions to provide necessary systems and services, such as decentralised trading platforms, for metaverse operational activities. This research review would serve as a basis for future studies to make the industry more viable and compliant with current requirements.

Keywords: *Metaverse, Augmented Reality (AR) Technology, Banking Industry, Mixed Reality (MR) Technology, Virtual Reality (VR) Technology*

Introduction

The virtual reality realms have evolved remarkably since the concept of metaverse was initially coined in 1992 together with the advancement of 3D (Dionisio et al., 2013). The Metaverse creates a completely engrossed and economically viable virtual ecosystem for the users as a revolutionary approach where individuals can connect, collaborate, and work. It is widely accepted that the recent investments made in the Metaverse by prominent media organisations and other industries anticipate the beginning of an era of change for the internet as a whole (Narin, 2021). The integration of Mixed Reality (MR) and Augmented Reality (AR) facilitates effective service expansion by creating a virtual digital interface with real-world experiences that encourage many industries. It is anticipated that information technological advances, such as chatbots, wearable devices, biometry, smart speakers, VR/AR, and Artificial Intelligence (AI), which have radically altered our daily activities, will also be implemented to oversee our fiscal affairs. To mitigate the termed bank rates, fully linked automated services need to be devised. Furthermore, market liberalisation is predicted to boost requirements for

1 Research Scholar, Department of Commerce Indira Gandhi National Tribal University, Madhya Pradesh

2 Professor, Department of Commerce Indira Gandhi National Tribal University, Madhya Pradesh

innovations in the banking sector in the future (Vergallo & Mainetti, 2022). It is equally crucial for banks to remain updated with technological advances. So, to provide customers with quick transactions and time-saving benefits, the banking industry closely monitors technological advancements to ensure the security of their deposits and transactions (Srivastava & Dhamija, 2021).

The practical applications of virtual and simulated devices that enable the banking services and their users to engage in a much more interesting and immersive way is technically referred to as the introduction of the metaverse in the banking industry. It forms a cybernetic ecosystem where deposits, long and short-term borrowings, and other forms of investment opportunities are offered completely in a digital realm (Saad et al., 2023). To make metaverse banks a reality, several revolutionary technologies are deployed for incorporating the metaverse and online banking operations (Koohang et al., 2023). The banking industry possesses the potential to employ metaverse either through blockchain or by designing innovative business frameworks. A virtual environment that promotes participation and collaboration is essential for this industry to establish a strong connection with its customer base and for this, the metaverse plays a crucial part in reaching out to customers (Golf-Papez et al., 2022). Users can access their financial transactions and records using a metaverse banking process if something seems fraudulent with their financial records. Past research shows that the study on metaverse in the context of medical education, finance, gaming, and advertisements (Shen et al., 2021) has been conducted in significant numbers but the current study on the metaverse banking industry is limited and majorly based on the conceptual framework. This study reviews existing research related to the metaverse in the banking industry by adopting a Systematic Literature Review (SLR) and focusing on the objectives framed as below;

1. To determine the prevailing studies of the application of Metaverse in the banking industry;
2. To examine the roles of Metaverse in the banking industry to facilitate different services from the existing studies.

Systematic Literature Review (SLR) Method

The literature reviews lay the groundwork for scholarly studies. Education, computer sciences, information technology, and medical subject represents some of the domains that have deliberated and established standards for carrying out high-quality literature reviews. A structured approach to carrying out reviews of literature can improve the studies' validity, consistency, and clarity (Xiao & Watson, 2019). SLR applies a more stringent and structured review technique than narrative reviews. The effective implementations of this research approach in the social sciences opened the doors for its extension to other domains (Thome et al., 2016). To find every study that has been done in response to a certain subject, search algorithms for systematic reviews need to be created. As a result, a cautious search technique is required rather than a specific one. Many easily accessible search tools on websites have been discovered to be exceptionally accurate in comprehending specific study designs retrieved from library databases (Nightingale, 2009).

Research Methodology

The researchers applied the Systematic Literature Review (SLR) approach to locate and assess relevant articles associated with specified study objectives and recent trends. The most recent studies on Metaverse banking were scrutinized using SLR processes. The Google Scholar database was considered a source of information for the search procedure. The keywords used for specific searches were "Metaverse banking", and "banking" and "Metaverse". At the initial stage, articles were chosen using direct search and forward snowballing (article search through citations) that have both abstract and title or any of them. In the second stage, articles were preferred according to the criteria of inclusion as stated below;

Inclusion Criteria

- Articles' title with keywords "Metaverse banking", and "banking" and "metaverse"
- Articles published in the years 2022 and 2023
- Articles associated with research objectives
- Only Full-fledged quality papers

Exclusion Criteria

- Duplication in articles
- Publications in other languages apart from the English language

The below figure-1 explains a Systematic Literature Review (SLR) process adopted in the study

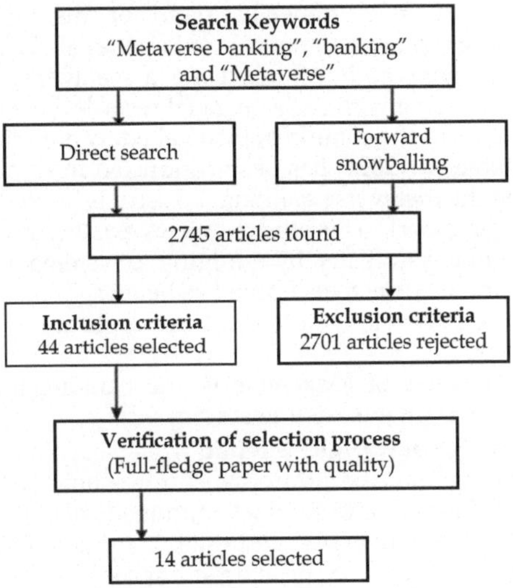

Fig. 1: Systematic Literature Review (SLR) process
Source: Compiled by the authors

Results

Based on the SLR process, 14 research articles are explored signifying related studies on Metaverse banking. Table 1 provides a brief overview of the documents obtained for the current study, including the topic, reference, objective, journal source, methodology, research type, and citation of the identified work. Different kinds of publications were examined for this process such as conference papers, review articles, and book chapters.

The result showed that the studies on Metaverse banking were mostly conducted in the years 2022 and 2023 because the banking sector has recently been engaged in a thorough examination regarding the possibility of banks offering services to their clients in the Metaverse. (Vakiti & SL, 2023). The banking industry is now at its initial stage of operating Metaverse in its services because the method that was highly used by past researchers was a qualitative study and was conceptual.

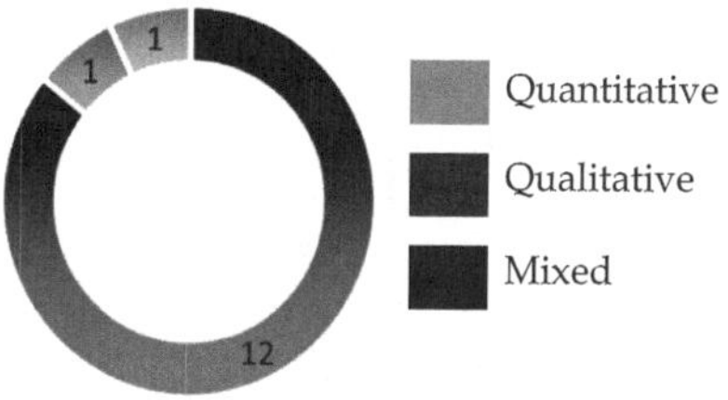

Fig. 2: Research methods adopted by the researchers

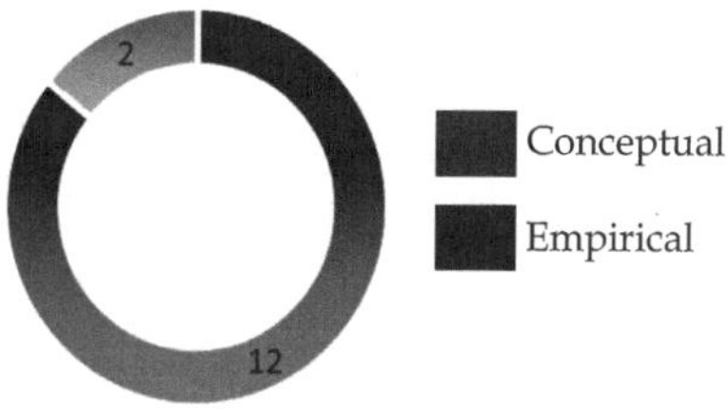

Fig. 3: Research type opted by the researchers

Table 1 presents a brief overview of obtained articles for the present study that contains a topic, reference, objective, journal source, methodology, research type, and citation of specified paper.

Table 1. Brief overview of selected articles

Research topic	Refer-ences	Research objec-tives	Journal source	Re-search meth-od	Re-search type	Cita-tion
Banking in Metaverse - Opportunities and Challenges	Sarkar S. (2023)	• Exploring the oppor-tunities for banking through the Metaverse • Providing strategies to overcome challeng-es in Metaverse for banks	The Man-age-ment Ac-countant Jour-nal	Quali-tative	Con-cep-tu-al	3
Devising an Indonesian Legal Architec-ture for Metaverse Banking: Chal-lenges and Op-portunities	Prata-ma K. J. (2023)	• Disproving viewpoints on legal framework related to Metaverse banking	Journal of Central Banking Law and Institutions	Quali-tative	Con-cep-tu-al	1
Big Data and Metaverse Revolu-tionizing the Futuris-tic Fintech Indus-try	Yathi-raju N. & Dash B. (2023)	• Exploring the ad-vantages of Metaverse and Big Data • Identifying the ways to transform fintech through Metaverse	International Journal of Computer Science & Information Technology	Quali-tative	Con-cep-tu-al	2
FinTech Ena-blers, Use Cas-es, and Role of Future Internet of Things	Bhat J. R. et al. (2023)	• Discussing the trends of fintech enablers • Presenting a model for Metaverse banking	Journal of King Saud Universi-ty - Com-puter and Infor-mation Scienc-es	Quali-tative	Con-cep-tu-al	23
MetaMoney: Explor-ing the Intersection of Virtual Worlds and Financial Systems	Kumar S. et al. (2023)	• Reviewing Metaverse appli-cations in financial services • Conceptualizing the integration of finance with Metaverse	Available at Social Science Research Network	Quali-tative	Con-cep-tu-al	0

Metaverse for Public Good: Embracing the Societal Impact of Metaverse Economies Metaverse for Public Good: Embracing the Societal Impact of Metaverse Economies	Naqvi N. (2023)	• Exploring the use cases of Metaverse in multiple sectors • Examining the strat-egies for Metaverse and its influence on society	The Journal of The British Blockchain Association	Quali-tative	Con-cep-tu-al	0
The Applica-tion of Artificial Intelligence in Metaverse: A New Challenge on Personal Data Protection in the Financial System	Sautun-nida L. et al. (2023)	• Evaluating the influence of Metaverse on the performance of banking companies	In Islamic Sustainable Finance, Law and Innovation: Opportu-nities and Challenges, Springer	Quali-tative	Con-cep-tu-al	0
A Study to An-alyse the Im-pact of Using the Metaverse in the Banking Industry to Augment Perfor-mance in a Competitive Environment	Saad A. A. et al. (2023)	• Evaluating the influence of Metaverse on the performance of banking companies	In Applying Metalytics to Measure Cus-tomer Experi-ence in the Metaverse, IGI Global	Quan-ti-ta-tive	Empir-ical	4
The Metaverse and Islamic Financial Contracts: The Case of Ijarah	Saad A. A. et al. (2023)	• Examining the Metaverse trends and their integration with the business brands	F1000Re-search	Quali-tative	Con-cep-tu-al	0
The Future In-novation of Fintech in the Metaverse Banking: Re-view	Vakiti J. L. & SL T. D. (2023)	• Addressing the advancements of Metaverse banking through fintech	International Research Jour-nal on Ad-vanced Sci-ence Hub	Quali-tative	Con-cep-tu-al	0
Marketing Strate-gies of Banks in the Period of Metaverse, Blockchain, and Cryptocurrency in the Context of Consumer Behavior Theories	Ozkay-nar K. (2022)	• Discussing the marketing strategies for the technologies to be adopted in the banking sector	International Journal of In-surance and Finance	Quali-tative	Con-cep-tu-al	6
Metaverse in Banking: An Initiative for Banking Transforma-tion from Emerging Country Prospective	Sahoo D. & Ray S. (2023)	• Finding out the influence of Metaverse banking transactions on customers • Understanding the ways to create custom-er trust on Metaverse banking	Academy of Marketing Studies Journal	Mixed	Empir-ical	0

Metaverse and Banking Indus-try – 2023 The Year of Metaverse Adoption	Dubey V. et al. (2022)	• Discussing the ways to enhance the financial operations of banks through Metaverse	Technium	Quali-tative	Con-cep-tu-al	10
Metaverse Applica-tions in Smart Cities: Enabling Technolo-gies, Opportunities, Challenges, and Future Directions	Yaqoob I. et al. (2023)	• Reviewing the Metaverse technolo-gies and their feasibil-ity around different industries	Internet of Things	Quali-tative	Con-cep-tu-al	0

The banking in metaverse enables an individual to attend a virtual investor meeting that the bank has arranged and can easily discuss their investment intentions with an avatar financial expert. The Metaverse is another technological tool that banks can use to train their staff affordably and successfully. Banks can go over and beyond in promoting inclusivity and diversity by matching each client with a virtual assistant who is from a similar background. All of these strengthen the bond between people, foster a stronger feeling of connection, and eventually aid in retaining customers while boosting revenue (Sarkar, 2023). The following figure explains different metaverse services provided by the banking industry.

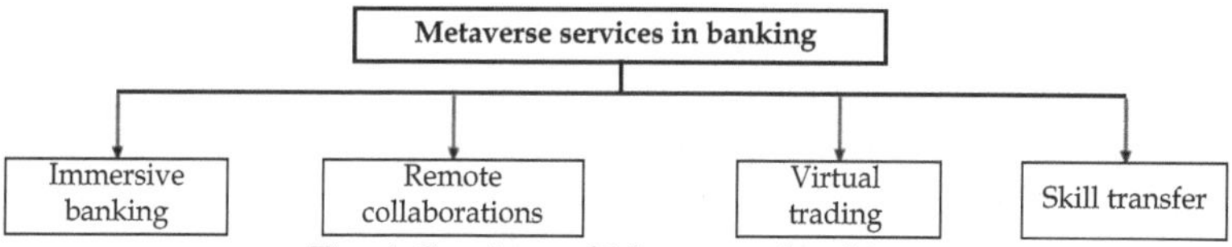

Fig. 4: Services of Metaverse banking
Source: (Bhat et al., 2023)

Discussions

The banking industry has always been quick to pick up on new trends. We have experienced how banks are embracing digitalization to transition from a paper-based to a paperless system. Branchless banking, which does not have actual branches, is another motivator. This paved the door for digital banks to open during the pandemic in 2020. Additionally, given how quickly technology is developing in only two years, banks will be shifting into the Metaverse. The forecasting for 2023–2028 indicates that banks and digital businesses will work together more; innovative rules will be implemented; and the adoption from industries other than financial services will automatically rise. Financial institutions can establish virtual locations in the Metaverse where clients can visit in their avatar form and receive services. VR and AR technology will be used to introduce mixed-reality experiences in this emerging field. The necessity for actual branch locations will disappear as a result of VR and AR technologies, which will enable customers to engage in financial transactions in a more personalised and exclusive way. By the end of this decade, 50% of banks globally are expected to embrace virtual reality (VR) or augmented reality (AR) as an additional channel for employee engagement and client transactions. (Kumar et al., 2023). Among the most notable features of Metaverse banking are virtual branches, virtual financial counselors, virtual product demos, and so forth.

In 2022, JP Morgan and HSBC were among the first institutions to open their Metaverse offices. Other banks that followed included Sygnum, Union Bank of India, Bank of Poland, and others (Naqvi, 2023). Kookmin Bank, based in South Korea, has introduced a virtual bank where customers can communicate with the avatar of the bank employee. With the MS HoloLens holographic headset, traders can view data as three-dimensional graphics thanks to a virtual workstation created by Citi. Customers may conduct banking operations and view records in virtual reality through an app developed by BNP Paribas. In Decentraland, JP Morgan Bank has launched a virtual club called Onyx Club. The Sandbox Metaverse is where Siam Commercial Bank has constructed its headquarters. A virtual lounge named Uni-Verse has been introduced by the Union Bank of India. To learn more about the bank's offerings, customers can select their avatar and enter the lounge. Only PCs and laptops can access the service. Kia.ai, an Indian company, has created a Metaverse called Kiyaverse specifically for Metaverse banking. Leading Swedish digital bank Mercobank has made its intention to join the NFT market public. Additionally, the bank is testing a digital asset security programme. Germany's Commerzbank has applied to Bafin for a local cryptocurrency license to store cryptocurrency assets.

In 2022, Accenture conducted a survey and found that 67% of global banking executives think that the Metaverse would benefit their companies. Furthermore, by 2030, 47% of bankers predict that customers will use AR and VR as another medium for financial transactions. To prosper in this new market, banks must carefully plan their approaches to guarantee lower costs for services, improved emotional connections, and flexibility in response to change while maintaining the capacity for additional innovation. The banking's requirement for branding is another reason to investigate the Metaverse. Growing more and more connected to the Metaverse is the tech-savvy Generation Z. To ensure their continued accessibility in the Metaverse, the banks must also remain reachable. Through this strategy, banks will be able to find new consumers in the Metaverse. Virtual reality simulations of different consumers would be quite approachable.

Conclusion

This study reviews the existing research on Metaverse banking by adopting the SLR process on the Google Scholar database. 14 research articles were identified for review to comply with the objectives once the selection criteria were performed. This research identifies the trends of Metaverse banking studies through the publication year. The researchers found that the majority of studies were conducted in the year 2023 following 2022 because the idea of catering services to customers through Metaverse banking has been thoroughly considered in these years. From the literature review, the researchers observed that the banking industry is now at its initial stage of operating Metaverse in their services because the method which was highly used by past researchers was a qualitative study and was conceptual.

The second objective of this study relates to examining the roles of Metaverse in banking. Although electronic systems have made banks readily accessible to everyone, virtual transactions within the Metaverse would establish an entirely different virtual banking ecosystem. Recently, there has been an ongoing and gradual rise in the acceptance of Metaverse in the banking industry since the technology delivers additional benefits to banks such as cost savings, quick communications, security enhancement, and feasible transactions. With Metaverse, it is also practicable to construct virtual assets that resemble conventional assets comprising securities, commodities, and paper currency. The potentiality of Metaverse to merge social networks with AR technology will revolutionize the banking industry by delivering pleasant experiences to customers.

Implications

Firstly, the industry personnel must switch themselves to contemporary technological advances to train their workforce and deal with customer services. Secondly, government institutions should grant necessary systems and services such as decentralised trading platforms for Metaverse operational activities. Lastly, this literature review can serve as a basis for future studies to make the industry more viable and compliant with current requirements.

Limitations

Since the present study emphasised reviewing the banking-related Metaverse research, future researchers may study the Metaverse in the context of other specific industries or professions such as education, healthcare, tourism, and marketing. This research adopts mainly Google Scholar as a source for SLR; databases comprising Scopus and Web of Science can additionally be applied to yield more findings. Future studies can opt for other literature review techniques and empirical-based findings by taking data from users and banking industry employees regarding Metaverse usage.

References

1. Bhat, J. R., AlQahtani, S. A., & Nekovee, M. (2023). FinTech Enablers, Use Cases, and Role of Future Internet of Things. *Journal of King Saud University-Computer and Information Sciences*, *35*(1), 87-101.
2. Dionisio, J. D. N., Iii, W. G. B., & Gilbert, R. (2013). 3D Virtual Worlds and the Metaverse: Current Status and Future Possibilities. *ACM Computing Surveys (CSUR)*, *45*(3), 1-38.
3. Dubey, V., Mokashi, A., Pradhan, R., Gupta, P., & Walimbe, R. (2022). Metaverse and Banking Industry–2023 The Year of Metaverse Adoption. *Technium*, *4*(10), 62-73.
4. Golf-Papez, M., Heller, J., Hilken, T., Chylinski, M., de Ruyter, K., Keeling, D. I., & Mahr, D. (2022). Embracing Falsity Through the Metaverse: The Case of Synthetic Customer Experiences. *Business Horizons*, *65*(6), 739-749.
5. Kumar, S., Sureka, R., Lucey, B. M., Dowling, M., Vigne, S., & Lim, W. M. (2023). MetaMoney: Exploring the Intersection of Virtual Worlds and Financial Systems. *Available at Social Science Research Network*, 1-26. https://ssrn.com/abstract=4400979
6. Naqvi, N. (2023). Metaverse for Public Good: Embracing the Societal Impact of Metaverse Economies. *The Journal of The British Blockchain Association*, *6*(1), 1-17.
7. Narin, N. G. (2021). A Content Analysis of the Metaverse Articles. *Journal of Metaverse*, *1*(1), 17-24.
8. Nightingale, A. (2009). A Guide to Systematic Literature Reviews. *Surgery (Oxford)*, *27*(9), 381-384.
9. Ozkaynar, K. (2022). Marketing Strategies of Banks in the Period of Metaverse, Blockchain, and Cryptocurrency in the Context of Consumer Behavior Theories. *International Journal of Insurance and Finance*, *2*(1), 1-12.
10. Pratama, K. J. (2023). Devising an Indonesian Legal Architecture for Metaverse Banking: Challenges and Opportunities. *Journal of Central Banking Law and Institutions*, *2*(1), 1-24.
11. Saad, A. A., Rehan, R., Abukakar Usman, A., & Salaudeen, A. O. (2023). The Metaverse and Islamic Financial Contracts: The Case of Ijarah. *F1000Research*, 1-14. https://doi.org/10.12688/f1000research.131519.1
12. Sahoo, D., & Ray, S. (2023). Metaverse in Banking: An Initiative for Banking Transformation from Emerging Country Prospective. *Academy of Marketing Studies Journal*, *27*(4), 1-15.

13. Sarkar, S. (2023). Banking in Metaverse Opportunities and Challenges. *The Management Accountant Journal, 58*(1), 63-67.
14. Sautunnida, L., Zain, N. R. M., Zakri, I. M. M., & Yahya, A. (2023). The Application of Artificial Intelligence in Metaverse: A New Challenge on Personal Data Protection in the Financial System. In *Islamic Sustainable Finance, Law and Innovation: Opportunities and Challenges*, 117-126, Springer Nature. https://link.springer.com/chapter/10.1007/978-3-031-27860-0_10
15. Seth, D., Gupta, M., & Singh, B. J. (2022). A Study to Analyse the Impact of Using the Metaverse in the Banking Industry to Augment Performance in a Competitive Environment. In *Applying Metalytics to Measure Customer Experience in the Metaverse*, 9-16, IGI Global. https://www.igi-global.com/chapter/a-study-to-analyse-the-impact-of-using-the-metaverse-in-the-banking-industry-to-augment-performance-in-a-competitive-environment/309300
16. Shen, B., Tan, W., Guo, J., Zhao, L., & Qin, P. (2021). How to Promote User Purchase in Metaverse? A Systematic Literature Review on Consumer Behavior Research and Virtual Commerce Application Design. *Applied Sciences, 11*(23), 1–29.
17. Srivastava, K., & Dhamija, S. (2021). Paradigm Shift in Indian Banking Industry with Special Reference to Artificial Intelligence. *Turkish Journal of Computer and Mathematics Education, 12*(5), 1623-1629.
18. Thome, A. M. T., Scavarda, L. F., & Scavarda, A. J. (2016). Conducting Systematic Literature Review in Operations Management. *Production Planning & Control, 27*(5), 408-420.
19. Vakiti, J. L., & SL, T. D. (2023). The Future Innovation of Fintech in the Metaverse Banking. *International Research Journal on Advanced Science Hub, 5*(5), 474-482.
20. Vergallo, R., & Mainetti, L. (2022). The role of Technology in Improving the Customer Experience in the Banking Sector: A Systematic Mapping Study. *IEEE Access, 10*, 118024-118042 https://doi.org/10.1109/ACCESS.2022.3218010
21. Xiao, Y., & Watson, M. (2019). Guidance on Conducting a Systematic Literature Review. *Journal of planning education and research, 39*(1), 93-112.
22. Yaqoob, I., Salah, K., Jayaraman, R., & Omar, M. (2023). Metaverse Applications in Smart Cities: Enabling Technologies, Opportunities, Challenges, and Future Directions. *Internet of Things*, 1-19. https://doi.org/10.1016/j.iot.2023.100884
23. Yathiraju, N., & Dash, B. (2023). Big Data and Metaverse Revolutionizing the Futuristic Fintech Industry. *International Journal of Computer Science & Information Technology, 15*(1), 1-13.

3

Financial Services and the Metaverse: Opportunities and Challenges

Dr. Jagadeesh H[1] *& Dr. Satish Modi*[2]

Abstract

This article explores the growth of the Metaverse idea, the emergence of the Metaverse myth, continuing innovation activities about the advancement of the relevant technologies, and the real financial development of those companies, or funds, that are connected to the Metaverse. While contrasting the Metaverse with the current state of the Internet, it explores some of the business model breakthroughs and others that are anticipated to arise. One of the most intriguing investing topics for the upcoming ten years seems to be the metaverse. The financial industry is being shaped in the metaverse by more investments than at any point before as well as other underpinning financial operations. As they aim for comprehensive capital exposure, investors are not just investing in the metaverse but also in related markets, which are changing as a result. The conclusions offer potential directions for further investigation. Incorporating the metaverse into the business model of a financial institution presents several challenges with control of the information or regularisation issues, although there are many benefits and the metaverse continues to be in the early stages in the sense of technological development or application possibilities. We all concur that the metaverse still has a way to go before realizing all of its potential from both a technological and commercial perspective.

Keywords: *Metaverse, financing, technology and business*

Introduction

As widespread adoption of metaverse technology occurs across the entire BFSI industry, the age of metaverse financial services has arrived. Live entertainment, video games, and social media now dominate metaverse use cases, but there is also a lot of room for financial services. Neal Stephenson introduced the concept of a metaverse in his science fiction novel "Snow Crash" (Evans et al., 2022) over thirty years ago, but it has only been in the past few years that substantial efforts have been made to implement it. The debut of the virtual environment Second Life in 2003 marked the beginning of appearances to a sizable audience. The idea changed during the ensuing years, mostly in the gaming industry (Cao, 2022). Only 30% of businesses will have services or goods prepared for this new market by 2025, according to Gartner, and only one out of every four individuals will make use of an average of an hour each day there. This evolution has been influenced by several causes, including new technology advancements and the emergence of other related advances in the appropriation and exchange of virtual assets.

1 Assistant professor, Department of Political Science, Government First Grade College Gauribidanur, Chikkabalpur district, Karnataka

2 Assistant Professor, Department of Commerce, Indira Gandhi National Tribal University, Amarkantak M.P

The thrust of the COVID-19 epidemic, along with blockchains, cryptocurrencies, and Non-Fungible-Tokens (NFT), demonstrated the significance and viability of transferral operations in a virtual environment. Additionally, the creation, the money invested in, and the knowledge of the Metaverse were expedited by Facebook's significant stake in it, a major Big Tech that even modified the name to Meta to clearly emphasize its commitment. Facebook altered the name of its business and invested more than $10 billion in the Metaverse's development in 2021 alone (Henz, 2022; Kraus et al, 2022).

In reality, based on the Wall Street Journal, it presently only has 200,000 active users each month, which is far less than the 500,000 people it aimed to reach this year as well as its initial target of 300,000 current users by February 2022. Additionally, according to the same source, no more than 10% of Horizon World's venues or areas are visited by a minimum of 50 people. In other words, just 1,000 of the 10,000 locations present in this metaverse receive an average of 50 visits. The fact that people stop using the application after an initial month is another important development. We ask whether financial institutions and their clients are ready for this paradigm change in light of this information and transfer our attention to the realm of financial services. Therefore, the greatest obstacle for financial services organisations at this early stage is to study the metaverse's various potentials and test its use in various use cases rather than diving in with a predetermined plan. It's unlikely that major banks or insurers will make the switch to these virtual worlds anytime soon given the unpredictability of a technology like this.

The Metaverse and the Financial Sector

Over the next three to five years, the energy sector aims to invest roughly 18% of its digital investment expenditures in the metaverse, followed by the automotive, machinery and assembly (17%), high technology (17%), tourism (15%), and media and entertainment (15%) sectors. Depending on the degree of disruption, the total accessible market (TAM) for the metaverse in the US might reach USD 8.3 trillion. Millions of individuals exposed to the interactive digital environment have the potential to significantly change how they live and work in the future. That ecosystem is anticipated to be powered by NFTs. Every morning, a fresh metaverse-related headline greets us. There is a constant flow of stories and news coverage, with both positive and negative news stories being common. Because of the current degree of interest, it appears necessary to provide new content on the topic constantly.

In this regard, the majority of the headlines and communications come across the center on two main subjects: (1) immersive technology (platforms, devices, fresh investment in the market, new participants, etc.); and (2) unresolved questions that are typical in a stage as early as the one we are presently in. With this study, we aim to offer a novel or additional approach, either in terms of potential responses to certain of the questions we ask ourselves now, or, more importantly, in terms of real-world use cases, a less researched field. Let's concentrate on the financial sector and how it might benefit from the metaverse in future generations and during these early stages. The financial sector aids people in achieving their objectives, following their aspirations, and safeguarding their most important possessions, but it does not serve as an end in and of itself. The financial sector offers options that, typically from an economic perspective, help us accomplish goals that are challenging for us. And the things we cherish and need most are typically the ones that are hardest for us to obtain.

The metaverse offers the financial sector some opportunities. It might be applied to encourage a sense of intimacy with the subject or to facilitate activities that aid clients in achieving their objectives. Similarly, it might help people comprehend the tools the organization gives its customers access to accomplish that goal. And why not, it might even aid the worker in his day-to-day performance. All of this is done with a strong emphasis on experience, which is one of the core tenets of the metaverse. The technical aspects of the Metaverse have received some attention in the literature up to this point (Dwivedi, 2022), and various definitions have been put forth (Sparkes, 2021; Ball, 2022), however the economic angle, the actual spread of the technology, and the current state of the Metaverse's potential business model are still understudied. This article will examine some of these issues critically while attempting to comprehend the current state of affairs in the various industries, looking at the level of interest expressed and the investments generated, as well as summarising a few of the business models Innovations (BMI) which have so far emerged in the various fields linked to the Metaverse.

This paradigm has a wide range of potential applications in the future, but the metaverse might be helpful now. For instance, it could play a crucial role in boosting awareness campaigns and enhancing the company's inventive axis visibility. Whatever the case, we are still a long way from fully understanding everything that the current situation might offer the financial sector and society at large. The following portions of the report will have some opinions on all of this. We will proceed, however, with the caution of those who approach a notion as obviously radical as this using an as-yet-constrained perspective. information that can be added to business innovation roadmaps and used to help decide strategically on transaction activity occurring within the metaverse domain. metaverse potential. Industry leaders use our unique tools and services for business excellence to unleash new opportunities for company growth and unrivaled returns on investment.

Issues and use cases specific to the Banking Sector

We frequently contrast the idea of the metaverse with that of novel virtual worlds and full immersion, but in reality, we have been utilizing this kind of technology for generations without categorizing it as belonging to the metaverse. For instance, the video gaming industry has made enormous strides recently, and the younger generations are accustomed to exploring expansive and practically unlimited virtual worlds. Therefore, it does not appear that this describes what the metaverse is or what is causing the information storm to develop around it. The numerous creative definitions of the Metaverse that can be explored in both the academic literature and the tech-related press demonstrate the ground-breaking originality it represents. The Metaverse can be described in a variety of ways, including as a thing or a service that exists at a location, or even a specific point in time. An infinite number of models (digital representations of people) can participate in social, political, economic, and cultural activities in the three-dimensional virtual environment known as the Metaverse. The Metaverse needs to be examined analytically as a result of its three basic parts: software, content, and hardware (Kaddoura, and Husseiny, 2023).

According to Chen and Zhang (2022), the Metaverse is predicted to alter educational systems (immersive education), increase opportunities for professional and social networking, change the healthcare system (leading to multifaceted medical information standards, and social information fusion to, telemedicine, and online health management), and improve transparency in the evaluation of second-hand markets and product quality. Nearly all industries that might gain from direct, despite virtual, user contact may be impacted, however, as with many fundamental advances, we are unable to foresee the full range of potential future applications at this time. The metaverse does more than just provide us with a new channel. It brings with it the idea of a digital possession, a brand-new thing of want for which users of these sites are prepared to fork over the money, occasionally with insane glee. if tracking patents is the most effective approach to gauge innovation. Patents are acknowledged as an accurate measure of innovation, if not at the aggregate level, even with the reasonable caveat that they do not account for all innovations created (Acs et al., 2002; Burhan et al., 2017). The Metaverse is unquestionably gaining significant economic interests from a variety of viewpoints with these various uncertainties, the fiscal options we already stated, and the less-than-positive impressions expressed by many commentators (Narin, 2021). As a result, we have all seen extremely major changes in industries like real estate and the arts, along with the growth of a variety of consumer items that some people are even prioritizing over their actual physical counterparts. The emergence of a new market is caused by the rise of this brand-new transnationality, which is frequently backed by the virtual currencies of these platforms. a market where a wide range of solutions work well and where there are still many things to come. A market that many organizations have dared measure by supplying real-world vertigo numbers.

Possible use cases for the Banking Industry in the Future

After examining the basic challenges at the core of the present debate and taking into consideration the metaverse's immaturity and beginnings, we'll discuss several potential courses for action and use cases that banks could take in the short- to medium-term. The target audience of the experience will be split into internal and external customers (workers and people who want to be), to create a preliminary classification of these scenarios of use. In the sector right now, there are examples of the initial initiatives directed at both. Many other businesses from traditional non-tech industries are looking at the Metaverse primarily as users in addition to the numerous companies that are providing technologies and equipment for it. One can start with branding and marketing as one of the main drivers for businesses joining the Metaverse (Rauschnabel, 2022). Joining the Metaverse increases visibility for both big and small brands because it can be seen as a novel advertisement perspective (Kim, 2021; Taylor, 2022). Consider the Metaverse to be the future frontier for shopping online as this is particularly relevant for platforms used for e-commerce. This is a related prospect (and economic opportunity). The sellers may look for ways to show their tangible goods to customers in novel, comprehensive, and engaging ways to boost both customer loyalty and product demand (Jeong et al., 2022).

The metaverse can present chances that are intriguing to investigate, from reaching out to new customers to devising tactics to boost awareness and offer visibility, marketing, and growth. The majority of market-wide activities to date are concentrating on this client profile.

1. Gaining and keeping a new client: If reaching younger consumers is one of our entity's goals, the metaverse may serve as a helpful tool for businesses looking to increase target user traffic. Customers are the ones who adapt to technology advancements the fastest, so providing experiences based on what they want to do might be a great approach to draw attention to our business and attract potential customers.

2. Improving financial literacy: Few clients are truly aware of all their bank may provide them due to the range and occasionally complexity of the range of services and goods offered by financial institutions. Professional advice delivered via the branch network or remote support services has traditionally been crucial. In this sense, and particularly for the younger generations, making use of immersive scenarios that mimic real-world problems for which the financial sector might offer answers can be a significant area of work that facilitates essential information about goods and services.
3. Increasing brand recognition and placement within the bank's primary target client segments: In our always-connected world, it can be challenging to get customers to focus on a particular product or service since they are always being exposed to stimuli through various communication channels. In this regard, it is satisfying to witness the effects that the developments and efforts that are being introduced in this new arena are having on diverse entities on a global scale. The return on the investments made will probably be substantial in terms of notoriety.
4. Commercial development/expansion strategies: As we've already mentioned, most geographies, notably the more complex ones, which are frequently among the most lucrative for business entities, are constrained by the typical financial environment of a corporation. Through the metaverse, that would be feasible to reveal how these products function and the value they offer differently, making it easier for people to comprehend their dangers and advantages. This creates a chance for banks as well. Additionally supporting an axis like sustainability could enhance the point of view and make it more appealing to particular customer types.
5. Employee education/awareness: One easy technique to increase efficiency using metaverse is to promote self-learning of specific procedures when traditional methods are not efficient or if the training expenses necessary to duplicate certain conditions are high. For instance, it might be possible to replicate some parts of the office system without being physically present.
6. Enhancement of process efficiency: Employees may encounter procedures that call for complex information processing, spatial vision, or simulations to make decisions. Immersive environments, such as those offered by the metaverse, can streamline some of these procedures by permitting the relocation of particular actions and considerably lowering the cost of some expenses. The usage of this new technology could help reconcile and enhance working conditions as some of these processes are compatible with teleworking methods.
7. Employee socialization: In the corporate world, remote employment is already commonplace. The metaverse can be a wonderful addition to the low-cost organization of meetings, conferences, workshops, work groups, and events for geographically distributed teams.

The replication of real-world business models, but with the addition of fresh content via the Metaverse platforms, such as sustainable Metaverse tourism, augmented reality (AR), lifelogging, mirror worlds, and virtual worlds, as suggested by Smart (2007) (Go & Kang, 2022; Koo et al., 2022; Gurosy et al., 2022). The route through the metaverse is made up of various access points and phases rather than being singular or linear. Numerous businesses have already started to develop projects in the sectors of augmented reality and virtual reality, as well as initiatives involving artificial intelligence and machine learning. We must not disregard blockchain-related proof of concept (PoC) efforts or genuine initiatives. Naturally, we can't help but bring up a few interesting Metaverse applications that could help society as a whole.

Transforming Shortcomings into Strengths

Other barriers must be added, including the costly nature of devices (glasses, the headsets, powerful equipment, etc.) or regulation, in addition to some crucial factors, such as those stated above (uncertainty about the short-term potential of this technology, confined Money invested approximation through examples of concept instead of through real exercises). These factors combine to make the metaverse an actuality that is still an ongoing goal for practically every industry, not only insurers and financial services firms.

Company providers can, however, focus on other areas to make sure they are prepared to provide their goods and services in the metaverse when the time comes.

1. As previously noted, interoperability will be a major force in the development of the metaverse. It is a notion that is strongly related to our perspective on Financial Liquid Ecosystems, in which we hold that only businesses will have a relevant position in these spaces if they expose their systems to third parties and connect with those of others. The metaverse will be an additional component of the ecosystems. Therefore, all the efforts that companies are currently taking to lay the groundwork for "their metaverse" will be crucial for when the new reality manifests, which, as experts point out, will most likely happen in no less than ten years.
2. Users need security in their operations and transactions, just like they would in another virtual environment. To succeed, insurance companies must be able to provide clients with security across the full spectrum of activities they engage in within the metaverse (virtual identity, personal data protection, protection for making payments or renewals, etc.). The opposing side of this coin is how insurance might develop fresh goods and services to safeguard their clients against those dangers. In this regard, we examine many particular situations in the article where companies could develop new products related to the growth of the metaverse.
3. Ethics and data use: As the metaverse and all of its accompanying technologies take off, financial institutions will have more capacity to gather consumer data. As a result, the creation of interactions that are distinct from the ones that are now available allows for the collection of a large amount of data that consumers currently are unwilling to share with insurers in the metaverse. As a result, insurers will need to evaluate their usage of such data. Companies will need to know what to do with the data generated by, for instance, gamification actions or actions that continuously track a user's activity. Utilising that data ethically and transparently will be essential to developing fresh, engaging experiences in the realm of the metaverse.
4. Connection to users: The emotional underpinning of the technology in the metaverse is one of its greatest strengths. Since the advent of social networks, this has been abundantly evident that users are motivated by factors like group participation, peer acknowledgment, or the need to demonstrate to others what they have accomplished. The metaverse is a fusion of various technologies, some of which are based on senses like sight. However, the emotions that a person exhibits in response to something (a commercial, an event, a service) are as crucial. With the use of technology like facial

recognition or machine learning, businesses may be able to read customer emotions virtually instantly.

It starts with a straightforward explanation of the Metaverse and makes educated guesses about possible evolutions of the multiple/single Metaverse conclusion and the centralization/decentralization division. Additionally, it offers an outline of the Metaverse's actual financial results. The actual technological barriers and financial setbacks, however, shouldn't be taken for granted because a more comprehensive Internet experience is soon to arrive. But when it does, all the major concerns about Internet 2.0—privacy, identity, content filtering, and market tipping—might resurface, albeit in a more drastic way. To prevent the potential that the Metaverse, with its numerous wonders, has bad effects on society, consumers, and markets, it is crucial to comprehend what is coming and to be prepared to prepare for it.

Conclusion

Many of the technologies that make up the metaverse are not new, even though it is portrayed to us as such. For instance, the video gaming industry has advanced significantly in recent years, and the younger generations are now used to exploring expansive and practically unlimited virtual worlds. Furthermore, the benefits of this technology are not exclusive to the entertainment industry. When financial organizations like banks or other firms invest in the creation of a metaverse, both customers and staff stand to gain. This is especially true when the customer's view is that regular interactions with the agent are not necessary. Some benefits for the consumer include enticing and acquiring new customers, boosting awareness of the portfolio of goods and services, positioning the brand, and garnering the public's interest in a society overrun with stimuli. On the inside, the metaverse can encourage self-learning, draw in talent, increase process efficiency, and promote socialization between staff members.

The key takeaway from this paper's comparison between World Wide Web 2.0 and the Metaverse is that the latter requires a more advanced infrastructure, technologies, and tools to provide users with an entirely satisfactory experience. For their development, implementation, and widespread adoption, they will need a significant investment of time and money. The current perception of the Metaverse as having low quality and, occasionally, a lack of engaging content and engagement can only be dispelled if there has been a major increase in user numbers, which can only occur in the context of an experience of the highest caliber. Incorporating the metaverse into the business model of a financial institution presents many challenges with control of information or regularisation issues, although there are many benefits and the metaverse continues to be in the early stages in the sense of technological development or application possibilities. But the metaverse won't disappear any time soon. From our perspective, its use will continue to rise.

References

1. Acs, Z. J., Anselin, L., & Varga, A. (2002). Patents and innovation counts as measures of regional production of new knowledge. *Research policy, 31*(7), 1069-1085.
2. Ball, M. (2022). The metaverse: and how it will revolutionize everything. Liveright Publishing.
3. Burhan, M., Singh, A. K., & Jain, S. K. (2017). Patents as proxy for measuring innovations: A case of changing patent filing behavior in Indian public funded research organizations. *Technological Forecasting and Social Change*, 123, 181-190.
4. Cao, L. (2022). Decentralized AI: Edge Intelligence and Smart Blockchain, Metaverse, Web3, and DeSci. *IEEE Intelligent Systems, 37*(3), 6-19.

5. Chen, D., & Zhang, R. (2022). Exploring Research Trends of Emerging Technologies in a Health Metaverse: A Bibliometric Analysis. Available at SSRN 3998068.
6. Dwivedi, Y. K., Hughes, L., Baabdullah, A. M., Ribeiro-Navarrete, S., Giannakis, M., Al-Debei, M. M., & Wamba, S. F. (2022). Metaverse beyond the hype: Multidisciplinary perspectives on emerging challenges, opportunities, and agenda for research, practice and policy. *International Journal of Information Management*, 66, 102542.
7. Evans, L., Frith, J., & Saker, M. (2022). The Roots of the Metaverse. In *From Microverse to Metaverse: Modelling the Future through Today's Virtual Worlds* (pp. 15-24). Emerald Publishing Limited.
8. Go, H., & Kang, M. (2022). Metaverse tourism for sustainable tourism development: tourism agenda 2030. Tourism Review, (ahead-of-print).
9. Gursoy, D., Malodia, S., & Dhir, A. (2022). The metaverse in the hospitality and tourism industry: An overview of current trends and future research directions. *Journal of Hospitality Marketing & Management*, 1-8.
10. Henz, P. (2022). The societal impact of the Metaverse. *Discover Artificial Intelligence*, *2*(1), 19.
11. Jeong, H., Yi, Y., & Kim, D. (2022). An innovative e-commerce platform incorporating the metaverse to live commerce. *International Journal of Innovative Computing, Information and Control, 18*(1), 221-229.
12. Kaddoura, S., & Al Husseiny, F. (2023). The rising trend of Metaverse in education: challenges, opportunities, and ethical considerations. *PeerJ Computer Science, 9*, e1252.
13. Kim, J. (2021). Advertising in the Metaverse: Research agenda. *Journal of Interactive Advertising, 21*(3), 141-144.
14. Koo, C., Kwon, J., Chung, N., & Kim, J. (2022). Metaverse tourism: conceptual framework and research propositions. *Current Issues in Tourism*, 1-7.
15. Kraus, S., Kanbach, D. K., Krysta, P. M., Steinhoff, M. M., & Tomini, N. (2022). Facebook and the creation of the metaverse: radical business model innovation or incremental transformation?. *International Journal of Entrepreneurial Behavior & Research, 28* (9), 52-77. Electronic copy available at: https://ssrn.com/abstract=4382717 The Metaverse: technology, financing and economics 29 Robert Schuman Centre of Advanced Studies.
16. Narin, N. G. (2021). A content analysis of the metaverse articles. *Journal of Metaverse, 1*(1), 17-24.
17. Park, S. M., & Kim, Y. G. (2022). A Metaverse: Taxonomy, components, applications, and open challenges. *IEEE* Access, 10, 4209-4251.
18. Rauschnabel, P. A., Babin, B. J., Tom Dieck, M. C., Krey, N., & Jung, T. (2022). What is augmented reality marketing? Its definition, complexity, and future. *Journal of Business Research, 142*, 1140- 1150.
19. Smart, J., Cascio, J., Paffendorf, J., Bridges, C., Hummel, J., Hursthouse, J., & Moss, R. (2007). A cross-industry public foresight project. In Proc. Metaverse Roadmap Pathways 3DWeb, 1-28.
20. Sparkes, M. (2021). What is a metaverse, New Scientist, 251, (3348). Stephenson, N. (1992). Snow crash. Penguin Random House.
21. Taylor, C. R. (2022). Research on advertising in the metaverse: a call to action. *International Journal of Advertising, 41*(3), 383-384.

4

She's Empowered: An Examination of Socio-economic Status and Perception of Tribal Women in Sonbhadra's SHGs

Aditi Sarawagi[1] *& Dr. M. Sanjoy Singh*[2]

Abstract

SHGs help women in all spheres of empowerment, but they also have some challenges associated with it. Sonbhadra, being the highest tribal-dominated district of Uttar Pradesh faced various impediments which have been addressed by SHGs. The study aims to assess the socio-economic status of tribal women in Sonbhadra's SHGs and examine how these factors influence their perceptions of the groups. Data from 106 tribal women beneficiaries of SHGs were collected using multi-stage sampling. Questionnaires with both open-ended and close-ended questions were used for data collection. A reliability test was carried out on the factors considered, followed by correlation analysis and ANOVA using SPSS 23. The findings indicate that participation in SHGs leads to an improvement in the socio-economic status of tribal women, reflected in increased income and savings, and there is a significant association between socio-economic factors and perceptions related to esteem and psychological needs. However, the study did not find a significant relationship between economic and social factors and financial perception. Tailored programs focusing on education, healthcare, and employment opportunities can uplift their socio-economic status and foster holistic empowerment. Strengthening SHGs through ongoing training, capacity building, and mentorship is vital to sustain their impact.

Keywords: *Socio-economic, tribal women, perception, self-help groups, empowerment*

Introduction

India's rich cultural diversity and socio-economic tapestry are intertwined with different tribal populations, each of which contributes a distinct thread to the nation's social fabric. The tribal women of Sonbhadra are a vital but frequently marginalized minority in India's broad socio-cultural environment. Sonbhadra, a district in Uttar Pradesh, has long been home to a variety of indigenous communities, each with its heritage, traditions, and challenges (Chattopadhyaya, 2008). Tribal women have traditionally faced various impediments to empowerment, reinforced by deep-rooted patriarchal traditions and socio-economic inequities, despite repeated initiatives to alleviate their socio-economic concerns (Meera & Yekta, 2021). Sonbhadra's indigenous populations, including the Gonds, Bhuiya, Chero, Patari, and others, have a long history of marginalization, exclusion, and exploitation (Verma, 2013). Poverty, illiteracy, and a lack of basic services have exacerbated their vulnerability and limited their prospects for growth and development. Among this already marginalized community, indigenous women

[1] Research Scholar, Department of Commerce Indira Gandhi National Tribal University Amarkantak, Madhya Pradesh

[2] Assistant Professor, Department of Commerce Indira Gandhi National Tribal University Amarkantak, Madhya Pradesh

face numerous layers of prejudice (Weaver, 2022). Because of the intersectionality of gender and ethnicity, they are more vulnerable to socio-economic exploitation and violence inside their homes and in the larger society. In different parts of India, Self-Help Groups (SHGs) have arisen as a revolutionary vehicle for addressing gender disparities and poverty (Tiwari & Thakur, 2007). These community-based organizations, primarily comprised of women, provide a platform for collective savings, microcredit access, and skill-building possibilities. SHGs empower women to transcend traditional gender roles, attain financial autonomy, and increase their decision-making authority within their families and communities by building solidarity and collaboration among their members (Meenai, 2003). SHGs empower women by fostering financial independence and social cohesiveness, as well as encouraging collective action (Kumar et al., 2018). As a result, these organizations play a critical role in altering indigenous women's standing within their communities and, perhaps, in society at large. The emergence of SHGs in Sonbhadra represents a positive movement in recognizing indigenous women's capacity as change agents. These organizations help women gain access to financial resources, allowing them to invest in income-generating enterprises and escape the cycle of poverty. Furthermore, SHGs foster information sharing, provide training in a variety of livelihood skills, and empower women through workshops on health, sanitation, and gender rights (Suguna, 2006). SHGs have been promoted as a tool to alleviate poverty and empower women by the government, non-governmental organizations (NGOs), and development agencies (Jain & Jain, 2012). Despite the broad adoption of SHGs, the impact of these programmes might vary greatly depending on the environment and unique issues encountered by the target community. However, a thorough investigation of the dynamics of tribal women's empowerment within the framework of Sonbhadra's SHGs remains relatively unexplored.

Understanding the complex relationship between socio-economic circumstances and indigenous women's perceptions of SHGs is therefore critical to promoting a more complete and inclusive approach to women empowerment. This study work aims to fill a key information gap by diving into the complexities of tribal women's socio-economic situation and perceptions of SHGs in Sonbhadra. The article will attempt to analyze the influence of SHGs on the empowerment process and the subsequent changes in tribal women's perceptions within their communities. A review of tribal women's socio-economic situation and perceptions inside SHGs is a critical step toward constructing an inclusive and equitable society in which the full potential of every individual, regardless of gender or ethnicity, may be realized. Only by doing such an in-depth and empathetic study can we expect to establish a more powerful and just future for indigenous women, moving them from the periphery to the forefront of growth and development.

Brief Description of the Study Area

Sonbhadra district, located in the south-eastern edge of Uttar Pradesh and renowned as the "energy capital of India," is the state's second biggest district. The district has a total area of 6905 sq. km. The rural area is 6779.6 sq. km., while the urban area is 125.4 sq. km. Sonbhadra is one of Uttar Pradesh's most backward districts in terms of economic, social, and political development. This district was rated second in terms of area, 51st in terms of population, and 52nd in terms of literacy (64 percent) in the state. The total population of the district is 1,862,559, where males are 971,344 and females are 891,215. The Gond, Kharwar, Paharia, Agaria, Panika, Patari, Bhuiya, Chero, and other notable tribal tribes have lived in this area since the dawn of civilization. The total tribal population of the district is 385,018 where males are 197,825 and females are 187,193 (Census, 2011). They have a very unhappy existence as a result of their social and economic backgrounds, as well as a lack of political support (Gupta & Bilas, 2017). The district's literacy rate (64%) is lower than the state average (67.7%) and it ranks 22nd in the state in terms of sex ratio (918), which is higher than the state average of 912 females per thousand males. The total main and marginal workers are 730,399 while non-workers are 1,132,160. Of the main and marginal workers, 19.31% are cultivators, 50.83% are agricultural laborers, and 4.03% are workers in the household industry (Census, 2011).

Review of Literature

Numerous studies have been conducted to examine the socio-economic state of indigenous women in Sonbhadra, showing a picture of fragility and marginalization. According to Kirmayer et al. (2009) and Hentschel & Waters (2002), poverty, illiteracy, and a lack of access to healthcare and basic utilities are common among indigenous women. The study emphasized the importance of focused interventions to overcome these differences and increase indigenous communities' well-being. Also, Sieder & Sierra (2010) have highlighted the necessity of recognizing the intersections of gender and ethnicity in maintaining socio-economic gaps among tribal women. They found that indigenous women endure additional prejudice, resulting in limited access to resources and decision-making authority. However, Kuokkanen (2011) emphasized the importance of property rights for indigenous women in Sonbhadra, since land ownership is critical to their economic stability and social prestige. SHGs have been widely explored and recorded for their revolutionary potential in empowering women. Kapoor (2019) and Singh (2016) found that SHGs improved women's economic independence, financial decision-making, and entrepreneurship. This research showed how SHGs assist women to gain access to loans, invest in income-generating businesses, and break free from poverty. Additionally, some studies have emphasized the function of SHGs in boosting social empowerment and creating female solidarity. Padmaja & Bantilan (2007) concluded that tribal women's engagement in SHGs boosted their social capital and expanded their social networks, allowing them to defy established gender norms. Suguna (2006) and Khan (2015) stated that SHGs serve as forums for capacity building, skill upgrading, and promoting gender rights awareness. Conversely, SHGs encounter several hurdles in their efforts to empower indigenous women, despite their revolutionary potential. According to Parida & Sinha (2010), the long-term sustainability of SHGs is dependent on aspects such as group dynamics, leadership, and external assistance. Internal disagreements and a lack of timely credit were recognized as important barriers to SHG's performance. Kumar & Kumar (2020) also noted how socio-cultural norms and a load of family chores frequently limit tribal women's active engagement in SHG activities. Furthermore, as observed by McCallum (2014), indigenous women's susceptibility is exacerbated by a lack of access to information and resources, restricting their capacity to make informed decisions.

Participation of tribal women in SHGs has resulted in small but important changes in their communities' views. According to Arora (2016) and Mahmud et al. (2012), indigenous women's position within households increased as they attained financial independence and actively participated in decision-making. This newly found agency elicited favorable responses from male family members, resulting in enhanced gender dynamics in the household. Brahma et al. (2019) found that SHGs served as forums for discourse and collective action, opposing patriarchal norms and practices. Cheston & Kuhn (2002) states that as indigenous women rose to the position of community leaders, their efforts were recognized and respected, instilling a sense of empowerment and respect among peers and community members. Several government programmes and policies have been put in place to alleviate the socio-economic issues that indigenous women confront in Sonbhadra. Abrol et al. (2020) and Khaki (2018) examined the efficacy of several government programmes, including the National Rural Livelihood Mission (NRLM) and the Pradhan Mantri Jan Dhan Yojana (PMJDY). The study emphasized the favorable effects of these programmes on financial inclusion, livelihood possibilities, and women's empowerment. The importance of non-governmental organizations (NGOs) and civil society in empowering tribal women in Sonbhadra cannot be underscored. NGOs play an important role in mobilizing and organizing SHGs, offering training, and enabling links to financial institutions, according to studies by Devi et al. (2014) and Sarkar & Singh (2006). These organizations have been critical in bridging the gap between government policy and the ground realities encountered by tribal women, guaranteeing the efficient implementation of empowerment programmes. Furthermore, Kilby (2010) emphasized the importance of community-based interventions by NGOs in breaking conventional gender norms and supporting women's leadership. These organizations have been able to raise knowledge about women's rights and generate a collective feeling of agency among indigenous women through interacting with local communities.

Statement of Problem

The tribal community of Sonbhadra has its own distinctive cultural and social aspects but they are very backward in the view of socio-economic conditions for centuries. They share 20.67 percent of the total population of the district yet they have remained outside the realm of the general development process due to their habitation in forests and hilly tracts. Several initiatives have been taken for the improvement in the socio-economic status of the community women but the sustainable result was not obtained. Microfinance through SHGs helps improve the socio-economic status of the poor, especially women. The microfinance intervention has been found beneficial in some regions and in other regions, not many benefits have been observed. The perception and experiences of tribal women participating in Self-Help Groups (SHGs) in Sonbhadra are influenced by their socioeconomic status, yet there is a lack of comprehensive research addressing this relationship. The existing literature fails to explore how factors such as income, employment, savings, access to resources, and social support systems affect the perception of tribal women toward SHGs in Sonbhadra.

Objectives of the Study

1. To check the socio-economic status of Sonbhadra's SHG's tribal women.
2. To examine the influence of socio-economic status on the perception of SHG's tribal women.

Research Methodology

Sample Design

Tribal women of Sonbhadra's SHG were targeted for the study, for which the list of beneficiaries of Ghorawal and Robertsganj block was gathered from the NRLM office in Sonbhadra. Of 2607 tribal beneficiaries, a list of 500 tribal women beneficiaries was made available. Response from 180 women beneficiaries was gathered. Women who were part of an SHG for more than 1 year have been considered for the study. Therefore 106 responses were considered for the study as they meet the study's requirements. More participation of target respondents is limited by various factors, including unavailability, time constraints on the part of the borrowers, respondents' locations, and misinformation. Multi-stage sampling technique was used for the data collection.

Variables considered for the Study

Economic factors such as income, employment, savings and investment, the improved purchasing power of fixed and current assets, and other facilities such as improvement in food consumption patterns and loan availability were considered. Social factors such as decision-making power, the standard of living, interpersonal relationships, social recognition, etc. were considered. Financial perception, perception of esteem needs, and psychological needs were also taken. Economic and Social factors are formative independent variables, while Perception-related factors are reflective dependent variables.

Tools and Tests

The questionnaire consisting of both open-ended and close-ended questions was used to examine the stated objectives. A reliability test was carried out on the factors considered for the study over the 212 respondents. The scale is considered reliable if the coefficient equals or exceeds 0.70 (Kilic, 2016). Further examination was carried out based on the Cronbach Alpha score. The relationship between social factors, economic factors, and factors related to perception was analyzed using correlation analysis. Additionally, the inferential statistics F-test was used to observe significant differences between the respondents' social, and economic factors and perception. SPSS 23 was used to carry out statistical tests.

Results and Discussions

Of 106 women beneficiaries, 68.8% of women fall within the middle-aged group. 90.6% of women were married, and the rest were widows or unmarried. Regarding their education, 80.2% of women were educated, of which 53.8% got primary education. 19.8% of women were not educated, but they could sign. Farmers and farm laborers constitute 47.1%, and industrial labor constitute 21.7%. 16% of respondents are self-employed, and have business experience of more than five years belonging mainly to 'Generation X.' Regarding monthly family income and savings before and after joining SHG, 59.4% of women have monthly family income before joining SHG in the range of 5001-10000, and rest have income below 5000. After joining SHG, 86.8% of women have income in the range of 5001-10000, and 11.3% in the range of 10001-15000. 88.7% of women had savings of less than 1000 before joining SHG, but after joining SHG, 83.9% of women had savings of more than 500, 31.1% in the range 1501-2000.

Table 1: Reliability test on factors undertaken for the study

Particulars	Total no. of Items	Cronbach's Alpha
Economic	15	0.899
Social	8	0.926
Financial Perception	3	0.992
Perception of Esteem Needs	2	0.713
Perception of Psychological Needs	3	0.817

Sources: Compiled from SPSS

To ensure the reliability of the study, a Cronbach's Alpha test was conducted to assess the consistency of the questions framed for each factor. Based on the results, which indicated values higher than 0.7 for all factors, it can be concluded that the variables and factors are reliable. Kaiser-Meyer-Olkin Measure of Sampling adequacy was 0.812 which is greater than 0.5, and Bartlett's Test of Sphericity was significant at 0.000.

H01: No significant relationship exists between the economic and social factors and factors related to perception.

Table 2: Correlation of the factors considered

		Financial Per-cep-tion	Perception of Esteem Needs	Perception of Psychological Needs	Eco-nomic Factors	Social Factors
Financial Perception	Pearson Correlation	1	.915**	.810**	.306**	.351**
	Sig. (2-tailed)		.000	.000	.001	.000
Perception of Esteem Needs	Pearson Correlation	.915**	1	.921**	.453**	.497**
	Sig. (2-tailed)	.000		.000	.000	.000
Perception of Psychological Needs	Pearson Correlation	.810**	.921**	1	.596**	.640**
	Sig. (2-tailed)	.000	.000		.000	.000
Economic Factors	Pearson Correlation	.306**	.453**	.596**	1	.946**
	Sig. (2-tailed)	.001	.000			.000
Social Factors	Pearson Correlation	.351**	.497**	.640**	.946**	1
	Sig. (2-tailed)	.000	.000	.000	.000	
**. Correlation is significant at the 0.01 level (2-tailed).						

Source: Primary data

Table 3 shows the correlation coefficient among economic and social factors is highest (0.946), followed by the perception of psychological and esteem needs (0.921). The correlation coefficient between economic factors and financial perception is the lowest (0.306) indicating the low association between the variables. However, since the calculated significance value is 0.000, which is less than the threshold limit of 0.05, the null hypothesis is rejected, and we say that there exists a significant correlation between the independent and dependent variables.

H02: Socio-economic factors do not influence factors related to perception.

Table 3. ANOVA Economic factor as an independent variable is considered

		Sum of Squares	df	Mean Square	F	Sig.
Financial Perception	Between Groups	290.590	36	8.072	1.105	.354
	Within Groups	503.901	69	7.303		
	Total	794.491	105			

Perception of Esteem Needs	Between Groups	641.745	36	17.826	1.690	.031
	Within Groups	727.850	69	10.549		
	Total	1369.514	105			
Perception of Psychological Needs	Between Groups	1611.823	36	44.773	2.183	.003
	Within Groups	1414.904	69	20.506		
	Total	3026.726	105			

Source: Primary data

Table 4. ANOVA Social factor as an independent variable is considered

		Sum of Squares	df	Mean Square	F	Sig.
Financial Perception	Between Groups	247.518	25	9.901	1.448	.110
	Within Groups	546.973	80	6.837		
	Total	794.491	105			
Perception of Esteem Needs	Between Groups	708.580	25	28.343	3.430	.000
	Within Groups	661.014	80	8.263		
	Total	1369.594	105			
Perception of Psychological Needs	Between Groups	1782.717	25	71.309	4.586	.000
	Within Groups	1244.009	80	15.550		
	Total	3026.726	105			

Source: Primary data

The ANOVA result shows that the significance value of the perception of esteem needs and perception of psychological needs is less than 0.05, which means that the economic factor and the social factor influence the perception of esteem needs and perception of psychological needs, and therefore we will reject the null hypothesis. The significance value of financial perception is more than 0.05, and hence we will accept the null hypothesis and say that the economic factor and the social factor do not influence financial perception.

Measures to Improve Socio-Economic Status of Women

1. **Access to Quality Education:**
   Girls and women should be given free or subsidized quality education (Alderman et al., 2003). The focus should be made on providing scholarships, school infrastructure improvement, and awareness

campaigns so that enrolment can be encouraged which will break the cycle of poverty (Glewwe & Muralidharan, 2016) and promote socio-economic development.

2. **Skill Development and Vocational Training:**
   Providing women with skill development and other vocational training such as training in agriculture, crafts, entrepreneurship, and modern trades can enhance their employability and income-earning potential (Barooah & Dedhia, 2015).

3. **Financial Inclusion:**
   Providing increased access to banking services, micro-credit, and saving facilities for facilitating financial inclusion is crucial for empowering women economically (Steward et al., 2012). SHGs can play a significant role in linking women to formal financial institutions.

4. **Livelihood Diversification:**
   Supporting the establishments of income-generating activities such as small-scale enterprises, handicrafts, and cottage industries can encourage livelihood diversification beyond traditional occupations which will enhance income opportunities for women (Hartl, 2009: Sheheli, 2012).

5. **Social Safety Nets:**
   Food security schemes, old-age pensions, and widow support, such social safety net programs can provide a safety net for vulnerable women and their families (Barkat-e-Khuda, 2011; Holmes & Jones, 2013).

6. **Gender Sensitization:**
   Conducting gender sensitization workshops and awareness campaigns within communities can challenge traditional gender norms and promote gender equality (Makama, 2013).

7. **Infrastructure Development:**
   Investment in infrastructure development including roads, water supply, sanitization facilities, and electricity can improve living conditions and facilitate economic activities (Soltani et al., 2021).

8. **Strengthening SHGs:**
   Continuous training, capacity building, and mentorship support should be used to strengthen SHGs (Sharma & Kumar, 2016). Women's leadership within SHGs should be encouraged and linking them to the market opportunities must be ensured.

9. **Government Support:**
   Government policies and programs should be tailored to address the specific needs of the women, taking into consideration their unique socio-cultural contexts and vulnerabilities.

10. **Monitoring and Evaluation:**
    Regular monitoring and evaluation of socio-economic development initiatives are essential to assess their effectiveness and make necessary adjustments for sustained impact.

Conclusion & Suggestions

The path of tribal women in Sonbhadra's Self-Help Groups (SHGs) exemplifies the resilient spirit of empowerment. The purpose of this study was to investigate the socioeconomic position and perceptions of tribal women involved in SHGs, to reveal the transformational influence of collective action. The findings of the study reveal that participation in SHG helps in improving the socio-economic condition of tribal women as it increases their income and saving and there is a great association between the socio-economic factor and factors related to perception. Socio-economic status influences the perception of the tribal women beneficiaries of SHGs. If the socio-economic status of women improves, their perception towards SHGs also improves and vice-versa, which will affect the number of people joining SHGs, and also affect the credit facility they will seek.

Policymakers and development practitioners must devise tailored initiatives that address the unique issues encountered by indigenous women in Sonbhadra. Tailored programmes aimed at improving access to education, healthcare, and employment opportunities can improve their socio-economic condition and encourage holistic empowerment. It is critical to assist SHGs by providing ongoing training, capacity building, and mentorship. Building leadership skills and encouraging women's active involvement in decision-making processes should be prioritized. To overcome deeply ingrained gender stereotypes, tribal tribes should implement awareness campaigns and sensitization programmes. To develop support for gender equality and women's empowerment, these activities should include men, women, and community leaders. Collaboration between government agencies, non-governmental organizations (NGOs), civil society, and other stakeholders is critical for the success of women's empowerment projects. Partnerships may be strengthened to increase the effectiveness of programmes and promote greater coordination in addressing the different needs of indigenous women.

Limitations

The sample size of individuals from Sonbhadra SHGs is one of the study's key limitations. We had to work with a limited number of participants due to logistical and time restrictions. The in-depth exploration of certain aspects of tribal women's empowerment has not been done due to time constraints. The study was limited to tribal women in Sonbhadra and may not completely represent the particular issues experienced by tribal women in other geographies or cultural contexts. As a result, the findings may not be completely relevant to tribal women in other areas of India or various socio-cultural contexts. The study considered limited variables. Further studies can be done considering other variables such as political factors, barriers faced, etc.

References

1. Abrol, D., Khanna, J., Dutta, K., Sambyal, R. (2020). Assessing the Impact of Government Schemes on Rural Development: A Study of Udhampur District (Jammu and Kashmir State). In: H. Chahal, V. Pereira & J. Jyoti (Eds.), *Sustainable Business Practices for Rural Development* (pp. 69-91). Palgrave Macmillan, Singapore. https://doi.org/10.1007/978-981-13-9298-6_5
2. Alderman, H., Kim, J., & Orazem, P. F. (2003). Design, evaluation, and sustainability of private schools for the poor: the Pakistan urban and rural fellowship school experiments. *Economics of Education review, 22*(3), 265-274. https://doi.org/10.1016/S0272-7757(02)00051-1
3. Arora, A. (2016). Assessment of financial literacy among working Indian women. *Business Analyst, 36*(2), 219-237.
4. Barkat-e-Khuda. (2011). Social safety net programmes in Bangladesh: A review. *The Bangladesh Development Studies, 34*(2), 87-108. https://www.jstor.org/stable/23339844

5. Barooah, N., & Dedhia, E. M. (2015). Study of socio-economic status of women engaged in handloom weaving and measures for enhancing their sustainability. *International Journal of Research in Social Sciences, 5*(4), 653-665.
6. Brahma, J., Pavarala, V., & Belavadi, V. (2019). Driving social change through forum theatre: A study of Jana Sanskriti in West Bengal, India. *Asia Pacific Media Educator, 29*(2), 164-177. https://doi.org/10.1177/1326365X19864477
7. Census of India. (2011). *Uttar Pradesh-Series 10-Part XII A-District Census Handbook, Sonbhadra.* Directorate of Census Operations, Uttar Pradesh. Retrieved from https://censusindia.gov.in/nada/index.php/catalog/1294 on 08.08.2023.
8. Chattopadhyaya, I. (2008). Living Tradition: A Study of Prehistoric Rock-paintings and Indigenous Art from District Sonbhadra, Southern Uttar Pradesh, India. *Athens Journal of Humanities & Arts, 3*(4), 251-270. https://doi.org/10.30958/ajha.3.4.3
9. Cheston, S., & Kuhn, L. (2002). Empowering women through microfinance. *Draft, Opportunity International, 64,* 1-64.
10. Devi, S. S., Kumar, S., & Singh, J. (2014). Role of non-governmental organisations in formation and linkage of self help groups in Punjab. *Indian Journal of Economics and Development, 10*(2), 184-190. http://dx.doi.org/10.5958/j.2322-0430.10.2.047
11. Glewwe, P., & Muralidharan, K. (2016). Improving education outcomes in developing countries: Evidence, knowledge gaps, and policy implications. In E. A. Hanushek, S. Machin & L. Woessmann (Eds.), *Handbook of the Economics of Education 5,* 653-743. Elsevier. https://doi.org/10.1016/B978-0-444-63459-7.00010-5
12. Gupta, P., & Bilas, R. (2017). Socio-Economic Status of Scheduled Tribes in Sonbhadra District, Uttar Pradesh. *National Geographical Journal of India, 63*(03), 61-71.
13. Hartl, M. (2009, March 31-April 2). *Technical and vocational education and training (TVET) and skills development for poverty reduction–do rural women benefit* [Paper presentation]. FAO-IFAD-ILO Workshop on Gaps, trends and current research in gender dimensions of agricultural and rural employment: differentiated pathways out of poverty, Rome, Itlay.
14. Hentschel, J., & Waters, W. F. (2002). Rural poverty in Ecuador: assessing local realities for the development of anti-poverty programs. *World Development, 30*(1), 33-47. https://doi.org/10.1016/S0305-750X(01)00099-7
15. Holmes, R., & Jones, N. (2013). *Gender and social protection in the developing world: Beyond mothers and safety nets.* Bloomsbury Publishing.
16. Jain, D., & Jain, B. (2012). Does microfinance empower rural women? Empirical study in Udaipur District, Rajasthan. *Researchers World-Journal of Arts, Science and Commerce, 3*(2), 76-89. https://ssrn.com/abstract=1911140
17. Kapoor, S. (2019). Entrepreneurship for economic and social empowerment of women: A case study of a self help credit program in Nithari Village, Noida, India. *Australasian Accounting, Business and Finance Journal, 13*(2), 123-142. http://dx.doi.org/10.14453/aabfj.v13i2.8
18. Khaki, A. R. (2018). Effectiveness of financial inclusion programs: a case study of Jammu and Kashmir state. *International Journal of Financial Innovation in Banking, 2*(1), 29-47. https://doi.org/10.1504/IJFIB.2018.092418
19. Khan, M. I. (2015). Women empowerment, entrepreneurship, and capacity development. *Journal for Studies in Management and Planning, 1*(9), 43-56. http://internationaljournalofresearch.org/index.php/JSMaP
20. Kilby, P. (2010). *NGOs in India: The challenges of women's empowerment and accountability.* Taylor & Francis.

21. Kilic, S. (2016). Cronbach's alpha reliability coefficient. *Psychiatry and Behavioral Sciences, 6*(1), 47-48. 10.5455/jmood.20160307122823
22. Kirmayer, L. J., Sehdev, M., Whitley, R., Dandeneau, S. F., & Isaac, C. (2009). Community resilience: Models, metaphors and measures. *International Journal of Indigenous Health, 5*(1), 62-117.
23. Kumar, D., & Kumar, D. (2022). Gender Matters: Reappraising the Issues of Equity, Participation and Ownership in Watershed Management. *Contemporary Voice of Dalit*. Advance online publication. https://doi.org/10.1177/2455328X211063068
24. Kumar, R., Suar, D., & Mishra, P. (2018). Characteristics for the effectiveness of women's self-help groups in bihar. *VOLUNTAS: International Journal of Voluntary and Nonprofit Organizations, 29*, 1283-1299. https://doi.org/10.1007/s11266-018-9995-9
25. Kuokkanen, R. (2011). Indigenous economies, theories of subsistence, and women: Exploring the social economy model for Indigenous governance. *American Indian Quarterly, 35*(2), 215-240. https://doi.org/10.5250/amerindiquar.35.2.0215
26. Mahmud, S., Shah, N. M., & Becker, S. (2012). Measurement of women's empowerment in rural Bangladesh. *World Development, 40*(3), 610-619. https://doi.org/10.1016/j.worlddev.2011.08.003
27. Makama, G. A. (2013). Patriarchy and gender inequality in Nigeria: The way forward. *European scientific journal, 9*(17), 115-144.
28. McCallum, M. J. L. (2014). *Indigenous women, work, and history: 1940-1980, 16*. Univ. of Manitoba Press.
29. Meenai, Z. (2003). *Empowering rural women: An approach to empowering women through credit-based self-help groups*. Aakar books.
30. Meera, M., & Yekta, K. (2021). The Challenges to Political Participation of Women in Afghanistan: Historical and Cultural Perspectives. *Asian Studies, 9*(1), 65-91. https://doi.org/10.4312/as.2021.9.1.65-91
31. Padmaja, R., & Bantilan, M. C. S. (2007). *Empowerment through Technology: gender dimensions of social capital build-up in Maharashtra, India* (No. 577-2016-39200). http://oar.icrisat.org/id/eprint/3036
32. Parida, P. C., & Sinha, A. (2010). Performance and sustainability of self-help groups in India: A gender perspective. *Asian Development Review, 27*(1), 80-103.
33. Sarkar, A. N., & Singh, J. (2006). Savings-led micro-finance to bank the unbankables: Sharing of global experience. *Global Business Review, 7*(2), 271-295. https://doi.org/10.1177/097215090600700206
34. Sharma, P. K., & Kumar, S. (2016). Leading Strategies for Microfinance Institutions and Service Support to Self Help Groups (SHGs) to Strengthen Inclusive Growth–A Study of Bareilly Division of Uttar Pradesh. *Research Journal of Social Science & Management, 5*(12), 194-203.
35. Sheheli, S. (2012). *Improving livelihood of rural women through income generating activities in Bangladesh* (Doctoral thesis). https://doi.org/10.18452/16588
36. Sieder, R., & Sierra, M. T. (2010). *Indigenous women's access to justice in Latin America*. Chr. Michelsen Institute. http://hdl.handle.net/11250/2436094
37. Singh, U. (2016). Impact of Micro Credit on Women Empowerment: A Case Study of Dholpur District of Rajasthan. *International Journal of Management and Development Studies, 5*(4), 81-93.
38. Soltani, M., Kashkooli, F. M., Souri, M., Rafiei, B., Jabarifar, M., Gharali, K., & Nathwani, J. S. (2021). Environmental, economic, and social impacts of geothermal energy systems. *Renewable and Sustainable Energy Reviews, 140*, 110750. https://doi.org/10.1016/j.rser.2021.110750

39. Stewart, R., Van Rooyen, C., Korth, M., Chereni, A., Da Silva, N. R., & De Wet, T. (2012). *Do micro-credit, micro-savings and micro-leasing serve as effective financial inclusion interventions enabling poor people, and especially women, to engage in meaningful economic opportunities in low-and middle-income countries?: a systematic review of the evidence*. EPPI-Centre, Social Science Research Unit, Institute of Education, University of London.
40. Suguna, B. (2006). *Empowerment of rural women through self help groups*. Discovery publishing house.
41. Tiwari, A. M., & Thakur, S. G. (2007). SHG-based microfinance programmes: Can they remove poverty?. In M. Chen, R. Jhabvala, R. Kanbur & C. Richards (Eds.), *Membership Based Organizations of the Poor* (pp. 177-193). Routledge.
42. Verma, A. K. (2013). Tribal 'Annihilation' and 'Upsurge' in Uttar Pradesh. *Economic and Political Weekly 48*(51), 52-59. https://www.jstor.org/stable/24478404
43. Weaver, H. N. (2022). Overcoming Prejudice and Discrimination Through Resilience of Indigenous Peoples. In E. P. Congree, D. Meister, S. C. Osborn & H. Takooshian (Eds.), *Behavioral Science in the Global Arena: Global Mental, Spiritual, and Social Health* (pp. 121-133). Information Age Publishing.

5

Encouraging the Growth of Microfinance on Employment Generation in Umaria District

Dr. Parmeshwar Singh Maravi[1] *& Dr. Ashish Mathur*[2]

Abstract

In this paper, the influence of microfinance on the creation of jobs in the Umaria district of Madhya Pradesh is examined. After joining SHGs, it also analyses socio-economic factors including age, marital status, education, business experience, income & employment, significant sources of income, women's status in society, etc. Data from 270 borrowers in the chosen area were gathered using the multistage random sampling procedure. Using SPSS 22, the variables were analyzed using average, percentage, factor analysis, correlation analysis, and regression analysis. Age, education, and loans from SHGs were discovered to be the most important characteristics and to have a greater impact on employment, with a substantial positive association between these variables and the performance of microfinance. This study highlights how timely and appropriate loan assistance provided by microfinance assists rural women in creating jobs. They can launch their microbusinesses and take advantage of several prospects for a better life thanks to microfinance. Policies should be developed to enhance educational possibilities and supportive and promotional services for the development of rural women to have a more substantial impact.

Keywords: *SHGs, microfinance, employment generation, performance and growth*

Introduction

Microfinance has recently become recognized as a potent tool for empowering women, especially those in rural areas. Microfinance programmes help women become more empowered by improving their socioeconomic standing overall and their ability to make decisions at the family level. The world's poorest 79 million people had access to microfinance services by the end of 2000. As a result, microfinance can significantly advance gender equality and support women's access to better working conditions and sustainable means of subsistence. Today, the majority of emerging nations, including India, place a greater focus on the advancement of women as business owners and their active participation in national development. If given the necessary resources, including the necessary finance, a suitable climate, and enough resources in general, women can be successful and better entrepreneurs. Studies on rural women have demonstrated their superior commercial skills. They have been found to use credit more effectively than men. People look for menial work to survive because of poverty and unemployment (Adepoju, 2006). Given that they have the least access

1 Assistant Professor, Department of Commerce Government Adarsh College, Dabrauha, Umaria, Madhya Pradesh

2 Professor, Department of Management Central University of Haryana, Haryana

to and the least control over the majority of economic resources, women are disproportionately affected by the negative effects of poverty and unemployment. Because of this, a sizeable portion of women, especially in rural regions, engage in irregular, seasonal, and informal work. The majority of them (Najeeb et al., 2020), particularly in developing countries like India, rely on farming as a source of income. Their well-being is hampered by poor educational backgrounds, cultural norms and traditions, and male members' influence over women's decisions (Lakwo, 2007). Without rural areas, India's total development is impossible. It has been emphasized, nonetheless, that women can be lifted out of poverty and have their standard of living raised by providing them with financial assistance (Khandker, 2005; Li et al., 2011) and, in turn, by encouraging their entrepreneurial endeavors (Bruton et al., 2013). For women in developing nations, earning through self-employment has gradually grown more appealing as a source of income, particularly through home-based entrepreneurial activities (Adom & Anambane, 2019). However, these small firms' expansion is hindered by a lack of readily available credit, a lack of capital, a dearth of modest loans, and collateral limitations (Das, 2000; Kasali et al., 2015; Singh & Kaur, 2021).

One such initiative that has emerged as a potent weapon for women's empowerment is microfinance. According to the available literature, the majority of research on microfinance has been done in the southern part of the nation, with Thane District receiving very little attention in this area. It is a modest attempt to examine how microfinance contributes to women's empowerment and how satisfied women are with microfinance. Around 94.07 percent of loans disbursed to recipients are to women, according to the Status of Microfinance (2022). Given that women make up the majority of microfinance recipients, it is important to look at how microfinance has affected rural women's capacity to find employment. The issue is whether microfinance initiatives effectively empower participants by providing opportunities for revenue generation. As a result, for the current study, information and data from rural women beneficiaries of microfinance in the Umaria District of Madhya Pradesh were obtained to assess how the programme improved the lives of the women beneficiaries and provided chances for work.

Review of Literature

According to Kumari et al. (2019), the microfinance sector offers a dynamic strategy for enhancing lower-level groups' sources of income, which eventually aids in the eradication of poverty. It also presents a plan for the effective management of small enterprises through the empowerment of disadvantaged female entrepreneurs. This study also identified the requirement for the construction by the governing bodies of a structure to ensure easy access to the credit facilities of micro-finance units.

The importance of the role performed by the microfinance sector in addressing societal poverty was examined by Sohn & Ume (2019). This paper discusses the significance of the efforts taken in the form of credit facilities to ensure that poverty is reduced at the macroeconomic level of the economy. It has been found that female recipients of micro-banking are more effective than their male counterparts, hence some specific activities should be put in place with a focus on them to continue viable growth in the sector.

According to an investigation by Ali & Mughal (2019), financial help provided by microfinance institutions can only produce positive outcomes when it is combined with business management expertise. This study has brought attention to how important it is to give small business owners the managerial and non-managerial skills they need to take full advantage of the growth potential offered by the financial benefits of a microbanking system.

Sussan & Obamuyi (2018) have highlighted the role that microfinance institutions play in enabling aspiring business owners to the point where they can ensure the expansion and development of their enterprises. The outcome has also acknowledged the significance of non-financial services provided by MFIs for significantly influencing the improvement of a company enterprise as a whole.

Hussain et al. (2017) analysis of the microfinance sector's effects on the economy brought attention to the sector's importance. Research has explicitly looked at how the microfinance sector affects the group of people who live in poverty. The research claims that to combat poverty and raise people's standards of living, the microfinance industry has notably increased its assistance in the areas of income, housing infrastructure, education, agriculture, health safety, and food security.

The impact of the contribution of microfinance banks or institutions on the SME sector has been studied by Taiwo et al. (2016). The amount of aid and support given to small firms by the microfinance industry has been debated. The study has talked about the effect that giving businesses the right amount of financial and non-financial support in every way conceivable has on their ability to expand.

By providing them with the necessary support and adequate guidance regarding cutting-edge practices, market trends, and cutting-edge technologies that need to be implemented in the business, microfinance institutions are important in facilitating the growth of micro-entrepreneurs, according to Ferdousi (2015). The idea is that small-scale businesses gain from microfinance sectors by receiving financial assistance and sound business training so they may develop their skills and establish a long-term business structure. This study has highlighted the significance of focusing on clients' services in maximizing entrepreneurs' potential.

Ali et al. (2015) investigated how numerous factors, including income growth, improvements in business operations, and educational attainment, affect people's quality of life. The financial and non-financial services obtained through microfinance organisations are crucial to the overall development and advancement of society.

According to Fwamba et al. (2015), the microfinance sector has broadened the scope of its services to include advice and savings rather than sticking to the more conventional strategy of providing simple financial services. It has proven to be a tremendous tool for women who own businesses. They are now actively participating in the decision-making process. This has significantly increased their morale because it gives them a way to meet their needs and gain their independence by expanding their capacities, which in turn motivates them to perform and manage a variety of jobs within the organisation.

According to Modi et al. (2014), different microfinance segments play a role in improving the lives of underprivileged rural women. Furthermore, it has shown how some particular elements, such as the socioeconomic level, the ability to make one's own decisions, a supportive parenting style, and the role of women in society and the family all help to raise society's standard of living. The study's conclusions simply focus on how the government and microfinance institutions can create the required regulations to greatly enhance the social and economic conditions of low-income rural women entrepreneurs.

The government must actively participate in resolving the problems that microfinance banks encounter, according to Awojobi (2013), to ensure that their financial services are easily accessible. It has acknowledged that the government's responsibility is to make sure microfinance organisations have the resources they require to efficiently carry out their lending operations. This study has also contributed to determining the benefits of microfinance on female entrepreneurs' ability to start businesses and increase their sources of income.

The microfinance sector was portrayed by Adhikari & Shrestha (2013) as a social transformation agent. It has been revealed how crucial the microbanking industry is for promoting social and economic stability. Micro-banking institutions' efficient fund-mobilization efforts, which in turn considerably strengthen the empowerment of women company owners and allow them to raise their social status, play a part in this stability.

According to Nwankwo et al. (2013), the introduction of the microfinance business into the economy became necessary as a result of the ineffectiveness of the banking system's non-addressing and resolving the financial needs of the impoverished parts of society. The concept of micro-banking offers people new ways to address their financial needs and strengthens their ability to establish sustainable companies. The report has also offered some suggestions for dealing with the problems preventing microbanking from operating effectively.

The overall contribution of microfinance to raising an economy's level of sustainability has been examined by Imai et al. (2012). It has been observed that the active involvement of microfinance businesses in an economy greatly lowers the level of impoverishment in that nation. The frequency of poverty in society and the portfolio of microfinancing were found to be related, according to the study. The level of poverty is eventually demonstrated by unemployment, which is caused by a decreased GDP and loan portfolio. As a result, it is thought that the micro-banking industry has significantly influenced the country's capacity for handling its finances.

Yahaya & Osemene (2011) developed the idea of supporting micro-banking systems in society since they assist in creating a mechanism to reach out to and support small-scale business owners. It has also highlighted the importance of governing bodies developing a system to help small business owners grow their companies. The research indicates that the microfinance business greatly contributes to improving the conditions of society's most vulnerable communities through affordable funding, money mobilisation, and opportunities for employee development.

Okpara (2010) noted the impact that specific circumstances play in producing poverty as well as the need for micro-financial help in limiting these effects. In two stages, the effect of micro-credit facilities has been measured. The poverty rate initially increases little with a decreasing rate, but later on, it shows a sharp reduction as a result of the ongoing expansion of credit services provided by the microfinance sector. This effect amplifies the need for a framework to be put in place to support the growth of the microfinance sector of the economy.

Prajapati et al. (2022) identify the empirical data on the socioeconomic status of microfinance for poverty reduction and empowerment of tribal women by SHGs. The study's findings revealed a distinction in tribal women's position before and following their use of microfinance in SHGs. Additionally, the financial framework has failed to express how to meet the needs of the underprivileged tribal population, notably the tribal women.

According to Kurmanalieva et al. (2003), the purpose of microfinance in financial systems, whether they be global or local, is to provide financial services and a sizable flow of capital to economically disadvantaged communities that are frequently ignored by the formal banking sector.

Nevertheless, MFIs have expanded to support entrepreneurial ventures that will lead to endogenous growth and reduce poverty, which are issues that traditional approaches like foreign aid and government-run programs have failed to solve (Khavul 2010).

Microfinance has a reputation for serving underserved and disadvantaged groups like women, the elderly, individuals with disabilities, and those seeking only to meet their most basic requirements (Hansen et al. 2020). Moreover, microfinance could have a positive impact on society as a whole. Although eradicating poverty was the initial objective, microfinance also offers some energizing opportunities for expanding markets and promoting social change (Armendariz & Morduch 2010).

Objectives of the Study

1. To determine the socioeconomic factors that affect rural women.
2. To investigate the effects of microfinancing on rural women's employability.

Research Methodology

The main objective of this study has been to examine how microfinance has affected its recipients. How the borrowers' level of living has altered has been demonstrated through the success of microfinance and the creation of jobs. For sample collecting, villages of the microbusiness were taken into account as the deprived rural group prevails, tending to separate physical, social, and demographic characteristics. 300 replies from the list were collected using multistage random sampling for this reason. 270 respondents had submitted a total of 90 responses, had finished at least one year of the post-loan phase, and were still in the middle of the loan payback cycle. In this study, appealing loans, education, training participation, income, employment, microenterprise activities and duration have all been regarded as independent variables. When examining the effect of microfinance on employment generation, which is our dependent variable, performance has been seen as a mediator. Based on the Cronbach Alpha score, the questions have been retained for further analysis. Correlation and multiple regression analyses have been used to investigate the impact of microfinance on employability. Also, substantial differences in the responses' performance, numerous impacts, and socio-demographic characteristics have been seen using the inferential statistics F-test.

Results and Discussion

The demographic profile of the recipients is shown in Table 1. 65.6% of the 270 female recipients are in the middle age range. The remaining women were widows, leaving 93.7% of them in a union. 54.4% of women had some form of education, while 23% had only an elementary education. Despite having no formal education, 45.6% of women could sign. 73% of self-employed and salaried women have one year or more of business experience, and 35.2% of women have five years or more of business experience. After joining a SHG, 75.6% of women had a monthly family income between Rs 500 and Rs.1000, while 30.0% and 28.9% of women had a monthly family employment schedule of 26 to 30 days and 11 to 15 days, respectively. The remaining 37.8% of women joined the group by their persuasion, the influence of friends or neighbors, or the influence of the group leader, who influenced 62.2% of the group's female members. Regarding status position, 76.6% of women believe that women in society have an ordinary to good status position. But 17% of women believe that women are in a low-status position.

Table 1: Profile of Beneficiaries

S. No.	Particulars	Category	Frequency	Percent
1	Age	Below 20	6	2.2
		21-30	85	31.5
		31-40	92	34.1
		41-50	65	24.1
		More than 50	22	8.1
2	Marital Status	Married	253	93.7
		Widow	17	6.3
3	Education	Illiterate but can sign	123	45.6
		Primary	62	23
		Secondary	43	11.9
		Higher Secondary	42	11.5
4	Business Experience	No Business Experience	73	27
		1-3 years	42	15.6
		3-5 years	60	22.2
		More than 5 years	95	35.2
5	Income after joining SHG	Less than 4000	23	8.5
		4001-8000	139	51.5
		8001-12000	65	24.1
		12001-16000	27	10
		More than 16000	16	5.9
6	Employment after joining SHG	Upto 7 days	11	4.1
		8-16 days	78	28.9
		17-21 days	48	17.8
		22-28 days	52	19.3
		Above 28 days	81	30
7	Key activities	Sewing	93	34.4
		Agro-based	46	17
		Livestock	17	6.3
		Trade	42	15.5
		Others activities	72	26.6
8	Who influenced you to join the group?	Self	15	5.6
		Group Leader	168	62.2
		Neighbors	37	13.7
		Others	50	18.5

9	Status of women's Position in the society	Very Bad	4	1.5
		Bad	46	17
		Average	117	43.3
		Good	90	33.3
		Very Good	13	4.8

Sources: Primary Data

Table 2: Reliability test on Factors considered for the study

Particulars	Total no. of Items	Cronbach's Alpha
Barriers	6	**0.890**
Livelihood	4	**0.898**
Perception	6	**0.926**
Reason of joining	6	**0.932**
Training Programme	6	**0.896**
Performance of Microfinance	6	**0.812**

Sources: Compiled from SPSS

Cronbach's Alpha was used to conduct the reliability test. The purpose of the test was to ascertain the dependability of the questions that were prepared for each element. Every factor's estimated value exceeded 0.7, indicating the validity of the factors and the associated variables. The Bartlett's Test of Sphericity was significant at 0.000, while the Kaiser-Meyer-Olkin Measure of Sampling Adequacy was 0.764. KMO is more than 0.5 in value.

H01: The impact of microfinance variables and microfinance performance are not significantly correlated

Table 3: Correlation analysis concerning factors considered in the study

Particulars	B	L	P	ROJ	TP
Barriers	1				
Livelihood	0.039				
Perception	.312**	.349**			
Reason of Joining	.265*	.254**	0.102		
Training Programme	0.017	.357**	.247**	0.121	
Performance of Microfinance	.432*	.654**	.646**	.619**	.599**

Sources: Primary Data Correlation is significant at the 0.01 level & 0.05 level (2-tailed).

The assessed significance value was 0.000, which is less than .05. The null hypothesis was ultimately rejected (Table 3). The many performance-impacting parameters that were taken into consideration for the study had a strong positive association.

H02: Between variables that are regarded as dependent and independent, there is no meaningful link

Table 4: Regression analysis examining how microfinance affects the creation of jobs

Model	Coefficientsa		
	β	t	Sig.
(Constant)	94.893	34.679	0.00
Education	3.032	4.893	0.00
Age	4.672	4.465	0.00
Key activities	1.463	2.899	0.010
Attended meeting	3.665	2.971	0.006
Loan through SHGs	6.573	2.087	0.000

Sources: Primary data

R = 0.529, R Square = 0.38, F = 31.426, Sig. 0.000b

Dependent Variable: Impact of microfinance on employment

R is correlated with other variables from the regression analysis because there is a substantial relationship between the variables that were taken into consideration. Table 4 shows that the impact of microfinance on employment is positively correlated with age, education, income-generating activities, meeting attendance, and a loan through an SHG (R=.529). However, the corrected R square value is .38, which implies that these factors only contribute 38% to the dependent variable—impact on employment—of the study. The analysis also demonstrates that attendance at meetings (= 3.66 p.05) has the least significant impact on the performance of microfinance, with age, education, and loans from SHG having the most influence (= 4.672, 3.032, & 6.57, p.05). According to the ANOVA results, the significant value was less than 0.01, indicating that independent variables may significantly predict the impact on employment at a 95% confidence level for a dependent variable.

Suggestions and Conclusion

The government should provide both the marketing infrastructure needed to advertise the items as well as the infrastructure needed to train SHG members in microenterprises. For microenterprise-linked SHGs to properly and effectively advertise their products and services, they need to have a strong marketing network. To manage marketing tasks independently, they require institutional support for marketing and the necessary resources. To raise knowledge about starting micro-businesses, many enterprise development programmes need to be arranged.

When starting the micro-enterprise, it is important to do a thorough analysis of the available natural resources, skills, and potential. A concerned government official ought to give the SHG members guidance, support, and counsel. There is a lot of room for research in the microfinance and micro-enterprise sectors, including the issues that micro-enterprises, members of Self-help Groups, and government agencies encounter when processing microfinance to the various SHGs. Because the study is based on a small sample size and only represents a small number of rural locations in Umaria District of Madhya Pradesh, additional research on a larger scale is required to validate and corroborate the findings. Future research can also be conducted with the use of different factors besides income and consumption. Study on how microfinance has affected SHGs' cross-sectional business activity. Furthermore, it is a reality that the results of studies of this kind might change over time and from region to region. To establish programmes for the uplift of the underprivileged in society, policymakers occasionally find that these research and their conclusions are more helpful. Planners and policymakers interested in economic planning should take into consideration the research on microfinance and its effectiveness towards livelihood transformation in employment creation and empowerment. As was already established, the programme successfully encourages borrowers to become self-sufficient, employable, and to change their way of life. The increased support for borrowers is a benefit of microfinance services. They can launch their microbusinesses and take advantage of several prospects for a better life thanks to microfinance. The majority of the families in this study are joint families, which significantly increases the financial strain. Additionally, the majority of respondents are in their middle years and are aiming to develop significant financial independence. By encouraging people to take cautious risks, investigate different income sources, reach their full potential, and enhance their leadership and creative abilities, microfinance aids in people's promotion and management. The growth of SME owners will help strengthen the neighborhood's economy, and a lot more non-agricultural start-ups might be formed soon.

References

1. Abdallah Ali, M., Mughal, M., & Chhorn, D. (2022). Microfinance and poverty reduction: Evidence from Djibouti. *Review of Development Economics*. 26. 10.1111/rode.12856.
2. Adepoju, A. (2006). Internal and international migration within Africa. *Migration in South and Southern Africa: Dynamics and Determinants*, 26-46. https://doi.org/10.13140/2.1.4812.8969
3. Adhikari, D. B., & Shrestha, J. (2013). Economic impact of microfinance in Nepal: A case study of the Manamaiju Village Development Committee, Kathmandu. *Economic Journal of Development Issues*, 36-49.
4. Adom, K., & Anambane, G. (2019). Understanding the role of culture and gender stereotypes in women entrepreneurship through the lens of the stereotype threat theory. *Journal of Entrepreneurship in Emerging Economies, 12*(1), 100-124. https://doi.org/10.1108/JEEE-07-2018-0070
5. Ahmad, R. & Hussain, A. & Umer, M. & Parveen, K. (2017). Efficiency of Microfinance providers in Pakistan: An Empirical Investigation. *Review of Economics and Development Studies*. 3. 177. 10.26710/reads.v3i2.173.
6. Ali, S. I., Ali, A., & Subhan, F. (2015). Empirical Assessment of the Impact of Microfinance on Quality of Life. *Pakistan Business Review*, 719.
7. Armendariz, B., & Morduch, J. (2010). The Economics of Microfinance. Cambridge, MA: MIT Press.
8. Awojobi, N. O. (2013). Microfinance as a strategy for poverty reduction: The Nigerian experience. Berlin, Germany: Berlin School of Economics and Law.
9. Bruton, G. D., Ketchen Jr, D. J., & Ireland, R. D. (2013). Entrepreneurship as a solution to poverty. *Journal of Business Venturing, 28*(6), 683-689. https://doi.org/10.1016/j.jbusvent.2013.05.002
10. Das, M. (2000). Women entrepreneurs from India: Problems, motivations and success factors. *Journal of Small Business & Entrepreneurship, 15*(4), 67-81. https://doi.org/10.1080/08276331.2000.10593294
11. Ferdousi, F. (2015). Impact of microfinance on sustainable entrepreneurship development. *Development Studies Research, 2*(1), 51-63.
12. Hamad, R. & Fernald, L. (2015). Microcredit participation and women's health: Results from a cross-sectional study in Peru. *International journal for equity in health*. 14. 62. 10.1186/s12939-015-0194-7.
13. Hansen, N., et al. (2020). Microfinance Services and Women's Empowerment. In Handbook on Ethics in Finance, 1–22. New York: Springer.
14. Imai, K. S., Gaiha, R., Thapa, G., & Annim, S. K. (2012). Microfinance and poverty—a macro perspective. *World development, 40*(8), 1675-1689.

15. Kasali, T. A., Ahmad, S. A., & Lim, H. E. (2015). The role of microfinance in poverty alleviation: Empirical evidence from South-West Nigeria. *Asian Social Science, 11*(21), 183-192. http://doi.org/10.5539/ass.v11n21p183
16. Khandker, S. R. (2005). Microfinance and poverty: Evidence using panel data from Bangladesh. *The World Bank Economic Review, 19*(2), 263-286. https://doi.org/10.1093/wber/lhi008
17. Khavul, S. (2010). Microfinance: creating opportunities for the poor?. Academy of management perspectives, *24*(3), 58-72.
18. Kumari, P. & Azam, S., & Khalidah, S. (2019). The Effect of Microfinance Services on Poverty Reduction: Analysis of Empirical Evidence in Sri Lankan Perspectives.
19. Kurmanalieva, E., Montgomery, H., & Weiss, J. (2003). Micro-finance and poverty reduction in Asia: what is the evidence. In ADB Institute Annual Conference on 'Micro finance and poverty reduction', Tokyo December 2003.
20. Lakwo, A. (2007). *Microfinance, rural livelihoods, and women's empowerment in Uganda*. Leiden: African Studies Centre. https://repository.ubn.ru.nl/bitstream/handle/2066/56359/56359.pdf
21. Li, X., Gan, C., & Hu, B. (2011). The impact of microcredit on women's empowerment: evidence from China. *Journal of Chinese Economic and Business Studies, 9*(3), 239-261. https://doi.org/10.1080/14765284.2011.592352
22. Modi, A., Patel, K. J., & Patel, K. M. (2014). Impact of microfinance services on rural women empowerment: An empirical study. *IOSR Journal of Business and Management, 16*(11), 1-8.
23. Najeeb, F., Morales, M., & Lopez-Acevedo, G. (2020). *Analyzing female employment trends in South Asia* (Working Paper No. 9157). World Bank Policy Research Working Paper. https://ssrn.com/abstract=3541384
24. Nwankwo, O., Olukotu, G. A., & Abah, E. (2013). Impact of microfinance on rural transformation in Nigeria. *International Journal of Business and Management, 8*(19), 99.
25. Okpara, G. C. (2010). Microfinance banks and poverty alleviation in Nigeria. *Journal of Sustainable development in Africa, 12*(6), 177-191.
26. Prajapati, M., & Bhadouria, S. & Singh, M. (2022). Role of Microfinance in the Socio-Economic Status of Tribal Women A Case Study of Selected District of Madhya Pradesh. *Mekal Insight*, 4, 1-14.
27. Shelby, L. B. (2011). Beyond Cronbach's alpha: Considering confirmatory factor analysis and segmentation. *Human Biases of Wildlife, 16*(2), 142–148.
28. Singh, P., & Kaur, C. (2021). Factors determining financial constraint of SMEs: a study of unorganized manufacturing enterprises in India. *Journal of Small Business & Entrepreneurship, 33*(3), 269-287. https://doi.org/10.1080/08276331.2019.1641662
29. Sohn, W., & Ume, L. (2019). Impact of Microfinance on Poverty Alleviation: A Global Analysis. *Journal of Economics, 7*(2), 82-102.
30. Sussan, M. U., & Obamuyi, T. (2018). The impact of microfinance bank on entrepreneurship development in Nigeria. *Journal of Business and Economic Development Science Publishing Group, 3*(2), 51-61.
31. Taiwo, J.N., Onasanya, Y.A., Agwu, M.E., & Benson, K.N. (2016). The role of microfinance institutions in financing small businesses. *Journal of Internet Banking and Commerce.* 21,1-20.
32. Yahaya, K. A., & Osemene, O. F. (2011). Effectiveness of microfinance banks in alleviating poverty in Kwara State Nigeria. *Global Journal of Management and Business Research, 11*(4).

6

A Study on Women's Empowerment and Skill Development in Manipur

Dr. A. Victoria Chanu[1] *& Mabemma Thoudam*[2]

Abstract

The process of giving women greater economic, social, political, and legal autonomy is known as women empowerment. It assures that women have equal rights. It is a crucial tool for realizing development objectives and building a better community. In the culture we live in today, many women must find a way to support both their families' needs and their own. However, many women lack access to fundamental knowledge and abilities. As a result, they are forced to work for low pay. Therefore, it has become essential for women to acquire a marketable skill that will be a cornerstone of their overall development. The community and family as a whole will gain from the empowerment of women through skill development in addition to the individual women. In this approach, skill development centres are set up through appropriate organizations in various localities to offer skill development programmes to unemployed and underprivileged women, regardless of caste, ethnicity, or religion. This will raise their level of income, develop their knowledge and skills, boost their ability, and raise their standard of living. This study focuses on women's empowerment and skill development with particular reference to the state of Manipur.

Keywords: *Skill development, Women, empowerment, government programme, and policies*

Introduction

The last several decades have seen a significant increase in the importance of women's empowerment. Empowerment, in the words of the United Nations Development Programme (UNDP, 1994), is a procedure that transfers power from the powerful to the weak. There are currently roughly 3.1 million persons in India who seek skill development annually. According to the 11th Five-Year Plan (FYP11), an increase in annual capacity of almost 15 million percent is planned. The nation wants 500 million skilled individuals in its database as of 2022. Both domestically and internationally, Indian women have been particularly effective convicts. The findings also imply that initiatives to advance women's educational attainment, increase work prospects, and raise the marriageable age will contribute to their empowerment, at least in part. Devi (2018) stated that we aim to bring about institutional, individual, and policy change that would enhance the lives of women and girls around the world.

As part of its commitment to ensuring equal rights for women, India has ratified some international agreements and human rights instruments. The Constitution not only guarantees women's equality but also gives the State the authority to implement measures that positively discriminate against women. The development activities place a high priority on the empowerment of women. The

[1] Assistant Professor Department of Commerce Dhanamanjuri University (DMU), Manipur
[2] Research Scholar Department of Commerce Dhanamanjuri University (DMU), Manipur

district administration's stance on the advancement of women, particularly the underprivileged and the illiterate, has significantly changed. Training a woman benefits the entire family, the community, and the country. The current research focuses on women's empowerment in the domestic sphere, or, more specifically, their independence from other family members' control and their capacity to influence desired outcomes in the home. The following elements are part of the United Nations Development Fund for Women's (UNDFW) concept of women's empowerment. Gaining awareness and comprehension of gender interactions and potential changes. According to Batliwala (1974), empowerment is "the process of challenging existing power relations and of gaining greater control over the source of power". When the concept of male dominance and female subordination is challenged, women's empowerment is understood as the process and the outcome. Making it possible for women to have equal access to and control over resources (material, intellectual, and human).

Objectives of Women's Empowerment

1. To offer free reproductive and child health services to any customer, create a national network of public, private, and non-governmental organisations (NGOs) institutions;
2. Identifying gaps in the empowerment of women and the development of children and adolescents; expanding access to safe abortion care and opening more childcare facilities for working women;
3. By using energy-saving technologies to lessen the burden on women;
4. Creating an enabling environment through programme convergence.
5. To improve women's access to fuel, clean water, wood and fodder;
6. To create health management and health packages at all levels; and to raise the standard and accessibility of services for maternity and child health care.
7. To evaluate the results of programmes and policies that support women's empowerment.
8. To locate the data demonstrating the impact of women's empowerment on key development outcomes like health, education, fertility patterns, income levels, etc.
9. Organizing educational and empowerment programmes for girls and women;
10. Improving clinical and contraceptive delivery services;
11. Training resource people, animators, and trainers for activities visualised;
12. Conducting and promoting experiments, innovations, and research in the issues and programmes of rural women's empowerment;
13. Raising awareness among women for their development;
14. To encourage women to be genuinely ambitious and to dream for betterment;
15. To work towards organizing women to combat issues and challenges specific to them;
16. To incorporate socio-economic activities with consideration for environmental protection and health in light of rural women's concerns;

Skill Development for Women

Women have demonstrated their aptitude for community improvement. Women must therefore participate in skill development. They make up a considerable portion of the workforce, but the ratio of working women in the labor force as a whole is dropping. Many of them are employed in unofficial industries. This shows that women's workforce lacks skills and employment prospects. In India, the majority of women workers are currently unskilled. They can be encouraged to improve their life skills, which will enable them to find well-paying employment with improved living conditions and the self-assurance to provide for their families. They will become more capable and self-sufficient as a result. It has been determined that the idea of training and skill development needs to go beyond the teaching of technical and administrative abilities, with a greater emphasis on literacy, numeracy, political, and life skills. Some abilities that training facilities should teach for women's empowerment include: Business etiquette, language development, personality development, leadership, management, entrepreneurship, basic accountancy, and computer abilities are all included in the list of soft skills.

A national policy for "women empowerment" has been adopted by the Indian government to ensure the general advancement of women in the nation. Women are taught skills that help them stand on their own, support themselves, and advance in society. The Maharashtra government, on the other hand, has started "Skill Sakhi" to empower women. Their primary goal is to empower women in addition to providing them with career possibilities. They provide training in a variety of skills, including knitting, embroidery, tailoring, and the creation of things for home decor. Only when women work can the "Skill India" and "Make in India" missions be successful.

Review of Literature

Women's fundamental rights, which provide women the ability to take charge of their lives and, in turn, mark their impact in society, include being empowered and having access to the workforce. Due to the nature of women's jobs in India, skilling women presents a much bigger issue than skilling males. The majority of women in India are employed in low-wage, low-skill employment with little social security or job security (Kumar 2022). Their impact on the economy is essentially invisible. Men make up 63 percent more of the workforce in the informal sector globally than women do (58.1 percent). However, compared to men, a greater proportion of women workers in India are employed in the informal economy: 94% of women who work do so in unorganised industries. Statistics show the gender gap in terms of population, literacy, and employment as day labourers in agriculture, on construction sites, as microbusiness owners, or working from home. According to Parveen, R. (2023), gender discrimination is worse in the informal sector than it is in the formal sector, with women informal workers earning less than half as much as men. Women in our society have different training demands than men because women are responsible for taking care of the home, raising children, and occasionally working as low-wage labourers or subsistence farmers. Long-term development and sustainable livelihood are also improved by opportunities for income. The difference in pay between men and women has remained constant at 50% Klasen, (2018).

In an interactive session on skill development and tribal women's empowerment, Bartlova et al., (2021) stated, "Change should start in the family. We shall be able to accomplish anything if there is a widespread understanding of women's empowerment. affirming that women are naturally strong and capable of accomplishing anything. Women of all education levels can be empowered. Rights and obligations are intertwined. So, let's band together, do things together, and collaborate. The 2011 Indian population census indicates that women make up 48.04 percent of the population and have a literacy rate of 71.5 percent (Vijayabhaskar et al., 2021). Singh contends that women can achieve economic independence if they have the proper SD training (source: Singh 2018). To evaluate the impact of MGNREGA employment on women's empowerment, microfinance through self-help organisations, and occurrences of sexual harassment and interpersonal violence as indicators for women's empowerment, Rodrigurez collected annual district-level data across India (Rodriguez, 2022). The sustainability of women's entrepreneurship depends on efficient funding, accessibility, technical expertise, and up-and-reskilling up-and promote women's empowerment in general (Andriamahery & Qamruzzaman, 2022). Hariharan makes an effort to understand more about India's unique role in training for skill enhancement and female empowerment. Women frequently lack visibility in the context of improvement. According to Hariharan (n.d.), whereas education helps women arm themselves with the skills they need to find their way in the world, SD lessens gender inequities. Women are increasingly active in a variety of fields in India, including education, the arts and humanities, the service industry, sports, politics, the media, and science and technology, but their representation in the labour force as a whole is still underwhelming (Vyas, 2018). Hoxha, & Kleinknecht (2020) urged women's organisations to set the pace for the state's growth through skill development to strengthen the economy and address the issue of underemployment in the State. According to Unni, Jeemol, & Uma (2004), society's attitudes towards women need to alter in addition to their status and perception. There is a need to raise knowledge among unemployed rural women so that they can develop confidence and self-worth. According to Dhruba Hazarika (2011), women are the key to a nation's future growth. To succeed in this cutthroat environment, women must be empowered. According to Vijaya & Lokhandha (2013), increasing women's employability will result in higher output and income. Their ability to be more to a result of their confidence. Kittur Praveen (2014) concluded that to promote women's entrepreneurship, a particular training programme for female entrepreneur organizations was launched to programs their capabilities. Women need to navigate this society that is controlled by men, according to Mamta Mokta's (2014) research. Self-help organisations, non-governmental organisations (NGOs), governmental programmes, and microfinance institutions should inspire them to grow and be empowered. According to Prasanna Kumar (2014), we must pinpoint the regions in which women continue to experience issues and are unable to access resources, institutional knowledge, and basic education.

Statement of Problem

This study focuses on women's empowerment and skill development in Manipur. It discusses the initiatives taken by different groups to support women's empowerment and skill development in the region. Policies to support women politically, socially, and economically are also covered.

Objectives of the Study

The main objectives are:

1. To identify the essential abilities of women and promote them.
2. To study the role of skill development towards women empowerment in Manipur.
3. To suggest government policies and implement appropriate programmes to support the Skill Development of women

Research Methodology

Methodology Secondary data provides the foundation for the focus's research. To increase the inclusion of women in various sectors, the Indian government has implemented many regulations and programmes. Data from numerous research publications, websites, and essays are gathered here. There have been certain practices adopted by the organisations named. Between employment and labour, skill development is essential for boosting income and employment as well as for sustainable rural development.

Important SD Opportunities for Women in the Present Scenario

A strong society can be built by a competent, self-assured woman. What is concerning is that, regardless of how well a woman performs her job or performs on par with men, there may be instances where she is victimized. An Indian woman spends 25% of her time on daily tasks. However, a man only devotes 2.5% of his time to these pursuits. Only 35% of Indian women can use the Internet, according to a survey. To encourage women to use the internet and mobile phones, the Central Government is developing the Digital Saksharata Abhiyan (DISHA) and other platforms. Research from the National Institution for Transforming India (NITI) Aayog predicts that 75 million Indian women will likely enter the workforce in the next ten years. Women must therefore increase their learning at all levels and build their financial standing. Then and only then will we be able to end exploitation, social abuse, and wage inequality. Women can get employment or start their businesses with the support of the opportunities that come with literacy and SD. Women's skill development courses will promote employment and income options for women. In the current environment, every woman must possess at least one formal or professional competence. A capable woman can take the reins in running her family even if the main provider of income is unemployed. Not everyone may be able to work for the government, but a talented woman can labor to better her family's financial situation. A self-sufficient woman can not only become her family's financial pillar by working with confidence, but she can also serve as an inspiration for other, weaker women. A capable woman can play a significant role in advancing gender equality by working hard and transforming not only her family but also the global landscape. Women should have a variety of vocational skill training if they are to effectively utilize the numerous relevant skills that are ingrained in them. Due to the aforementioned factors, the government established CITSs and NSTIs all around the nation under the National Council for Vocational Training (NCVT) board to provide vocational SD training and provide chances for female trainers. Women are now able to earn equally to men and women thanks to this training. To become financially independent, boost her self-confidence, and hold a prominent status in the family and society, a woman gets admitted to numerous such trainings based on a minimal entry requirement. She then goes through various sorts of vocational training. Furthermore, the number of women trainers will rise daily if the government sets up hostels for the security of female trainees arriving from remote areas. By making it available to women in rural regions as well, the goal of vocational skill development training will be fully achieved. To promote home goods and assist sales, the Ministry of Micro, Small, and Medium Enterprises (MSME) works on behalf of the government, regional business owners, and SHGs. This encourages women around the world to start their businesses.

Although major gendered inequities still exist internationally, investing in women's economic empowerment is essential for achieving gender equality, ending poverty, advancing human development, and fostering inclusive economic growth (Hunt & Samman, 2016). Economic stability is crucial for women's independence. The likelihood that SD training will boost women's earnings and employment rates is high. Small-scale tasks with high skill levels include web design, whereas medium-scale tasks with high skill levels include plumbing repair, working as a receptionist, and home and agricultural work. She'll be able to pull it off. Additionally, women can receive training for non-traditional jobs like security guards, plumbing repairs, soldering, etc. Such jobs boost the proportion of women in the working class and offer them social and financial support. because women are good at seizing opportunities and are continually looking for them. No fi can afford to pass up the chances that present themselves. The state's rural economic productivity will be boosted through empowering women. Women's SD, upskilling, and reskilling give housewives the chance to start their businesses and support their families. It is everyone's responsibility to acknowledge and support a woman's abilities if she is to become independent and self-sufficient. Women take up all of the tasks of the household and every career in this situation, according to Vijayabhaskar et al. (2021). It is true that in the future, just "leaders" will be popular rather than male or female leaders. Women's management of their personal and professional lives is reimagined by SD. The woman should therefore make an effort to learn at least one skill. According to research by Diwakar & Ahamad (2015), SD can significantly improve family production, employment, and chances for money generation for many rural poor people and women. To combat intergenerational thinking, promote occupational and sectoral segregation, and challenge discriminatory norms, the main recommendations are to ramp up norm reform efforts. SD teaches women about internal power, decision-making authority, control over material possessions, physical and intellectual capital, and ability-based power. The time will soon come when housewives will earn a living and vice versa, based on their suitability and needs. A woman with good weapons can live a self-sufficient life.

Suggestion

Despite being the biggest and fastest-growing nation, India still falls behind other nations in terms of how easily women can obtain skills. The following are ideas for how to make things better: Women's policies need to be strengthened by providing more seats for them

Women's empowerment through skill-building programmes will give them greater opportunities. Digital platforms might be utilized for this.

Women can develop skills in a variety of industries for greater empowerment, including Banking and financial services

The following industries are represented: management, pharmaceuticals, the hospitality sector, the travel and tourism sector, the telecom sector, information technology, the media sector, and the childcare sector.

Conclusion & Recommendations

There is a road plan for women's emancipation. Women play a crucial role in society. "The best indicator of a country's progress is how it treats its women." Social acknowledgment of them and their increased participation in socio-economic and political matters are therefore crucial. Everyone should step forward to ensure that women have equal standing in all walks of life. Women have been an oppressed group throughout history despite making up half the world's population. Most countries around the world have treated women as second-class citizens, although other nations view women as superior in the home and community. Women are compelled to remain the dominating group around the globe, especially in the least developed countries, due to religious, cultural, and physical norms. Worldwide discrimination against women is well documented. Because of male dominance, women's participation in practically all fields has been reduced, even in the most industrialized countries with the best human rights record in the world. Women are treated as "prisoners" in many nations since they are prohibited from participating in many social and political activities (Meenu Agrawal, Shobana Nelasco, 2009) Planning professionals, managers, and social scientists from all over the world have begun deliberating and coming up with solutions to the access and empowerment issues that arise in a stratified society like ours. Gender issues are taking precedence over other sensitive issues in this direction, such as poverty, class conflicts, communities, ethnic issues, etc. Gender equity is still an important issue in guaranteeing an egalitarian development, just as it has been for thousands of years of human civilization. Beyond its epistemological aspects, gender issues undoubtedly incorporate other elements like the production relationship, educational access, regional distribution, job requirements, marital system, and even physical and physiological deficiencies. (2009) Ram Naresh Thakur The current discussion will be situated within the perspective of the development of sustainable agriculture for women. Women's engagement in moving across castes has proven essential to the sustainability of agricultural growth. (Junofy Antorozarina & Shobana Nelasco, 2009) The issue of women's empowerment has been thrown into a very complex, integrated situation, and we need to identify and confirm the areas where they are still far from enjoying the bare minimum of privileges. Access to resources, institutions, the decision-making process, and information, among other things, is crucial for enabling women to feel empowered, self-assured, and included in the mainstream social processes.

Gender-responsive skill-development programmes are needed for women, who are equally as capable as males. Socioeconomic development depends on the social, economic, educational, political, and legal empowerment of women. If given the chance, women are capable of managing. They must be handled with dignity, respect, and fairness. All that is required is a focused effort in the correct direction that only focuses on releasing women from all types of wickedness. India is moving more and more towards a "knowledge economy," hence it must concentrate on skill advancement. These abilities must apply to the new economic environment. An effective talent is needed to transform its demographic dividend. Development is promoted by empowerment. It is a staged process created by active elements in a specific society. Women would be able to develop confidence, realize their potential, and improve their self-esteem via empowerment. The development of skills can upend the nation's socioeconomic system. Women should have the sophistication to recognize when they need to alter to better themselves. The ancient notion about women's frailties, incompetence, and vivacity to reach the heights of acknowledgment needs to be dispelled to empower women in all domains. Both males and females need to change their mindsets. Therefore, it is crucial to give women nurturing care and guidance for them to advance, live peacefully, and ensure their futures. For more people to take appropriate action in this respect and for women to participate in these activities on an equal basis with their male counterparts, efforts should be made to improve skill development in the state.

References

1. Agrawal, M. (Ed.). (2009). *Women Empowerment and Globalization: A Modern Perspective*. Kanishka Publishers.
2. Andriamahery, A., & Qamruzzaman, M. (2022). Do access to finance, technical know-how, and financial literacy offer women empowerment through women's entrepreneurial development?. *Frontiers in Psychology, 12*, 776844.

3. Anuradha, R. V., & Reddy, G. L. (2013). Empowerment of rural women through vocational education and training. *Conflux Journal of Education ISSN*, 2320-9305.
4. Bartlova, M., Shurr, J. V., Dienstbier, J., Kalouskova, T., Soukupova, V., Sorm, M., & Francíkova, D. (2021). *Premodern History and Art Through the Prism of Gender in East-Central Europe*. Rowman & Littlefield.
5. Devi, S. (2018). Women empowerment in rural sector. *International Journal of Research in Social Sciences, 8*(4), 881-889.
6. Diwakar, N., & Ahamad, T. (2015). Skills development of women through vocational training. *International Message of Applied Research, 1*, 79-83.
7. Hazarika, D. (2011). Women empowerment in India: A brief discussion. *International Journal of Educational Planning & Administration, 1*(3), 199-202.
8. Hoxha, S., & Kleinknecht, A. (2020). When labour market rigidities are useful for innovation. Evidence from German IAB firm-level data. *Research Policy, 49*(7), 104066.
9. Kittur. P, (2014). Development of Rural Women Entrepreneurs through Workshop Training, *Research Journal of Management Sciences, 3*(2), 15-18.
10. Klasen, S. (2018). The impact of gender inequality on economic performance in developing countries. *Annual Review of Resource Economics, 10*, 279-298.
11. Kumar, S. (2022). The Skilling Imperative in India: The Bridge Between Women and Work.
12. Mokta, M. (2014). Empowerment of women in India: A critical analysis. *Indian Journal of public administration, 60*(3), 473-488.
13. Parveen, R. (2023). Vocational Skill Development Imperative for Women Empowerment in India. *Journal of Women Empowerment and Studies (JWES) ISSN: 2799-1253, 3*(03), 15-24.
14. Prasanna, K. (2014). Rural Women Empowerment in India, *Asian Journal of Multidisciplinary Studies, 2*(1), 2321-8819.
15. Ram, N. T. (2009). Rural women empowerment in India in empowerment of rural women in India.
16. Rodriguez, Z. (2022). The power of employment: Effects of India's employment guarantee on women empowerment. *World development, 152*, 105803.
17. Singh, A. K. (2018). Skills development of women through vocational training-case study of CSR initiatives of a public sector undertaking. *International Journal of Research in Social Sciences, 8*(10), 285-298.
18. SobhReddy, N. C. (2014). Rural women empowerment and entrepreneurship development in India. *International Journal of Business and Administration Research Review, 3*(5), 125-127.
19. Unni, J., & Rani, U. (2004). Technical change and workforce in India: skill biased growth?. *Indian Journal of Labour Economics, 47*(4), 683-692.
20. Vijayabhaskar, N. (2021). Opportunities And Challenges Of Women Entrepreneurship In Hyderabad Karnataka Region Of Karnataka State. *IJRAR-International Journal of Research and Analytical Reviews (IJRAR), 8*(1), 18-24.
21. Vyas, A. (2018). The impact of skill development on women empowerment. *International Journal for Advance Research and Development, 3*(1), 8-11.

7

A Study of MSMEs' Contributions to Skill Development in Manipur

Dr. Loitongbam Kirankumar Singh[1] *& Dr. Th. Priyokumar Singh*[2]

Abstract

The Self-help Group operating independently as innovative and proactive anti-poverty initiatives are examined in this paper. To maintain the growth of the entire economy and the SHG programme in particular, a stable macroeconomic environment, as well as the macroeconomic and financial sectors, are crucial. The business owners were chosen using a multi-stage purposive sampling technique. The final sample size consisted of 210 respondents, who were chosen from the total. The most relevant descriptive and statistical methods, such as the basic percentage and ANOVA test, were employed to analyze the data, which was administered using SPSS 21.0. The results showed that the significance values for all factors except for the establishment's year, industry, current turn oversize, and respondent age are less than 0.05 at the 5% level of significance. The findings suggest that there are no appreciable differences between men and women in terms of the elements that discourage, require, encourage, and motivate independent enterprises. There is no difference in all of the parameters when the estimated value is bigger than the 0.05 level of significance. It is possible to distinguish between the opinions of various stakeholders on the involvement of SHGs in the factors that encouraged skill development through innovators of both categories in larger social issues, showing their perceived positive perception of quality indicators on increasing employment and income opportunities for the workforce.

Keywords: *Skill development, SHGs, enterprise and employment*

Introduction

Governments of various nations typically give their citizens the freedom to develop their skills while taking into account the demands and future goals of their respective nations as well as the current scenario. India is a sizable nation with the second-largest population in the world. Even when additional non-traditional and commercial farming opportunities are available, the microfinance sector has emerged as a key driver behind the inclusion of underserved people by the present financial service providers (Mammen & Paxson, 2000). The microfinance sector in India is fragmented, with more than 3000 microfinance businesses (Sharma, 2015). Digital advances have increased opportunities, given us better communication channels, and increased productivity for individuals, groups, and governments. The international microfinance industry is rapidly growing as a result of technological advancements in the banking sector. The microfinance industry is more effective overall when information technology is used (Daowd et al., 2021). Banks and microfinance organizations have made significant contributions to the

[1] Faculty, Bachelor of Business Administration, D. M. College of Commerce, Dhanamanjuri University, Imphal, Manipur

[2] Assistant Professor, Department of Economics, D.M. College of Commerce, Dhanamanjuri University, Imphal, Manipur

development of the use of IT for the loan process, which makes the job easier and helps the organizations broaden the scope of their services (Harelimana, 2017). The industry will be able to benefit greatly from the country's movement through regular sessions, awareness initiatives, and workshops that train clients on how to use IT services. Microfinance interventions are widely acknowledged as a powerful strategy for reducing poverty and enhancing the socioeconomic standing of rural poor people. Micro-finance is making progress in India as well in eradicating poverty and empowering rural women. Microfinance has primarily been a supply-driven and contemporary strategy through the network of cooperatives, commercial banks, regional rural banks, NABARD, and NGOs. The growing significance of the economic contribution that women are making to support the local economy should alert policymakers, as should micro, small, and medium-sized firms and those demonstrating the rising proportion of women in self-employment (Smith, 1999). It is now acknowledged that many newly independent people started small businesses, and by 1997, 95% of all businesses were micro-businesses (Clark, 1995). The elimination of unemployment and the reduction of poverty were acknowledged as two of the primary goals of economic planning for the nation during the fifth five-year plan. In light of this, ending poverty has become a crucial goal for developing nations, notably India. Numerous initiatives to eradicate poverty have been started in previous five-year plans. A new enterprise is related to the innovative and dynamic process of entrepreneurship. An entrepreneur is a change catalyst who creates job possibilities for others. The prevailing economic, social, religious, cultural, and psychological variables in culture have a substantial impact on the emergence of entrepreneurs in that community. Researchers examined the variables that affected the development of sample men's and women's entrepreneurial skills. These elements were then categorized as "motivational factors": An individual's motivation is what drives them to take independent action. The individual may be motivated internally or outside. To establish a business, motivation is crucial. An entrepreneurial individual takes the initiative to realize a self-set future vision objective to fully realize one's purpose in life and share the results with others.

Motivating aspects:

The motivating aspects in some ways make it easier for entrepreneurs to continue to thrive in their industry. Even if someone has a great company idea, women entrepreneurs will not succeed unless they are supported by social, financial, and emotional networks on all sides. Therefore, it is necessary to support a variety of forces and variables. While self-confidence was the most important facilitative element, this aspect helped SHGs since non-SHGs' priorities varied. Women tend to seek entrepreneurship because they need to be financially independent.

Compulsory Elements:

Some women may have been forced to engage in risky activities for a variety of reasons. It was revealed that some circumstances forced business owners to launch their ventures. Both of these categories chose entrepreneurship due to compulsive motives. It has been noted that both group members were obliged to choose microenterprises due to "economic compulsions," "dependency situations," and "unemployment."

Discouraging Barriers: Initially, many barriers stopped women from having careers outside the home. Numerous studies have shown that "lack of finance," particularly "working capital," is a significant issue at every stage of an enterprise's development.

Review of Literature

According to Keishnaraj and Maithreyi (2005), microfinance is one technique for combating poverty. Through social mobilization with various entry points, such as the elimination of illiteracy, access to basic healthcare, removal of social ills, resolution of social conflict, and environmental protection through thrift and credit, they have facilitated the organization of SHGs for a common cause. NABARD created and promoted the SHG model. Smaller groups (SHGs) with 15 to 20 members raise modest sums of money to open unusual bank accounts in their names. The organizations often get together and lend members small sums of money to cover small but urgent needs. Peer pressure is increased and proper use of cash is ensured by the open decisions made in group meetings. The group receives loans from microfinance organisations, and it is up to the group to repay the debts. Policymakers in both industrialized and developing nations are paying increasing attention to the topic of women's and men's entrepreneurship. Entrepreneurial endeavors by both men and women play a significant role in expanding job opportunities and promoting economic growth (Costanza et al., 2003). Since the 1980s, policymakers and development organisations in developing nations have made women's entrepreneurship one of their main priorities. According to Nilufer (2001), an entrepreneur is somebody who possesses the aforementioned traits and applies them to create and manage a business. Entrepreneurs are business builders; they recognize potential new businesses Using their resources and borrowed money, they start businesses where none had ever been before, accept the dangers involved, and profit as a reward for their efforts. recognizing the concepts discussed above, one might define an entrepreneur as "a person who brings all the required resources for innovation, production, and renovation while considering the associated risks." In their article, Manimekalai and Rajeshwari (2001) emphasized how the granting of microloans by NGOs to women's SHGs had aided the groups in achieving a certain level of economic and social empowerment. It has grown in its ability to take charge, organize itself, and manage a variety of company operations, including obtaining financing, locating markets, identifying raw materials, and properly diversifying and modernizing. An ILO research defines entrepreneurship development as the integration of training and other support services into a structured programme to help people and groups who are interested in launching small companies. Entrepreneurship development is an endeavor that identifies challenges facing entrepreneurs and introduces solutions to those issues so that entrepreneurs can participate actively in the creative process. According to Kantor (2001), gender-sensitive policies and programmes openly acknowledge the differences between men and women and how these distinctions may affect a person's capacity to engage in entrepreneurship. Women's entrepreneurship development can be defined as gender-specific policies and programmes that are aimed specifically at women to benefit them within the current context of gender relations. However, other classifications have been applied to categorize organisation size. Dasgupta (2000) noted that the informal group approach to microfinance has produced some positive effects, such as the mobilization of savings by the underprivileged. Poor people's access to the necessary amount of appropriate credit, matching credit demand and supply, lowering transaction costs for lenders and borrowers, significantly improving recovery, ushering in a new era of subsidy- and corruption-free credit, and remarkably empowering poor women are all factors. Similarly, this, Gurumoorthy (2000) argued that SHGs are a practical substitute for accomplishing rural development goals and enlisting community support for all rural development initiatives. SHG is a workable organisational structure for providing rural women with microcredit to help them become businesswomen and to encourage them to engage in entrepreneurial activity. The standing of women as participants, decision-makers, and beneficiaries in the democratic, economic, social, and cultural realms of life is improved through SHGs. They encourage women to actively participate in society's socioeconomic development. Through a case study on thrift groups in Assam, Ahmad (1999) emphasised the fact that women are approaching the government directly to demand their legal rights and to publicly air their problems. It showed the viability of Self-help Groups in North East India despite insurgency. Small and medium-sized businesses vary by country and are typically based on the number of employees or the value of assets, claims Kristin (1999). Gender has been a key organizing force of social life throughout history and cultures, according to Coltrane (1998). According to Goldner, Penn, Sheinberg, and Walker (1990), the construction of gender and gender difference is a universal principle of cultural life. Gender is one of the main constructs people use to organize their family relationships, identities, and life decisions.

Statement of Problem

One of the main goals of any planning for a national economy is the reduction of poverty. Therefore, it becomes crucial to design poverty alleviation policies and programmes that are situation-specific to provide a minimum income level for the rural poor, who make up a sizeable portion of the national population in developing countries. Since the development of Technology and the application of modern technologies, microfinance has experienced tremendous change (Rajendran & Raya, 2011) and is an important tool for empowering rural and indigenous women. Thirty years after Yunus' revolutionary idea, microfinance is spreading around the world. It is fast evolving as a result of the many new opportunities, especially as a result of innovations (Bakker, Schaveling, and Nijhof, 2014). The study was conducted in Manipur to evaluate the effects of microfinance on the socioeconomic circumstances of SHG members, with the majority of significant socioeconomic issues mostly caused by unemployment and poverty. The beginning of planned economic development through several five-year plans brought diverse development and welfare under focus, and women have historically been seen as lesser family members. Government, NGOs, and international organizations have all adopted numerous such programmes for socioeconomic development. However, the results of all these efforts have not been sufficient. This collection of businesses offers an administrative framework for combining resources such as capital, labour, technology, and the market, as well as for promoting the participation of men and women and their influence on the development of skills in self-employment and other sources of income. The following particular goals guided the conduct of this investigation.

Objectives of the Study

1. To identify the demographic characteristics of independent SHGs that owned and operated enterprises.
2. To analyze the elements that promoted the growth of entrepreneurial skills in both groups.
3. To evaluate the effects of microfinance on the socioeconomic status of SHG members in terms of business barriers and different entrepreneurship-related aspects.

Hypotheses

There is no difference between male and female entrepreneurs in the demographic factors.

The elements that discourage, need, encourage, and motivate entrepreneurship in men and women have not changed.

Research Methodology

The district, block, villages, and entrepreneurs were chosen using a multi-stage purposive sampling technique. They were chosen because their diversification into entrepreneurial work through skill development was representative. Manipur's Valley district was selected as the focus of the study. Inconvenient to the researchers who held the key to MSMEs activity, 210 working SHG employees from manufacturing and services activities in four districts made up the sample for this study. Working entrepreneurs are represented in the sample under their size and the goals of the study. There are now nine districts in Manipur. Imphal East, Imphal West, Bishnupur, and Thoubal, four districts in the valley, were chosen for the current study. To improve the socio-demographic situation of the population and build any development strategy to generate new employment prospects through participation in work and research while developing their skills. It is descriptive research. It is based on both primary and secondary information gathered from those business owners, the former using an interview schedule. The publications and reports operating at the district, state, and federal levels were the sources of the secondary data. The study's acquired data was gathered, tabulated, processed, and interpreted. Various performance assessment methods and statistical techniques, including average, percentage, t-test, and ANOVA, were used to evaluate the data using the SPSS 21 software.

Results and Discussion

Self Help Groups a microfinancing strategy, are a novel innovation in credit delivery methods designed to improve income-generating activities. The scheme provides small loans to low-income individuals so they can engage in self-employment activities and improve their quality of life (Rahman, 1995; Hussain, 1998; and Morduch, 2000). For those who are the poorest, notably women, it is the most effective anti-poverty strategy (Micro Credit Summit, 1997). It is acknowledged that microfinance helps the poor by increasing their income, reducing their vulnerability, and smoothing out their consumption. Microfinance can help break the cycle of poverty by assisting the world's impoverished in as little as one generation (Maheswaranathan & Kennedy, 2010).

Table 1: Results of Demographic Variables with Men and Women Enterprises

Variables		Gender		Total
		Men	Women	
Age	Up to 30 years	11	17	28
	36-40 years	19	20	39
	41-45 years	52	53	105
	above 45 years	19	19	38
Literacy	High school	35	30	65
	Higher Secondary	28	38	66
	Graduate and above	39	38	79

Number of working employee	Up to 15	49	55	104
	16-25	43	48	91
	26-30	7	2	9
	Above 30	2	4	6
Type of industry	Manufacturing	38	42	80
	Services	21	24	45
	Agricultural and allied	12	9	21
	Handloom and handicraft	17	26	43
	Food and beverage	11	10	21
Income of the busi-ness	10,001-20,000	15	13	28
	20,001-30,000	19	26	45
	30,001-40,000	39	38	77
	More than 40,000	28	32	60

Sources: Primary Data

The key demographic factors that traditional civilizations use to determine social standing are shown in Table No. 1. The majority of working men and women are typically between the ages of 41 and 45. The table shows that only 12 and 16 SHG members, respectively, are still active up to the age of 35. They are actively participating in SHGs. According to their educational histories, the majority of the sample entrepreneurs had access to higher education. The majority of respondents discovered that men and women had higher secondary and graduate academic levels than the entire sample. The maximum proportion of working employees, up to 15 members, is 50 males and 54 women. The least amount of working employees over 30 was revealed by 3 men and 3 women. The sector of the industry is for the income bracket of SHG-affiliated men and women. The majority of respondents between 39 and 41 work in manufacturing, while the least number of respondents are employed in agricultural-related fields. 21 men and women work in the food and beverage industry; the remaining sample responses are dispersed throughout various other businesses. The respondents' standard of living can be determined by their income. The average monthly income of the 40 men and 37 women who responded was between Rs. 30001 and Rs. 40000. It showed that the respondents' medium income status was represented by members who made less money.

The ANOVA test values and significance for demographic factors and entrepreneurship in men and women are shown in the table. In the ANOVA comparisons between test values and significance values, accepting the null hypothesis for some variables is preferred. The results showed that, except for the establishment's year, industry, current turn oversize, and respondent's age, all factors have significance values that are less than 0.05 at the 5% level of significance. As a result, at a 5% level of significance, reject the null hypothesis and accept the alternative. Therefore, disregard the alternative hypothesis for the variable educational qualification and accept the null hypothesis at a 5% level of significance.

Ho1: No difference among the demographic variables between men and women enterprises.

Table 2: Results of hypothesis testing F-test

Groups of the Variable		Sum of Squares	df	Mean Square	F Value	P Value	Level of Significance
Year of the establishment	B G	1269.6	18	69.2	2.004	0.09	Significant
	W G	6721.11	191	34.867			
Type of industry	B G	87.14	28	3.212	1.622	0.011	Significant
	W G	287.03	181	1.762			
Current turnover size	B G	28.212	18	1.68	1.69	0.01	Significant
	W G	165.432	191	0.73			
Age of the enterprises	B G	22.438	18	1.451	1.59	0.027	Significant
	W G	137.635	191	0.801			
Educational Qualification	B G	10.456	18	0.62	0.741	0.745	Not Significant
	W G	125.659	191	0.64			

Sources: Primary Data

** Significant at 1% level, * Significant at 5% level.

Table No. 3 shows the findings of the hypothesis that there is a substantial difference between factors that discourage, compel, encourage, and motivate independent entrepreneurship and its dimensions among men and women. The significance level suggests that there are no appreciable differences between men and women in any of the contributing factors to independent entrepreneurship. In all the categories where the estimated value is more significant than the 0.05 level of significance, there is no difference between the groups of men and women.

Ho2: No change has been found among discouraging, compulsory, encouraging and motivational factors to enterprises in men and women.

Table 3: Results of hypothesis testing F-test

Groups of the Variable		Sum of Squares	df	Mean Square	F Value	P Value	Level of Significance
Discouraging Barriers	B G	0.135	1	0.139	1.142	0.279	Not Significant
	W G	23.876	208	0.14			
Compulsory Elements	B G	0.057	1	0.057	0.125	0.673	Not Significant
	W G	55.436	208	0.312			
Encouraging factors	B G	0.054	1	0.054	0.452	0.476	Not Significant
	W G	22.346	208	0.101			
Motivating aspects	B G	0.587	1	0.824	2.819	0.107	Not Significant
	W G	46.763	208	0.916			

Sources: Primary Data

** Significant at 1% level, * Significant at 5% level

By offering loans to the poor combined with inputs like skill development, training, and other support services, poverty can be decreased (Karmakar 2008). One will be pushed towards commercial endeavours as a result, opening the door to self-employment. This will probably create a base of revenue, which in turn will strengthen the populace. The rural poor's overall development would be facilitated by the surplus money from self-sustaining activities. According to the UNHCR (2011), "Meaningful livelihood interventions need multi-year strategic plans, with carefully sequenced and targeted interventions, in keeping with changes in people's attitudes towards working, investing, and hiring. Additionally, they must be adaptable enough to deal with changes in the market and regional policies, as well as build upon and support regional development objectives. Microfinance helps people and households build their financial capital so they can expand their employment opportunities and maintain their socioeconomic well-being. As a result, micro-finance has emerged as a paradigm shift in the growth process.

Conclusion

Microfinance organisations target the poor to help the majority of people who are economically and socially disadvantaged. SHGs and environmental management: According to the Rio Declaration (1992), "women have a vital role in environmental management and development," and attaining sustainable development depends on their full participation. To promote gender equality and female emancipation, reduce poverty, and ensure sustainable environmental management, the Millennium Development Goals recognize these needs. According to Farzaneh and Indira (2011), the participation of SHG members in development initiatives through SHGs can significantly raise societal awareness of environmental sustainability. The SME sector is most susceptible to economic instability because of its small size and lack of scale. Despite the widespread financial crisis in international markets, the SME sector experienced significant growth in the most recent fiscal year. The government also offered support for the initiatives that instructed all public sector banks to give small industrial units extra financial aid without the need for collateral security. The top body has started several assistance programmes for small and medium-sized businesses throughout the financial crisis, keeping in mind the importance of the small-scale sector in attaining long-term growth and poverty alleviation goals. The state government is providing SMEs operating there with the support they need to thrive, making it particularly alluring to small businesses. All of these strategies are available to small business owners who want to start their operations in the state and advance development. The findings showed that men and women both emphasised characteristics with significance levels below 0.05 for a 5% level of significance, except the establishment's year of operation, industry, current turn oversize, and respondent age. Repudiate the null hypothesis, then. It was discovered that financial limitations are the greatest impediment to entrepreneurship when comparing the effectiveness of barriers to independent entrepreneurship in men and women. However, it is interesting to note that there was no discernible difference between the elements across the two groups in terms of the dimensions of autonomous entrepreneurship and the characteristics that were mandatory, encouraging, or motivating to do so.

The path to achieving sustainable livelihoods and social development involves creating a channel for skill acquisition, empowering every segment of society by offering education and training through institutional setup, developing programmes and policies, and tying them exclusively to formal and non-formal fiscal institutions. When discussing skill development in a larger context, it is important to be explicit and to explain why, what, and how it is to be accomplished (e.g., through correct skill development, connecting young people with financial institutions, microcredit, self-help groups, etc.). Rural community-based skill development programmes should recognize that participants should leave with the knowledge necessary to address issues that may have arisen in the agricultural social system. Individuals should be able to improve their level of living and progress in terms of the Human Development Index by developing their skills. However, to create jobs, skills must be marketable and useful; otherwise, the programmes would encourage useless skills and exacerbate underemployment.

References

1. Ahmad, M.A., (1999). Women Empowerment: Self Help Groups, *Kurukshetra, 43* (5): 35-39. April.
2. Bakker, A., Schaveling, J & Nijhof, A. (2014). Governance and microfinance institutions. *Corporate Governance, 14*(5), 637-652 https://doi.org/10.1108/CG-03-2014-0032
3. Clark, P. (1995). *Business Development and the Poor:* The Strategy of Micro-Enterprise Assistance, available at: www.sbaer.uca.edu/docs/proceedings/95sbai01.
4. Coltrane, S. (1998). *Gender and families.* Thousand Oaks, CA: Pine Forge Press.
5. Costanza, G., Hrund, G. & Angela, M. (2003). *The Status of Statistics on Women and Men's Entrepreneurship in the UNECE Region*, Statistical Division, UNECE, Geneva.
6. Daowd, A., Kamal, M. M., Eldabi, T., Hasan, R., Missi, F., & Dey, B. L. (2021). The impact of social media on the performance of microfinance institutions in developing countries: a quantitative approach. *Information Technology & People, 34*(1), 25-49. https://doi.org/10.1108/ITP-03-2018-0135
7. Dasgupta, G. (2000). An informal journey through SHG's, *Indian Journal of Agricultural Economics, 56*(3), July-September.
8. Farzaneh, S & Indira, M., (2011). Empowerment of women through self help groups and environmental management: Experiences of NGOs in Karnataka state, India. *Journal of Human Ecology,* 34 (1): 29-40.
9. Goldner, V., Penn, P., Sheinberg, M. & Walker, G. (1990). *Love and violence:* Gender paradoxes in volatile attachments. Family Process, 29, 343-364.
10. Gurumoorthy, T.R., (2000). Self Help Groups Empower Rural Women, *Kurukshetra,* 48, 5. February.
11. Harelimana, J. B. (2017). The impact of information communication and technology utilization on the financial performance of microfinance institutions in Rwanda case study: Reseau Interdiocesain De Microfinance (Rim) Ltd, Rwanda (2011–2015). *Management and Organizational Studies,* 4(2), 13-28. https://doi.org/10.5430/mos.v4n2p13
12. Hussain, A. M., (1998). *Poverty Alleviation and Empowerment: The Second Impact Assessment Study of BRAC's. Rural Development Programme.* Dhaka: BRAC.
13. Karmakar, K. 2008. Trends in rural finance. *Indian Journal of Agricultural Economics, 63*(1): 14.
14. Kantor, P. (2001). Promoting women's entrepreneurship development based on good practice programmes: some experiences from the north to the south, *SEED Working Paper No. 9,* International Labour Office, Geneva.
15. Keishnaraj & Maithreyi, (2005). Growth and rural Poverty, *Economic & Political Weekly,* September 21.
16. Kristin, H. (1999). *Small and medium scale enterprises:* A framework for intervention, Small enterprise unit, Private sector development department, The World Bank, Washington, DC.
17. Maheswaranathan, S. & Kennedy, F. B., (2010). *Impact of Micro - Credit Programmes on Eliminating Economic Hardship of Women.* ICBI. Sri Lanka: University of Kelaniya. Retrieved from http://www.kln.ac.lk/uokr/ICBI2010/7.pdf.
18. Mammen, K., & Paxson, C. (2000). Women's work and economic development. *Journal of Economic Perspectives, 14*(4), 141-164.

19. Manimekalai, M. & Rajeswari, G., (2001). Nature and Performance of Informal Self Help Groups -A Case from Tamilnadu. *Indian Journal of Agricultural Economics, 56*(3): 453-454.
20. Micro-Credit Summit, (1997). *The Micro-Credit Summit: Declaration and Plan for Action.* Washington, DC: Grameen Foundation.
21. Morduch, J., (2000). The Microfinance Schism. World Development *28*(4): 617-629.
22. Nilufer, A. (2001). Jobs, Gender and Small Enterprises in Bangladesh: factors affecting women entrepreneurs in small and cottage industries in Bangladesh, *SEED Working Paper No. 14*, International Labor Office, Geneva.
23. Rahman, H., (1995). Mora Kartik: Seasonal deficits and the vulnerability of the rural poor. In H. Rahman, & M. Hossain (Eds.), *Rethinking rural poverty Bangladesh as a case study* (54-67). Dhaka: University Press Limited.
24. Rajendran, K., & Raya, R. P. (2011). Does Microfinance Empower Rural Women?–An Empirical Study In Vellore District, Tamil Nadu. *Indian Journal of Finance*, 5(11), 47-55.
25. Sarma, M., & Pais, J. (2011). Financial inclusion and development. *Journal of International Development*, *23*(5), 613-628. https://doi.org/10.1002/jid.1698
26. Smith, I. (1999). Micro solutions to macroeconomic change: rural management and human resources, *Journal of the Agricultural Manpower Society*, 1(4).
27. UNHCR (United Nations High Commissioner for Refugees). (2011). *Investing in solutions: A practical guide for the use of microfinance in UNHCR operations*. Geneva: UNHCR. .

8

MSMEs as ICT Adoption: Relationship and Management Implications

Dr. Bharat Nirwal[1] & Archana Eknath Thombre[2]

Abstract

Information and communication technologies (ICTs) have a big influence on how products and services are marketed as well as how they are made, how people work, and how businesses are run. Particularly in small and medium-sized organizations (SMEs), ICTs can increase levels of uncertainty and put a strain on the firm's knowledge and skill base, individual responsibilities, and relationships. This study examines the barriers or causes preventing the adoption of ICT. To analyze how these affect SMEs' management, interpersonal dynamics, and working practices. The results of this study could offer managers in SMEs more specific directions and recommendations. SMEs frequently lack the specialized knowledge, resources, and time to handle such pressing concerns, these ICT adoption issues place a particularly high burden on management and staff in smaller organizations. adoption of several technological elements, this study indicates that working employees will understand the perceived value of adopting new technology in the absence of personal contact, only technology can support an organization's ongoing operations.

Keywords: *SMEs management, ITC, adoption and organization*

Introduction

SMEs are challenging to define because there is no agreed-upon definition. SMEs are divided into groups based on their investment and the number of employees. SMEs play a significant part in the global economy's balanced growth (Sharma et al 2014). Particularly in small and medium-sized organizations (SMEs), ICTs have the potential to increase levels of uncertainty and put a strain on the firm's knowledge and skill base, as well as on individual roles and relationships. The degree to which SMEs are exposed to ICTs and how ready they are to adapt to technological change can differ. According to Ramsey et al. (2004), the structure and size of SMEs make the challenges they encounter special. However, SMEs are generally regarded as being more adaptable in terms of their structures, systems, and processes and encourage a stronger willingness to meet the challenges of innovation and change (Richie 2005). Therefore, it may come as a surprise that the evidence regarding SME adoption of ICTs suggests a slow response and limited progression (Smallbone et al., 2001; Dawn et al., 2002; Houghton & Winklhofer, 2004). In this paper, we investigate the seeming paradox between the anticipated responsiveness in adoption and the notion that SMEs are typically better equipped to react to and adapt to change. While our main goal is to look at how these affect SMEs' employees, management, relationships, and working practices, we identify the barriers or factors that prevent ICT adoption.

1 Assistant Professor, Department of Commerce Late Nitin College Pathri, Parbhani, Maharashtra

2 Research Scholar, Department of Commerce Nutan College, Selu, Parbhani, Maharashtra

The technological, application, and relationship perspectives on ICT adoption, is a conceptual framework that we develop in this study. The environment and rate of ICT adoption are appropriate for specific SMEs, not to provide it as a universal model and set of solutions because it is dependent on nature. The opportunities to propose viable solutions to problems raised in practice as a result of ICT adoption identify uncertainties and dangers. The ICT and Relationship Transformation explained, and its implications for SMEs are discussed. The study assesses their consequences for management, workers, and the workplace while outlining potential directions for future work.

SME adoption of ICT In both established and emerging economies around the world, the SME sector is seen as being extremely important. 18 million SMEs in the European Union (EU) are in charge of 67% of jobs and 59% of GDP. SMEs account for 55% of employment and 51% of GDP in the UK (SBS, 2005). Although there is disagreement about the exact definition of the word "SME," the UK has adopted the EU definition of an SME as one that employs less than 250 people. The focus of this study, however, is on SMEs with a designated person in charge of all or part of the organization's responsiveness to ICT development since we are interested in organizational responsiveness to ICTs. Our main standard for defining definition over firm size is this. Given the variety of technical components that can be included, the rate at which they are developing, and the emergence of new technologies offering major capacity shifts, defining ICTs continues to be difficult. Since the Internet is a conglomeration of several ICTs, Daniel et al. (2002) see ICTs as essentially a continuum of advances that companies must accept. The broad definition of ICTs that we use encompasses a variety of largely digital tools for gathering, organizing, storing, processing, and communicating information both inside and outside of an organization, SMEs. Governments recognized the significance of SMEs in the adoption of ICT, not only due to the importance of SMEs but also due to their perceived capacity for creativity, innovation, and adaptability. While the connection goal was easily met, only a small percentage of UK SMEs advanced past the second stage of adoption (online commerce) and even fewer made it to the e-business stage (Peet et al., 2002). This is in line with earlier studies, such as that by Ramsey et al. (2004), which revealed that the majority of SMEs simply possessed a website. A similar lack of development was discovered in Australian SMEs by Lawson et al. in 2003. It hasn't worked out as expected that SMEs will follow larger firms' lead in moving through the stages. Preece (2000), for instance, concluded that businesses 'do not utilise them for ordering delivery of products/services, within the supply chain, or for modifying business procedures' and that website usage was mostly marketing-related. In contrast, Brown & Lockett (2004) stated that small businesses should embrace important applications like management resource programmes and enterprise resource programmes more quickly since they could result in sizable increases in productivity and effectiveness. The low adoption rate has been investigated in terms of the impact of adoption barriers or variables slowing down adoption rates (Smallbone et al., 2001). Barriers differ from diffusion agents in that the former slow or stop adoption while the latter diffuses its impact. Research on the added value outcomes initially concentrated on knowledge acquisition and information search, as well as communications effectiveness and efficiency (DTI, 2000). Although Lumpkin and Dess (2004) state that "companies are still not clear how the Internet adds value," future study is anticipated to concentrate on other factors that may have a better added value potential. The three main groups of diffusion or barrier agents are as follows. The works of Levy and Powell (2000), and Levy et al. (2001), provide examples of the "strategic" category emphasizing the creation of strategic information systems to assist in positioning and integrating investments. This is crucial because others have acknowledged that adoption success and rate are affected by past failures to attain strategic benefits as well as unexpectedly lengthy timeframes. Another set of Barriers is the incompatibility with current channels and the effects that changing structures, processes, and connections will have on the firm as a whole (Houghton and Winklhofer, 2004). " According to Mehrtens et al., 2001; Hussin et al., 2002; the availability of key resources, readiness to adopt new technologies, and perceived benefits, the technological category includes a variety of formal and informal responses by organizations and employees to technology and its effects. Technical challenges and a lack of IT expertise are given further emphasis by Houghton et al. (2001) and Houghton & Winklhofer (2004), who note that these tend to slow adoption rates. Preece (2000) concludes that adoption is delayed by the size of the necessary "set-up costs," comprising financial and human capital, as well as the absence of expert assistance. The most important element is the perception of application complexity. A smaller percentage (56%) of the SMEs they studied were likewise at ease with low levels of complexity, compared to the 79% who were happy with extremely low levels of complexity. Applications with high and extremely high complexity, such as supply chains, e-commerce, and financial transactions, were not widely observed. They explain this finding to the lack of expert support (such as hardware, software, and application support organizations) available to larger firms but not in the same way to smaller businesses. The intricacy of the interactions, both internally and externally, is acknowledged in the third category of organizational, social, and behavioral difficulties. According to Ramsay et al. (2004), it is "well acknowledged that company and market structures may have to be re-invented for SMEs to get the full benefit of the Internet and Electronic Business". The processes involved in the SME are "by no means a simple linear development whereby observers can expect an incremental build-up of knowledge and expertise on ICT to be established," Southern & Tilley (2000) further state. Personal relationships or networks that spread information, self-assurance, and passion, however, may encourage the adoption process. The adoption and efficient use of ICTs are hampered by heavy workloads and a lack of spare capacity in many SMEs. Perceptions of greater risk and uncertainty are the main driving forces behind the majority of barriers. The adoption of new technologies and the effects it has on relationships and markets give rise to uncertainty. The inability to adapt, the importance of the negative outcomes, and the requirement to fundamentally alter organizational behavior and practices all contribute to risk perception. Organizations can respond to these developments in a variety of ways, including by creating new kinds of interactions and networks that are intended to lessen some of the risks and uncertainties (Brindley & Wright, 2005). Trust is a key component of efficient inter-organizational networks that address uncertainty and risk. According to Brindley & Wright (2005), networks, clusters, and partnerships that foster this quality can result in more successful ICT adoption. Trust is a crucial factor in adoption, whether it comes from SMEs themselves, their suppliers, or their clients. In what they referred to as an "E-Trust platform," Brown & Lockett (2004) expanded on this idea. Trust in a third party is a crucial prerequisite for SMEs adopting higher-level complexity e-business solutions.

Application Perspective

In that it depicts how technology is embraced and applied within the organisation, this perspective interacts with and complements the technical perspective. One of the most evident activities is the requirement to pay attention to how ICTs affect the production of goods and services. Unless technology is the main component of the product or service offering (such as an online auction service), ICTs often have an impact on the service dimensions. The goal of all of the work is to find processes for transforming resources that are more effective and/or efficient, and this calls for the use of suitable tools, to help in barrier development, evaluation, control, and management, information systems are often used. Such creation of systems may take place without regard to modifications to processes, resulting in management and control improvements due to the higher quality of the information. An expectation of specific structural developments inside the organization to reflect the changes would be connected to this spectrum of developments. Such structural developments, according to Ritchie and Marshall (1993), follow changes in systems, processes, and products. The obligation to engage in efficient human resource development, the fourth underlying strand, reflects the latter argument. In addition to the more traditional areas of education, training, and skills development, it is essential to foster a culture in the SME that is open to change in all facets and to the individual experiences of the employees. These are significant knowledge management and transfer enablers, both internally and externally, that are essential for the successful adoption of ICTs (Ramsey et al., 2004).

Relationship Perspective

In addition to providing a means of reducing the increased risk and uncertainty associated with the scope and dynamism of ICT advancements and the reactions generated by the competitive environment, this may be seen as creating a connection between the technical and application viewpoints. Numerous studies, including Das & Teng (2001), highlight the increasing exposure to diverse and more significant levels of risk and uncertainty associated with the implementation of ICT as well as the reality that most firms do not typically use logical methods for risk assessment and decision-making. The least obvious and covert of the three perspectives continues to be the relationships that exist among people and systems, both within and outside of the system, and also more fundamentally through their interconnections. The concept of internal and external adaptation acknowledges the relationship perspective as being externally oriented on the subject of connections with other parties (like consumers and vendors) and centered inside in terms of reviewing and renovating the connections within the organization on their own. The organization must therefore effort on inside and outside adaptation. In the context of this dual focus, logistics refers to the more transactional requirements for establishing connections that are appropriate for the interactions about routine procedures, outcomes, and sources. They could be connected to a single transaction, several transactions, or both, and they may be centered on an immediate time frame or a longer-term time frame. Although this may not always be immediately quantified using normal accounting methods, the primary performance measure would be the ability to show that the inputs and outputs have been enhanced. To secure the organization's future and meet its performance metrics, this process of communicating, exchanging information, offering guidance, and forming various forms of partnerships is becoming more and more crucial.

MSME During Covid 19

The main problem is job risk in every country. Many people are losing their employment as a result of the lockdown on the firms and the lack of training on working from home for the workforce. Large international organizations are still able to run with fewer employees because of their linkages through technology and the Internet. The lack of a sufficient technological infrastructure greatly hinders the use of technology in SMEs. If employees are unavailable to perform their duties and the business is having financial problems, it will be tough to keep them on board. Given that SMEs account for 68% of all jobs in Australia, job loss is quite likely (OECD, 2020). Due to financial constraints, SME owners and managers in countries like India, China, and Germany are unable to keep their employees on staff and pay them salaries as the lockdown period continues. 11 million employees in the US were created by SMEs; those 11 million jobs are now at risk (OECD, 2020). During March and April 2020, the job market for SMEs in New Zealand had a 4% fall.

The second major issue is concern over the workforce's health. The leadership of the company is at a loss as to whether to call workers in for work or not. Employees who live in remote areas are unwilling to take jobs due to health concerns. Dai, et al. (2020); Nurunnabi et al. Businesses share this concern for the well-being of their employees. They can't finish everything at home, even though they don't want to call in staff people if they don't have to. According to Schivardi (2020), the third major problem affecting SMEs is the financial crisis. The majority of small and medium-sized businesses are having trouble making ends meet. In India, only 6% of SMEs have enough cash to last them for the next three months, and 27% are in financial trouble. Kumar et al. (2020) In China, 85% of SMEs expect to run out of cash in a span of three months or less, and conditions may be worse. According to Kilpatrick et al. (2020), the issue of liquidity affects small and medium-sized firms significantly. The revenue has drastically decreased, which affects how those organizations function overall. The operations and output of the small enterprises have been suspended. Customers believe that businesses will reinvent themselves using technology. SMEs are requesting incentives from the government in many different forms, including tariff reductions. However, all of these taxes and tariff reductions will be advantageous if small enterprises reinvent themselves and try to achieve economies of scale in the COVID-19 environment. The fourth problem SMEs are dealing with during COVID-19 is the fall in sales and turnover. In every country, SMEs' sales and turnover are falling. The lockdown has harmed sales since customers' income levels have fallen as a result in various nations. Demand for goods and services used in manufacturing is steadily declining. The poor demand is having a negative influence on the company's sales and turnover. 69% of SMEs in the UK have serious cash flow problems, and 35% are hesitant to reopen. 2020 Petropoulos; In February 2020, 80% of SMEs in China stopped operating; in the United States, 70% of SMEs anticipate supply chain disruptions; and, in China, 80% of SMEs have experienced direct or indirect devastation (OECD, 2020).78% of SMEs in Canada reported a fall in sales; 60% of SMEs in Greece reported a decline in sales; 90% of SMEs in Thailand anticipate a decline in income; In India, the cash situation for SMEs is terrible, and 71% of SMEs in New Zealand have seen their profits affected (OECD, 2020). In India, only 6% of SMEs have enough cash on hand to cover expenses for the upcoming six months, 27% are already insolvent, and 20% have been financially strapped for less than a month. A drop in customer demand is the fifth major problem impacting SMEs, according to Beraha and Duricin (2020).

Technology Adoption

Technology 4.0 is increasingly becoming a solution supplier for SMEs in the ongoing COVID-19 epidemic. According to Akpan et al. (2020), artificial intelligence-based algorithms and models can help with speedy processing and reasoning. According to Moeuf et al. (2017), big data and artificial intelligence tools may both help SMEs with smart manufacturing. Artificial intelligence-based solutions and propensity models can help identify the client. Customers must come first, which causes problems for sales managers. Propensity models help them prioritize customers, increasing sales productivity (Gerner, 2020). Artificial intelligence and robotics can reduce the amount of physical contact at work. For speedy diagnosis and outcomes, businesses and hospitals can use artificial intelligence first. The adoption of technology 4.0 components like artificial intelligence by SMEs will enable remote work for their staff. Artificial intelligence can automate around 80% of routine tasks, such as emailing, obtaining important data, and data extraction (Malhotra, 2020).

Objectives of the Study

1. This study examines the barriers or causes preventing the adoption of ICT.
2. To analyse how these affect SMEs' management, interpersonal dynamics, and working practices.

Research Methodology

The research methods and strategy used in this study are based on an earlier literature evaluation on the use of technology in SMEs. The researchers have reviewed earlier studies on a variety of technical topics, including how they might improve the performance of SMEs and the factors that influence technology adoption. The problems SMEs face have also been highlighted in earlier research.

Summary and Conclusion

To explain why SMEs have adopted ICTs more slowly than anticipated, the research classified several obstacles and diffusion agents that were taken from a variety of past studies (Peet et al., 2002). The research was founded on the idea that employee skills and expertise, working practices, rather than technical or operational reasons, were more responsible for the inactive adoption of ICT. This notion was initially validated by research with an SME in mind. The technological, application, and relationship perspectives were taken into consideration when the ICT and Relationship Transformation Model was created to represent effective ICT adoption inside enterprises. The exploratory empirical inquiry of the two SMEs was built on the relationship viewpoint, which aimed to capture the aspects less thoroughly examined in earlier studies. The three views of the model were validated by data from both SMEs, although each one showed significant differences in effects. From a technological perspective, the manufacturer of hi-fi systems benefited from the intrinsic qualities of their goods and marketplace technology base, which supported technological advancement. The company made a conscious decision to create and reinforce this culture. Contrarily, the textile manufacturer lacked a deep understanding of ICTs, in particular the best techniques for their translation and embedding. While both cases show how the application perspective is appropriate for their product and service development, the hi-fi manufacturer actively sought these changes. In response to current ICTs or anticipation of future ICTs, there were equally obvious contrasts in the approach to human resource development. In particular, we observed that the textile company realized that to compete in a globally competitive market, large investments in the ICT knowledge and skills of the workforce were required, as well as structural changes and advances. Both firms established partnerships both inside and externally after realizing the significance of the relationship perspective. ICTs were used directly by the hi-fi company to assist individual staff in creating and overseeing these relationships with clients. The fundamental cultural tenet of the textile manufacturer was based on one-on-one interactions, which they saw as a particular source of competitive advantage in addition to being crucial for developing confidence and trust between the parties. Some ICTs, in their opinion, were a barrier to the support of such connections. ICT adoption that is successful places demands on personnel. Individuals may need to constantly learn new things, including skills, and information to be promoted and ingrained inside the company. These trends indicate the need for organisational learning and lifelong learning for individuals. These modifications to processes, systems, and structures must be accompanied by an ongoing human resource development programme. This presents a challenge for SMEs because of their constrained resource bases. This was accomplished by the hi-fi manufacturer, one of the SMEs under investigation, through a fundamental redesign of the support, manufacturing, and organisational processes. While this may increase risk and uncertainty for any given person, controlling these worries and perceptions is crucial for SME success. For one SME, new forms of connections that aimed to build trust and commitment offered a solution, whereas the more conventional relationships in the other SME slowed down progress. SME management has two challenges. First, there is a need to create and put into practice tactics meant to alter mindsets and instill a culture of readiness to adopt ICTs throughout the SME, supported by suitable plans for the development of human resources. The main obstacles are the SME's ability to access the essential information and skills, as well as the organisational flexibility to devote the necessary resources to achieving these goals. To do this, it is important to promote new approaches to relationships both internally and internationally while also acknowledging and overcoming the inevitable worries and uncertainties brought on by the adoption of ICT. Future research should focus on using the model in various circumstances (such as international or other industries) to evaluate the relative value of these elements. The findings from this research may offer managers in SMEs more specific direction and recommendations. These ICT adoption-related difficulties are especially demanding on management and staff in smaller organisations (Lumpkin & Dess, 2004), as SMEs frequently lack the specialized knowledge, resources, and time to deal with such pressing concerns.

References

1. Akpan, I. J., Udoh, E. A. P., & Adebisi, B. (2020). Small business awareness and adoption of state-of-the-art technologies in emerging and developing markets, and lessons from the COVID-19 pandemic. *Journal of Small Business & Entrepreneurship*, 1-18.
2. Beraha, I., & Duricin, S. (2020). The impact of COVID-19 crisis on medium-sized enterprises in Serbia. Economic Analysis, *53*(1), 14-27.
3. Brindley, C.S. & Wright, D.L. (2005), 'Personalised Relationship e-Marketing and the SME', in F. Zhao (ed.), Entrepreneurship and Innovation in e-Business (Australia: Royal Melbourne Institute of Technology University), forthcoming.
4. Brown, D.H. & Lockett, N. (2004). Potential of Critical e-Applications for Engaging SMEs in e-Business: A Provider Perspective, *European Journal of Information Systems* 13, 21–34.

5. Dai, R., Feng, H., Hu, J., Jin, Q., Li, H., Ranran, W. & Zhang, X.Z. (2020). The impact of covid-19 on small and medium-sized enterprises: evidence from two-wave phone surveys in china. Working paper.
6. Daniel, E., Wilson, H. & Myers, A. (2002). Adoption of e-Commerce by SMEs in the UK, *International Small Business Journal 20*(3), 253–270.
7. Das, T.K. & Teng, B. (2001). Strategic Risk Behaviour and Its Temporalities: Between Risk Propensity and Decision Context, *Journal of Management Studies 38*(4), 515–533.
8. Dawn, J., Peter, B., & Jasbir, D. (2002). Government support for e-readiness of small and medium sized enterprises (SMEs). In *Proceedings of the 35th Hawaii International Conference on System Sciences.*
9. Department of Trade and Industry (DTI) (1994). Competitiveness—How the Best UK Companies are Winning, Cm 2563 (London: The Stationery Office).
10. Gerner, M., (2020). Using AI to cope in the coronavirus era. [Online] Available at: https://www.raconteur.net/technology/artificial-intelligence/covid-19-ai-solutions/[Accessed 25 November 2020].
11. Houghton, K. A., & Winklhofer, H. (2004). The effect of website and e-commerce adoption on the relationship between SMEs and their export intermediaries. *International Small Business Journal, 22*(4), 369-388.
12. Hussin, H., King, M. & Grigg, P. (2002). IT Alignment in Small Firms, European *Journal of Information Systems 11*(2), 108–127.
13. Kilpatrick, J., Barter, L. & Dess, J., (2020). COVID-19 Managing cash flow during a period of crisis, s.l.: Deloite.
14. Kumar, R., Singh, R.K., & Dwivedi, Y.K. (2020). Application of industry 4.0 technologies in SMEs for ethical and sustainable operations: Analysis of challenges. *Journal of cleaner production*, 275, 124063.
15. Levy, M., Powell, P. & Yetton, P. (2001), Aligning IS and the Strategic Context, *Journal of Information Technology 16*(1), 133–144.
16. Lumpkin, G.T. & Dess, G.G. (2004). e-Business Strategies and Internet Business Models: How the Internet Adds Value, Organizational Dynamics *33*(2), 161–173.
17. Malhotra, S., (2020). Significance of AI for Small Businesses: Preparing for the New Normal. [Online] Available at: https://artificialintelligence.oodles.io/blogs/ai-for-small-businesses/ [Accessed 25 Novmeber 2020].
18. Mehrtens, J., Grigg, P. & Mills, A. (2001). A Model of Internet Adoption by SMEs', *Journal of Information and Management 39*(3), 165–176
19. Moeuf, A., Lamouri, S., Pellerin, R., Eburdy, R., & Tamayo, S. (2017). Industry 4.0 and the SME: a technology focused review of the empirical literature.
20. Nurunnabi, M., Alhawal, H. M., & Hoque, Z. (2020). Impact of COVID-19: how CEOs respond to SMEs recovery planning in Saudi Arabia. White Paper, 3.
21. OECD, (2020). Coronavirus (COVID-19): SME Policy Responses, s.l.: OECD.
22. Peet, S., C.S. Brindley & R.L. Ritchie (2002). The European Commission and SME Support Mechanisms for e-Business, *European Business Review 15*(5), 335–341.
23. Preece, K. (2000). North West e-Commerce Survey, UK.
24. Ramsey, E., Ibbotson, P., & McCole, P. (2008). Factors that impact technology innovation adoption among Irish professional service sector SMEs. *International journal of innovation management, 12*(04), 629-654.
25. Ramsey, E., P. Ibbotson, Bell, J. & Gray, B. (2004). A Projective Perspective of International "e"- Services, *Qualitative Market Research: An International Journal* 7 (1), 34–47.
26. Ritchie, B., & Brindley, C. (2005). ICT adoption by SMEs: implications for relationships and management. *New technology, work and employment, 20*(3), 205-217.
27. Schivardi, F., & Guido, R. (2020). A simple method to estimate firms' liquidity needs during the Covid-19 crisis with an application to Italy. *Covid Economics, 35*, 51-69.

28. Sharma, M. J., & Gill, M. G. (2016). MSME-An Emerging Pillar of Indian Economy. *International Journal of Research in Humanities & Soc. Sciences*, *4*(5).
29. Small Business Service (SBS) (2005). http://www.sbs.gov.uk/statistics/smedef.php (accessed March 6, 2005).
30. Smallbone, D., D. North, Vickers, I. & Roper, S. (2001). Innovation and the Use of Technology in Manufacturing Plants and SMEs: An Inter-regional Comparison, Proceedings 24th ISBA National Small Firms Conference: Exploring the Frontiers of Small Business (Hinckley, Leicestershire: ISBA), 289–308.
31. Smallbone, D., Piasecki, B., & Rogut, A. (2001). The implications of EU accession for Polish SMEs. *Environment and Planning C: Government and Policy*, *19*(3), 317-333.
32. Southern, A. & Tilley, F. (2000). Small Firms and Information and Communication Technologies (ICTs): Toward a Typology of ICT Usage, New Technology, Work and Employment *15*(2), 138–154.

9

Microfinance in India: Future Prospect & Sustainable Approach

Riya Goel

Abstract

Microfinance in India pertains to the provision of small-scale savings, credit, and insurance services to socially and economically disadvantaged segments of society. It is increasingly recognized as a potent tool for poverty alleviation. This working paper aims to present an overview of the current state of microfinance in India, tracing its evolution to date. The dominant prospect of microfinance lies in the Self Help Groups (SHGs) - Banks linkage program, which seeks to offer a cost-effective mechanism for delivering financial services to the impoverished. The paper puts forth practical suggestions to address the issues and challenges associated with microfinance in India. These suggestions aim to enhance the effectiveness and sustainability of microfinance, encompassing areas such as improving credit delivery practices, diversifying product offerings, addressing customer overlap, promoting enterprise loans, implementing effective mitigation measures, and finding ways to lower interest rates. By implementing these recommendations, it is possible to steer microfinance in India toward a more productive and impactful path.

Keywords: *Microfinance, Sustainability, challenges, sustainable growth*

Introduction

Microfinance has emerged as a powerful tool for poverty alleviation and financial inclusion in India. With a population of over 1.3 billion people, India is home to a significant number of individuals who lack access to traditional banking services. Microfinance institutions (MFIs) have played a crucial role in bridging this gap and providing financial services to the unbanked and underserved populations in the country. Microfinance in India traces its roots back to the 1970s when various grassroots organizations began experimenting with small-scale lending to low-income individuals and communities. The main objective was to empower the poor by offering them access to credit, savings, insurance, and other financial services. These early initiatives laid the foundation for the formal microfinance sector that we see today.

The turning point for microfinance in India came in the 1990s when NGOs and other nonprofit organizations started to adopt a more structured approach to micro-lending. The formation of Self-Help Groups (SHGs) became a popular model, where individuals from economically disadvantaged backgrounds would come together to form a group and pool their savings. These SHGs then became eligible to receive loans from banks and other financial institutions, enabling them to invest in income-generating activities. The formalization of microfinance gained momentum with the establishment of specialized microfinance institutions, such as Non-Banking Financial Companies (NBFCs) and Microfinance Institutions (MFIs), in the early 2000s. These institutions were regulated by the Reserve Bank

Assistant Professor, Department of Management Kalinga University, Raipur, Chhattisgarh of India (RBI) and allowed to provide microcredit to individuals and groups. They operated with the dual objective of financial sustainability and social impact, aiming to serve the financially excluded while maintaining responsible lending practices. Microfinance in India witnessed rapid growth and expansion during the 2000s, with increased participation from both domestic and international investors. The success of microfinance was driven by its ability to reach the unbanked population, particularly women, and its focus on small-ticket loans for income-generating activities. By providing access to credit, microfinance empowered borrowers to start or expand small businesses, generate income, and improve their standard of living. However, the sector faced challenges in the late 2000s, particularly with issues of over-indebtedness and aggressive recovery practices by some MFIs. This led to a regulatory overhaul, with the introduction of stricter norms by the RBI to ensure consumer protection and responsible lending. The revised regulations sought to strike a balance between the financial viability of MFIs and the welfare of borrowers. Today, microfinance in India continues to evolve, with a diverse ecosystem of MFIs, SHGs, and other financial intermediaries working towards inclusive finance. The sector has expanded beyond credit to include a range of financial products and services, such as savings, insurance, and remittances. Technological advancements, particularly the rise of mobile banking and digital platforms, have further accelerated the reach and efficiency of microfinance operations.

Review of Literature

Agarwal & Sinha (2019 in their study provide a comprehensive review of empirical studies on microfinance in India. It analyzes the impact of microfinance on poverty alleviation, women's empowerment, and economic development. The review highlights the positive outcomes of microfinance interventions while discussing challenges and areas for future research.

Kaur & Shishodia (2018) focus on the role of microfinance in empowering women in India. It examines the impact of microfinance on women's economic and social empowerment, highlighting the positive effects on income generation, decision-making, and household well-being. The study also discusses the challenges and policy implications for promoting women's empowerment through microfinance.

Roy (2017) in this review paper provides an overview of the microfinance sector in India. It discusses the historical background, evolution, and regulatory framework of microfinance in the country. The study also highlights the challenges faced by microfinance institutions and the potential for future growth and development.

Mohan & Bansal (2015) examines the existing research on microfinance in India. It discusses the various dimensions of microfinance, including access to credit, savings, insurance, and remittance services. The study also analyzes the impact of microfinance on poverty reduction, income generation, and financial inclusion.

Das & Bera (2014) provide an overview of the microfinance sector in India, focusing on its evolution, growth, and impact. It discusses the role of microfinance in poverty alleviation, financial inclusion, and women's empowerment. The study also examines the challenges faced by microfinance institutions and the need for effective regulation and supervision.

Tiwari & Goswami (2013) examine the existing research on microfinance in India, emphasizing its impact on poverty alleviation and inclusive growth. It discusses the role of microfinance institutions, the challenges faced by borrowers and lenders, and the need for effective governance and regulation. The study also highlights the potential for future research and policy implications.

Yadav et al. (2012) provide an overview of microfinance in India, focusing on its historical development, evolution, and impact. It discusses the challenges faced by microfinance institutions, the role of self-help groups and microfinance institutions, and the need for financial literacy and client protection. The study also emphasizes the potential for scaling up microfinance initiatives to achieve sustainable development.

Objectives of the Study

1. To identify the challenges in microfinance in India
2. To achieve sustainable development through microfinance
3. To find out solutions to microfinance challenges in India

Research Methodology

It is a descriptive study primarily relying on secondary data. The collection of secondary data originates from diverse sources such as journals, magazines, and reports. Therefore, the accuracy and reliability of the data are contingent upon the accuracy and reliability of the sources used.

Microfinance: An overview

Microfinance refers to the provision of financial services, including credit, savings, insurance, and other basic banking services, to individuals who are typically excluded from the formal financial sector. It is designed to address the financial needs of low-income individuals, particularly those in underserved or marginalized communities. The concept of microfinance emerged as a response to the lack of access to formal financial services faced by a large portion of the global population, especially in developing countries. Traditional banks often consider these individuals too high-risk or too economically vulnerable to be eligible for loans or other financial products. Microfinance aims to bridge this gap by offering tailored financial solutions to help individuals overcome poverty, start or expand small businesses, and improve their livelihoods. One of the key features of microfinance is its focus on providing small-scale loans, often referred to as microcredit. These loans are typically given to individuals who lack collateral or credit history, enabling them to engage in income-generating activities or invest in productive assets. Microfinance institutions (MFIs), which can include specialized microfinance banks, non-governmental organizations (NGOs), and cooperatives, play a central role in delivering these services. In addition to microcredit, microfinance encompasses other essential financial services. Microsavings accounts allow individuals to securely deposit and accumulate savings, fostering financial resilience and providing a safety net for emergencies. Microinsurance provides risk mitigation through affordable insurance products, protecting individuals from unexpected events such as illness, accidents, or natural disasters. Remittance services also fall within the scope of microfinance, facilitating the transfer of funds between migrants and their families. Microfinance has demonstrated significant potential for poverty alleviation and social impact. By providing access to financial services, it empowers individuals, particularly women, and promotes entrepreneurship and economic development at the grassroots level. Through responsible lending practices, financial literacy programs, and social intermediation, microfinance seeks to create a sustainable and inclusive financial ecosystem.

While microfinance has experienced notable successes, it also faces challenges. Issues such as over-indebtedness, high-interest rates, and inadequate regulation have been identified as potential risks. Responsible microfinance practices and effective oversight by regulators are essential to ensure that borrowers are not burdened with excessive debt and are treated fairly. Microfinance in India traces its roots back to the early 1970s when non-governmental organizations (NGOs) like the Self-Employed Women's Association (SEWA) and MYRADA initiated microcredit programs to address the credit needs of the poor. The microfinance landscape witnessed significant growth and diversification with the establishment of specialized microfinance institutions (MFIs) like SKS Microfinance and Bandhan Financial Services in the 1990s. The sector gained momentum with policy support from the Reserve Bank of India (RBI), leading to the formation of Self-Help Groups (SHGs) and the introduction of microfinance regulations. Overall, microfinance plays a vital role in fostering financial inclusion and enabling economic participation for marginalized populations. Its impact extends beyond financial services, contributing to poverty reduction, women's empowerment, and overall social and economic development.

Issues of Microfinance in India

Microfinance in India has faced various challenges and issues over the years. Some of the key issues include:

1. Over-indebtedness: One of the primary concerns in the microfinance sector is the issue of over-indebtedness. In some cases, borrowers take loans from multiple lenders without having the capacity to repay them, leading to a debt trap. This situation can arise due to aggressive lending practices, inadequate credit assessments, or lack of financial literacy among borrowers.
2. High-Interest Rates: Microfinance institutions often charge relatively higher interest rates compared to traditional banks. While this can be attributed to the higher costs of serving low-income clients, excessive interest rates can burden borrowers and hinder their ability to repay loans. It is crucial to strike a balance between the financial viability of MFIs and the affordability of borrowers.
3. Lack of Consumer Protection: Inadequate consumer protection mechanisms in the microfinance sector have been a matter of concern. Borrowers, especially those with limited financial literacy, may face issues such as unfair collection practices, hidden charges, or lack of transparency in loan terms. Strengthening consumer protection measures is necessary to ensure the fair treatment of borrowers.
4. Regulatory Challenges: The regulatory framework for microfinance in India has evolved, but challenges persist. Striking a balance between promoting financial inclusion and protecting consumers remains a complex task. Ensuring effective oversight and regulation of microfinance institutions, while avoiding excessive restrictions that may impede their operations, is a delicate challenge for policymakers.
5. Limited Reach to Remote Areas: Despite significant progress, microfinance services still struggle to reach remote and rural areas of India. Lack of infrastructure, logistical challenges, and a sparse population density make it difficult for MFIs to extend their operations to these regions. Expanding the reach of microfinance services to underserved areas is crucial for promoting inclusive growth.
6. Sustainability of MFIs: Achieving financial sustainability while serving low-income clients can be a challenge for microfinance institutions. Balancing social impact objectives with financial viability requires careful management of operational costs, loan portfolio quality, and access to funding. Ensuring the long-term sustainability of MFIs is essential to maintain their effectiveness in poverty alleviation.

Addressing these issues requires a multi-faceted approach involving regulatory reforms, capacity building, financial literacy programs, and responsible lending practices. Collaborative efforts by microfinance institutions, policymakers, regulators, and other stakeholders are necessary to create a more inclusive and sustainable microfinance ecosystem in India.

Measures to overcome challenges of Microfinance in India

To overcome the challenges faced by microfinance, several measures can be implemented:

1. **Strengthening Regulatory Framework:**
   Enhancing the regulatory framework for microfinance is crucial to ensure consumer protection and responsible lending practices. Regulators should establish clear guidelines and standards for MFIs, including interest rate caps, transparency in loan terms, and fair collection practices. Regular monitoring and enforcement can help maintain accountability and protect borrowers' rights.

2. **Promoting Financial Literacy:**
   Increasing financial literacy among borrowers is essential to empower them with knowledge and skills to make informed financial decisions. MFIs can collaborate with local organizations and implement financial education programs to educate borrowers on topics such as budgeting, savings, debt management, and understanding loan terms. Improved financial literacy can help borrowers avoid over-indebtedness and make better use of financial services.

3. **Encouraging Responsible Lending Practices:**
   MFIs should adopt responsible lending practices to prevent over-indebtedness and protect borrowers' interests. This includes conducting thorough credit assessments to ensure borrowers' repayment capacity, promoting reasonable interest rates, and implementing appropriate loan size limits based on borrowers' income levels. Implementing effective client protection mechanisms and grievance redressal systems can also enhance the credibility and trust of MFIs.

4. **Enhancing Collaboration and Coordination:**
   Collaboration among MFIs, banks, government agencies, and other stakeholders is crucial for the sustainable development of microfinance. Cooperation can lead to knowledge sharing, resource pooling, and coordinated efforts to reach underserved populations. Public-private partnerships can facilitate access to funding, technical assistance, and infrastructure development, thereby expanding the reach of microfinance services.

5. **Leveraging Technology:**
   Embracing technology can enhance the efficiency and reach of microfinance operations. Digital platforms and mobile banking solutions can enable easier access to financial services, streamline loan processing, and facilitate remote transactions. Fintech innovations such as digital payments, online loan applications, and credit scoring algorithms can help reduce costs, enhance convenience, and improve the overall customer experience.

6. **Encouraging Investor Confidence:**
   Maintaining investor confidence is crucial for the sustainable growth of the microfinance sector. Transparent reporting and financial disclosures by MFIs, adherence to social performance standards, and responsible management of

investor funds can help build trust and attract sustainable investments. Strong governance and risk management practices are essential to ensure the long-term viability of MFIs.

7. **Focus on Social Impact:**
Microfinance should continue to emphasize its social impact objectives alongside financial sustainability. Monitoring and measuring social outcomes, such as poverty reduction, women's empowerment, and livelihood improvement, can demonstrate the sector's contribution to sustainable development. Impact assessments and reporting can help align microfinance efforts with broader social and development goals.

By implementing these measures, the microfinance sector can overcome challenges, ensure responsible and inclusive financial services, and effectively contribute to poverty alleviation and economic empowerment.

Sustainability through Microfinance

Sustainability through microfinance refers to the long-term viability and effectiveness of microfinance institutions (MFIs) in providing financial services to low-income individuals and communities while achieving their social and financial objectives. Here are some measures to promote sustainability in microfinance:

1. **Financial Viability:**
MFIs should focus on achieving financial sustainability by maintaining healthy loan portfolio quality, managing operational costs efficiently, and diversifying their funding sources. This includes balancing income generation with prudent risk management practices, establishing adequate provisions for loan losses, and adopting sound financial management strategies.

2. **Portfolio Management:**
Effective portfolio management is crucial for sustainability. MFIs should emphasize responsible lending practices, including thorough credit assessments, proper loan sizing, and monitoring of borrower repayment capacity. This helps mitigate credit risk and reduces the likelihood of default, ensuring a healthy loan portfolio and sustainable operations.

3. **Diversification of Products and Services:**
MFIs can enhance their sustainability by expanding their range of financial products and services beyond microcredit. Offering savings accounts, microinsurance, and other tailored financial products meets the diverse needs of clients and generates additional revenue streams for MFIs. Diversification also helps mitigate risks and reduces dependence on a single product.

4. **Technology Adoption:**
Embracing technology can significantly contribute to the sustainability of microfinance. Digital solutions and mobile banking platforms streamline operations, reduce costs, improve efficiency, and enable better access to financial services. Technology can also facilitate data collection and analysis, enabling MFIs to make informed decisions, monitor performance, and enhance risk management.

5. **Social Performance Management:**
Aligning social objectives with financial sustainability is crucial for sustainable microfinance. MFIs should measure and monitor their social impact, including poverty reduction, women's empowerment, and community development. Social performance management helps MFIs demonstrate their positive contribution to society and attract socially responsible investors.

6. **Capacity Building:**
   Investing in the capacity building of MFI staff and clients is essential for long-term sustainability. Training and skill development programs improve the knowledge and expertise of MFI staff, enabling them to provide better financial services and effectively manage risks. Additionally, empowering clients through financial education and training programs enhances their financial literacy and promotes responsible borrowing and savings habits.
7. **Partnerships and Collaborations:**
   Collaborations with banks, government agencies, donor organizations, and other stakeholders can strengthen the sustainability of microfinance. Partnerships provide access to funding, technical expertise, and networks that support the growth and stability of MFIs. Synergistic collaborations can also lead to knowledge sharing, innovation, and the development of sustainable microfinance ecosystems.

By implementing these measures, microfinance institutions can ensure their long-term sustainability, enabling them to continue serving low-income populations, fostering economic development, and promoting financial inclusion. Sustainable microfinance is a crucial component of a resilient and inclusive financial system that contributes to poverty reduction and sustainable development.

Regulatory Framework and Prospects of Microfinance in India

The regulatory framework and prospects of microfinance in India are crucial considerations for ensuring the stability, sustainability, and continued impact of the sector. The Indian government and the Reserve Bank of India (RBI) have taken proactive steps to regulate and support the microfinance industry, recognizing its importance in financial inclusion and poverty alleviation. Let's delve into the regulatory framework and prospects in more detail.

Regulatory Framework

- **Microfinance Institutions (Development and Regulation) Bill, 2012:**
  The RBI proposed this bill to provide a comprehensive regulatory framework for microfinance institutions (MFIs). It aimed to regulate the activities of MFIs, establish mechanisms for their supervision, and ensure client protection. However, the bill is still under discussion and has not been enacted as of my knowledge cutoff date in September 2021.
- **Prudential Regulations for NBFC-MFIs:**
  The RBI has issued prudential regulations specifically for Non-Banking Financial microfinance institutions (NBFC-MFIs). These regulations address important aspects such as capital adequacy, lending rates, loan portfolio quality, and borrower eligibility criteria. They aim to ensure the stability and sustainability of NBFC-MFIs while protecting the interests of borrowers.
- **Priority Sector Lending (PSL) Guidelines:**
  The RBI has made it mandatory for banks to allocate a specified percentage of their total lending to priority sectors, which includes microfinance. This policy encourages banks to lend to microfinance institutions and promotes the flow of credit to underserved populations.
- **Small Finance Banks (SFBs):**
  The RBI has granted licenses to several SFBs, which are specifically designed to cater to the banking needs of underserved and unbanked segments, including microfinance clients. SFBs focus on providing financial services to small businesses, low-income households, and individuals in rural and semi-urban areas.

Future Prospects

- **Technological Advancements:**
The integration of technology, including mobile banking, digital payments, and online platforms, has the potential to revolutionize the microfinance sector in India. These advancements can enhance the efficiency, accessibility, and scalability of microfinance services, particularly in remote and underserved areas.
- **Financial Inclusion and Digital Transformation:**
Microfinance institutions can play a crucial role in advancing financial inclusion by leveraging digital technologies. By offering mobile banking services, digital wallets, and innovative lending solutions, microfinance can reach a wider customer base and reduce transaction costs.
- **Data Analytics and Credit Scoring:**
The availability of comprehensive data on borrower behavior, repayment patterns, and credit histories can enable MFIs to make more accurate credit assessments and offer tailored financial products. Data analytics and credit scoring models can enhance risk management, improve loan disbursal processes, and foster responsible lending practices.
- **Collaborations and Partnerships:**
Collaboration between microfinance institutions, banks, technology firms, and government agencies can create synergies and promote innovation in the sector. Strategic partnerships can help overcome challenges related to funding, technology adoption, capacity building, and knowledge sharing.
- **Client Protection and Social Performance:**
Ensuring robust client protection mechanisms and maintaining a strong focus on social performance are vital for the sustainable growth of microfinance. The sector needs to emphasize responsible lending practices, transparency, financial literacy programs, and grievance redressal mechanisms to build trust and maintain the confidence of borrowers and stakeholders.

The regulatory framework and prospects of microfinance in India are closely intertwined. With supportive regulations, technological advancements, and a focus on client protection, microfinance has the potential to further expand its reach, empower marginalized communities, and contribute to India's financial inclusion goals. By embracing innovation, fostering partnerships, and upholding social objectives, microfinance can continue to play a vital role in alleviating poverty and promoting inclusive economic growth.

Conclusion

Microfinance has emerged as a powerful tool for poverty alleviation and financial inclusion in India. It has played a crucial role in bridging the gap and providing financial services to the unbanked and underserved populations in the country. The sector has evolved over the years, starting from grassroots initiatives to the establishment of specialized microfinance institutions regulated by the Reserve Bank of India. Microfinance in India has demonstrated significant potential for poverty alleviation and social impact by providing access to credit, savings, insurance, and remittance services. It has empowered borrowers to start or expand small businesses, generate income, and improve their standard of living. However, the sector has also faced challenges, including over-indebtedness, high interest rates, lack of consumer protection, regulatory complexities, limited reach to remote areas, and sustainability of microfinance institutions. To address these challenges, several measures can be implemented. Strengthening the regulatory framework, promoting financial literacy, encouraging responsible lending practices, enhancing collaboration and coordination among stakeholders, leveraging technology, and focusing on social impact are crucial steps. Additionally, maintaining investor confidence and emphasizing financial viability through portfolio management, diversification of products and services, technology adoption, social performance management, capacity building, and partnerships can contribute to the sustainability of microfinance institutions. By implementing these measures, the microfinance sector in India can overcome challenges, ensure responsible and inclusive financial services, and effectively contribute to poverty alleviation, economic empowerment, and sustainable development. Microfinance will continue to play a vital role in fostering financial inclusion and creating a more equitable and resilient society for all.

References

1. Agarwal, R., & Sinha, D. (2019). Microfinance in India: A Review of Empirical Studies. *International Journal of Finance, Economics and Trade, 3*(4), 193-201.
2. Basheer, M. (2013). What Does Sustainable Development Means? - A Study on Different Dimensions of Sustainability. *IJRCM, 3*(10), 114-116.
3. Das, P., & Bera, A. (2014). Microfinance in India: A Review. *International Journal of Research in Commerce and Management, 5*(5), 30-34.
4. Devaraja, T.S., (2011). Microfinance in India - A Tool for Poverty Reduction
5. Ehsan, Nadia, (December 2011). Issues in the growth of Micro Finance Banks: Impact of Customer, Internal and External Environment, *Interdisciplinary Journal of Contemporary Research in Business, 3*(8).
6. Emerlson Moses, (2011). in his study An Overview Micro Finance in India, *International Referred Research Journal,* RNI-RAJBIL 2009/29954. *3*
7. Kaur, G., & Shishodia, D. (2018). Role of Microfinance in Empowering Women: A Review. *Asian Journal of Multidimensional Research, 7*(4), 174-182.
8. Microfinance - Current Status and Growing Concerns in India http://www.iitk.ac.in/ime/MBA_IITK/avantgarde/?p=475
9. Microfinance and Its Delivery Models. StudyMode.com. Retrieved 08, 2007, from http://www. study mode.com/essays/Microfinance-Its-Delivery-Models-119718.html
10. Mohan, R., & Bansal, S. (2015). Microfinance in India: A Review of Literature. *Journal of Commerce and Accounting Research, 4*(1), 63-68.
11. Roy, D. (2017). Microfinance in India: A Review. *International Journal of Business and Administration Research Review, 2*(6), 156-160.
12. Sarumathi, S. & K. Mohan, (2011). in their paper Role of Micro Finance in Women's Empowerment, *Journal of Management and Science, 1*(1), 1-10
13. Srinivasan, N., (2009). Microfinance India State of the Sector Report 2008, *Sage Publications,* New Delhi.
14. Sriram, M.S. & R.S. Upadhyayula, (2004). The transformation of the microfinance sector in India: experiences, options and future. *Journal of Microfinance, 6*(2), 89-112.
15. Tiwari, A., & Goswami, A. (2013). Microfinance in India: Literature Review. *International Journal of Marketing, Financial Services and Management Research, 2*(11), 101-113.
16. Yadav, M., & Yadav, S. (2012). Microfinance in India: A Review. *International Journal of Business and Management Tomorrow, 2*(5), 1-6

10

Self-Help Groups for Empowering Women in Selected Districts of Madhya Pradesh

Dr. Manisha Prajapati[1] *& Sangam Prajapati*[2]

Abstract

The purpose of the study is to examine the function of SHGs in promoting women's empowerment in a selected tribal district of Madhya Pradesh. The primary objective of the research is to find out how SHGs operate in terms of mobilizing savings, providing credit to those in need, managing group money, repaying loans, developing leadership, establishing links with banks, and examining the social benefits received by members. Field observation and structured questionnaire survey techniques were used to obtain and compile primary data. Information was also gathered through conversations and interviews with regional NGOs and government employees working at the grass-roots level. 150 SHGs are operating in tribal districts. The study shows that SHGs had established a new agenda for bank microcredit, which serves as a type of financial intermediation. Credits are needed for a variety of goals (domestic, paying off previous obligations, investing, etc. After joining the organization, SHG members engage in a variety of economic activities, including the collecting, processing, and marketing of small-scale wood products, their businesses, goat farming, and dairying. The SHG members profit from developing saving habits, financial independence, self-assurance, social cohesiveness, asset ownership, debt freedom, supplementary work, etc. SHGs have benefited the consolidation of the poor by promoting women's empowerment, social cohesion, and socioeconomic improvement.

Keywords: *SHGs, Empowerment, Microcredit and Financial Independence*

Introduction

The definition of empowerment is the process by which women assume control and responsibility for their decisions. According to Tandon (2016), the fundamental components of empowerment include agency (the capacity to set and pursue goals), awareness of unequal systems of authority, self-esteem, and self-assurance. Individual, household, community, and societal empowerment can occur at an order of different levels and is encouraged by providing supportive variables (like exposure to new activities that can increase capacities) and removing restrictive elements (like a lack of resources and skills). In this regard, microfinance combined with self-help groups helps to advance the empowerment of women. It is not only a powerful instrument for eradicating poverty but also a way to support the empowerment of the most oppressed groups in society, particularly women. It's old wine in a new bottle, claims (Bosch, 2002). It consists of a group of three to eight individuals who agree to take responsibility for the growth of the group as a whole. The Self-help Groups (SHGs) model was used in India to launch the first

[1] Assistant Professor, Government Model College, Dindori, Madhya Pradesh

[2] Student, M. Com 4th Semester, Department of Commerce, Indira Gandhi National Tribal University Amarkantak, Madhya Pradesh

microfinance banks in the 1980s. It is Bangladesh's version of the Grameen replication model. Over 3,00,000 SHGs are in operation in India. The idea of microfinance has yet to take off in India. but if it continues to spread its wings at this rate, very soon all of the poor houses will be within its reach. The Southern area of India has had the most success with microfinance; Andhra Pradesh has set a good example for the other states in this regard. The current study is an effort to examine how microcredit affects underprivileged women in a particular Madhya Pradesh district.

Since the 1970s, when the innovative concept of microfinance was first proposed, many countries have started microfinance. Asian MFIs are the most renowned entertainers on the planet among the original MFIs. Bangladesh and India had the most remarkable growth in the region. Even though many countries have tailored their microfinance models to fit their own economic, social, and geographic circumstances, all of them adhere to a few basic principles, such as the Self-help Group (SHG) model and the Joint Liability Group (JLG) model. Additionally, microfinance is playing a key role in some areas, including the economy, job opportunities, schooling, societal status, and so forth. A microenterprise is a type of unregistered independent business that is typically managed by a group or disadvantaged person. A microenterprise is typically described as a small, independently run business with five or fewer employees. Microbusinesses provide a substantial contribution to equity, social stability, and economic prosperity. One of the most significant opportunities for low-income people to break free from poverty and create self-sufficient employment and financial prospects with little training and education is the microenterprise division.

Context of Microfinance in Madhya Pradesh

According to Tendulkar 1's Round 66 analysis of the NSSO data, MP has a rural poverty rate of 37.8% and an urban poverty rate of 19.7%. The projections in this report are based on data from the "Progress out of Poverty Index (PPI) - A simple Poverty Score Card for India" and "Census 2011 statistics," as well as the observations and viewpoints of various stakeholders who were consulted individually and in two consulting meetings, as well as secondary data accessed from different sources. When determining the supply and demand for credit, consideration is given to the expansion of various types of groups, but primarily Self-help Groups. Weak, inactive, and overlapping groupings are taken into account. SHGs are more prevalent right now, but the JLG idea is also expanding in the state. About 70% of SHG members are thought to be poorer than the other members. Around 69.0 percent of India's rural poor lived in just five high-poverty states, including Madhya Pradesh, in 1999-2000, according to the Planning Commission study (2014). The second-largest Indian state, Madhya Pradesh has a population of 72 million people and a total area of 308,252 square km. It contains 55393 villages, 23412 panchayats, 318 blocks, 52 districts, and 341 tehsils. There are 931 females for every 1000 males in it. With a literacy rate of 75% and a poverty rate of 48.6%, Madhya Pradesh has an outstanding opportunity for advancement in terms of some human development metrics. Given that 68% of the people living in the state are considered to be poor, poverty and a lack of employment possibilities pose serious challenges for MP. Madhya Pradesh has a total population of 72626809, with men making up 51.1% of the number. A little more than 73.5 percent of its people reside in rural areas, and 26.5 percent do so in cities. The literacy rate is 70.6%, with males having an average literacy rate of 80.5% and females having an average literacy rate of 60.0%. According to Census 2011, employment in the state makes up 43.47 percent of the total population, with 71.9 percent of those being primary employees and

28.1 percent being marginal workers. A total of 31.2 percent of the workforce (main and marginal) is employed as cultivators, 38.6 percent as agricultural labourers, 3 percent in domestic industries, and 27.2 percent in other occupations.

The issues that the people confront include a lack of knowledge about banking and financial literacy, insufficient bank reach that results in an increased client per bank branch (23,000 per bank branch according to the 2011 Census), and a significant portion, or around 65% of the state's unbanked population.

Review of Literature

In his article, Osman (2000) noted that micro-finance initiatives cannot end poverty on their own. Microfinance programmes must be combined with additional, complementary programmes targeting the societal as well as cultural components of need, hardship, impoverishment, and dispossession in the fight to eradicate poverty. In her study, Kapur (2001) attempted to discuss, analyse, and provide answers to the difficult questions of why, despite every attempt and advancement, there remains so much prejudice against women, as well as what approaches, steps and actions should be taken to attain the anticipated outcome of empowerment. According to her, women's emancipation is much more likely to be accomplished if they have complete control over the businesses they run, businesses they can support economically and managerially without being reliant on outside help. According to Pattanaik's 2003 study, SHGs work tirelessly to improve the lives of tribal women as participants, decision-makers, and beneficiaries in the household, economic, social, and cultural realms of life. But because of issues like gender disparity, abuse, and female assault, various Self Help Groups are not set up correctly or efficiently. In her book, Malhotra (2004) explores why women start firms, how women's business organisations support entrepreneurs and the extent to which women participate in international trade. It covers the advantages and disadvantages of adopting microfinance to combat the feminization of poverty as well as the potential of microfinance programmes for empowering and employing women. The growth in women's earning levels and control over their finances, she claims, will eventually result in higher levels of financial autonomy. They open up opportunities for women to establish various social and political positions as well as access to networks, marketplaces, and ideas. Additionally, they raise women's engagement in financial and other home decisions, which increases spending on women's welfare. These factors also improve perceptions of women's contributions to household income and family welfare. One of the noteworthy trends of the late 20th century, according to Narasaiah (2004), is an increase in women's involvement in society. He believes that microcredit is crucial for empowering women. enabling women to reach maximum achievement in all areas of life is increasing. Cheston & Kuhn (2004) concluded that women had been extremely successfully reached by microfinance initiatives. This offers microfinance organisations a rare chance for deliberate action to empower impoverished women and lessen the possible harmful effects certain women may encounter. In his article, Manimekalai (2004) stated that NGOs must assist SHGs in properly managing their income-generating activities. The financial institution's employees should offer guidance and assistance to the women in choosing and carrying out successful income-generating ventures. He noted that the establishment of SHGs has improved rural women's confidence and sense of self-worth. In their edited book, Sahu and Tripathy (2005) state that women make up 70% of the world's poor. Access to financial services is crucial for reducing poverty and maximizing its effect on the expansion of the local and national economies. Self Help Groups (SHGs) have become the most important tool for empowering women and participative development. Due to socioeconomic limitations, rural women are one of society's most marginalised groups. They continue to be at the bottom and in a lower social hierarchy position. Through microfinance and the creation of Self-Help Groups, they can free themselves from the swamp that is poverty and unemployment. In his article, Das Gupta (2005) stated that "micro-finance reform" should take the place of "financial sector reform" as the new paradigm to be adopted. While it's important to make the priority sector leaner, microcredit that's required must be closely supervised. Space and scope must be carefully planned to create a market where microfinance services can compete. The RBI must build a sizable database to comprehend microfinance. In his study, Sinha (2005) found that microfinance significantly influenced the country's impoverished people's borrowing and savings. He claims that direct investment is the principal purpose of microcredit. Of course, certain flexibility exists, based on the household's credit standards in place at the time of loan distribution. According to certain studies, microfinance initiatives have impacted women in both positive and negative ways. How much microfinance helps women has been questioned by several scholars (Mayoun, 1996). Some claim that micro-finance projects keep funders' attention and money away from potentially more successful alternatives for reducing poverty (Rogaly, 1996). They also claim that women's attention is diverted from other more effective techniques for empowering males. Women's enhanced autonomy has occasionally only been a passing trend. Women who already have it better only gain from it. However, due to their limited starting resources, lack of skills, and lack of market exposure, the poorest women are typically the least equipped to benefit.

Objectives of the Study

The objectives of the study are

1. To evaluate the economic benefits that members received from joining SHGs.
2. To examine the social benefit that members experience.
3. To develop a suitable policy intervention suggestion for SHGs to function effectively.

Research Methodology

The study is an in-depth evaluation and statistical analytical study that is based on recent patterns and instances that have occurred in operational methods for microfinance. The study's exploratory nature required the use of secondary sources, most notably the Bharat Microfinance Report, the NABARD Annual Report, the Status of Microfinance in India, and others. The current study is all the women in Madhya Pradesh who have benefited from efforts to reduce poverty and empower the underprivileged. Data is gathered at the SHG level and the level of each beneficiary as part of the technique of data collection for the current study, which is separated into distinct layers. Therefore, the study included all areas that were inhabited by the state of Madhya Pradesh's sizable tribal community. For this study, Madhya Pradesh districts' 50% tribal population is taken into account.

Field observation and structured questionnaire survey methods were used to acquire primary data. Information was also gathered through conversations and interviews with local NGOs and government employees that work at the grassroots level. The original data acquired from the group was complemented with secondary data obtained from the files of SHGs, NGOs, and government agencies. The SHGs and their members provided information on a wide range of topics, including the membership's makeup, savings that were mobilized, loans that were disbursed, interest rates, recovery practices, assets developed, outside aid received, etc. In addition, a variety of books, newspapers, articles, journals, magazines, and websites were used as references. Each block's data has been processed separately, and averages are being taken for each block's data on the composition and characteristics of SHG members, SHG savings and loans, the economic and social benefits enjoyed by SHG members, etc. To determine the effectiveness of the SHGs in the study region, conclusions are drawn from the analyses acquired from various blocks that have been compiled and compared.

Purpose of Credit Utilised on Demand

After a savings account has been open for six months, the savings are often consolidated and used for intragroup lending among members. The members themselves pick the loan amount and number of loans based on their own needs.

Table 1 Purpose-wise Credit Demanded by SHG Members

Purpose	Dhar	Barwani	Dindori	Mandla	Jhabua	Overall
Domestic consumption	56.77	11.85	14.78	65.36	47.89	31.46
Health	4.31	5.46	8.76	0.14	2.12	4.59
Festivals	5.98	8.96	7.96	3.25	2.60	5.60
Repayment of old debts	14.87	10.54	10.87	5.21	10.46	10.93
Investment	11.79	13.21	10.96	14.37	7.19	11.43
Others	5.87	48.34	44.01	11.32	28.07	227.22

Sources: Compile by the Author

Table 1 shows the SHGs' requests for credit based on their intended use. It has been noted that the majority of the members have asked for credit for household spending. Barwani (57.66%) and Dindori block (67%) have the greatest percentages. A sizable percentage of SHG members have requested credit for additional uses. Dhar block has the lowest percentage (6.4%) while Barwani has the highest (43.04%). A little over 11.56% of the credit is required for investments. The SHG members wanted a part of the credit to pay off previous debts. For event and health-related expenses, a smaller percentage of the loan is required. It is evident from the table that a greater proportion of the loans requested by SHG members are used for domestic spending, followed by debt repayment and other uses.

Table 2 Economic Activities Covered by the SHG Members

Item	Dhar	Barwani	Dindori	Mandla	Jhabua	Overall
Collection and marketing of Minor Forest Products	73	58	39	69	58	61.00
Individual business	6	9	28	8	6	12.00
Goatery	8	0	11	17	12	11.18
Dairy	8	23	7	6	13	11.02
Others	4	6	13	4	6	8.00

Sources: Compile by the Author

The majority of the SHG members are involved in the gathering and processing of minor forest products, as shown in Table 2. Broom making, cashew, mahul, turmeric, tamarind, khalli (leaf plates), raw broom, amla, and other items are among these products. Some of the members have small enterprises, such as those that make pickles, bodi, papad, haldi powder, wax, bags, vegetable businesses, custom clothing, and pan shops. They also work in the dairy, dairy farming, and goat farming industries. Some people are doing other things. They are making sweets using milk, ghee, and other ingredients and earning a nice price because there is a high demand for milk goods. These activities bring in between Rs. 600 and Rs. 1000 each month for them.

Table 3 Benefits Derived by SHG Members (Multiple Responses)

Benefits	Dhar	Barwani	Dindori	Mandla	Jhabua	Overall
Habit of Savings	74.44	78.67	67.54	75.87	79.65	75.234
Economic independence	69.87	69.87	66.04	66.54	64.89	67.442
Self-confidence	88.00	84.92	83.75	79.68	80.54	83.378
Social cohesion	71.32	79.76	70.69	69.43	84.22	75.084
Asset ownership	52.81	53.24	23.78	55.63	57.59	48.61
Freedom from debt	38.78	65.29	74.04	65.54	60.00	60.73
Additional employment	23.68	33.79	42.84	38.49	59.86	39.732

Sources: Compile by the Author

The growth of self-confidence (83.378%) is one of the standout advantages mentioned by all the members, which is followed by saving habits (75.234%), economic independence (67.442%), social cohesion (75.084%), asset ownership (48.61%), debt freedom (60.73%), and additional employment (39.732%).

Table 4 Opinion of Beneficiaries Regarding the Increase in the Power of Decision Making

Types of Decisions	Opinion of Beneficiaries					
	Yes	%	No	%	Total	%
Purchase and Sale of Fixed Assets	60	40	90	60	150	100
Purchase and Sales of Current Asset	80	53.3333	70	46.6667	150	100
Purchase and Sales of Domestic Animal	84	56	66	44	150	100
Purchase and Sales of Ornaments	92	61.3333	58	38.6667	150	100
Purchase of Home Appliance	94	62.6667	56	37.3333	150	100
Purchase of Clothes	112	74.6667	38	25.3333	150	100
Improvement of Housing Facilities	70	46.6667	80	53.3333	150	100
Raising of Loan	62	41.3333	88	58.6667	150	100
Repayment of Loan	54	36	96	64	150	100
Saving and their investment	58	38.6667	92	61.3333	150	100
Education of their children	76	47.5	84	52.5	160	100
Participation in Social Activities	90	60	60	40	150	100

Sources: Compile by the Author

Classifications have been created to show how women SHG members feel about the increase in power of decision-making within and outside of their households. It demonstrates that, of all decisions made for the study to learn the SHG members' opinions regarding the rise in their power in decision-making within and outside of their family, the majority of them have expressed the opinion that their opinion was taken into account and they were given the freedom to make the decisions. The vast majority of sample respondents believed that their ability to buy and sell current assets, domestic animals, and ornaments, as well as participate in social activities and buy appliances for their homes and clothes, had risen. Additionally, the majority of SHG members believe that their opinions are not taken into account when decisions are made regarding the purchase and sale of fixed assets, the building and improvement of housing facilities, the raising and repayment of family loans, savings and investments, and the education of children. These show that the family members were given a lot of latitude in making significant decisions.

Suggestions

1. To take advantage of microcredit programmes, disadvantaged women must be literate and have some math knowledge.
2. Legal literacy, human rights education, and gender awareness training are crucial additions to microcredit for the empowerment of women. For the group to function well, the members should receive essential instruction and direction.
3. The SHG members should be more engaged, energetic, and proactive to activate their savings through collective actions. NGOs should serve as a facilitator and motivator in this process.
4. The office bearers in charge of the group should receive some financial rewards so they may participate more actively in its activities.
5. The bank ought to provide the SHG with sufficient credit to their requirements.
6. Banks in all blocks should continue to form and extend financial assistance to them in a uniform manner.
7. The banks' process for approving credit for SHGs should be easy and speedy.
8. Marketing infrastructure for SHG product sales might be developed.
9. Block-level periodic exhibitions may be planned where SHG items may be showcased.
10. The members may organize meetings and seminars where they will have the opportunity to share their opinions and be able to strengthen their group through interactions.
11. The creation of successful micro-enterprises is dependent on the district administration, professional associations, and nonprofit groups taking an active role in market access, product design, and skill training.

Conclusion

Regarding the impact of microfinance on the lives of the impoverished people it is meant to reach, there have been numerous reviews over the past couple of decades, both in India and overseas. The results have been contradictory and unclear; it has been observed that microfinance has occasionally created credit reliance and repeated responsibility and has provided a burden to the impoverished people who are living below the poverty line. Additionally, it has been questioned whether lending institutions are solely motivated by financial gain or whether their focus has always been on eradicating poverty. The Reserve Bank of India and the Government of India are eagerly awaiting the establishment of a strong administrative structure to oversee the miniaturized scale account industry, which will indirectly aid in the reduction of poverty. The programme owes this level of inclusion to its ability to train large numbers of rural residents, mobilise the government apparatus, and attract development organisations. Regarding financial support and budgetary concern for the base of the pyramid, this programme represents a powerful intervention. A programme for the promotion of livelihoods and poverty alleviation has evolved from a proven stage originally intended for expanding the efforts of banking administrations among the poor.

Policy Implication

To meet the increased business needs, group structure orientation is necessary. In the context of SHG, the shift towards microcredit must be seen in the long run, highlighting the necessity of deliberate policy implications in favor of assurance in terms of technological redundancy, the product market, and human resource advancement. The development of a creative and diverse microfinance industry is therefore necessary if women are to truly benefit from it. We need to implement a proactive plan for reducing poverty in the twenty-first century that is growth-oriented, people-centered, and appears to take into account the aspirations, dynamism, and involvement of women. Self-help organizations are expected to be a key component of this plan. However, the groupings must be structurally oriented to meet the needs of a new company. Under the SHG framework, the microcredit movement must be considered in the long run, which emphasizes the need for a conscious policy implication in favour of assurance in terms of technological support, the product market, and human resource development. Therefore, there is a need for the growth of a creative and diverse microfinance industry, which will significantly aid in the empowerment of women.

References

1. Bosch, E. (2002), *Micro-finance: New Wine in a New Bottle, A Supplementing Role for Cordaid and IICO*, March.
2. Cheston, S., & Kuhn, L. (2002). Empowering women through micro-finance UNIFEM http://www. opportunity. org/files. *Empowering% 20Women% 20Paper% 20FI NAL.*
3. Dasgupta, R. (2005). Microfinance in India: Empirical Evidence, Alternative Models and Policy Imperatives, *Economic and Political Weekly*, 19 March.
4. Government of India (2011). Census report.
5. Government of India (2014). Planning commission report.
6. Kapoor, Pramilla (2001), *Empowering the Indian Women*, Publications Division, Ministry of Information and Broadcasting, Government of India.
7. Malhotra, M. (2004). *Empowerment of Women: Microfinance and women empowerment, 2.* Isha Books.
8. Manimekalai, K. (2004). Economic empowerment of women through Self-Help groups. *Third Concept, February, 1.*
9. Mayoux, L. (1999). Questioning virtuous spirals: micro-finance and women's empowerment in Africa. *Journal of International Development, 11*(7), 957.
10. Narasiah, M.L. (2004), *Women and Microcredit*, Sonali Publications, New Delhi.
11. Osman, K. (1999). Microfinance institutions: an effective weapon in the war against rural poverty. *Muslimedia, January, 16.*
12. Pattanaik, S. (2003). Empowerment through SHG: A case study of Gajapati district. *Smaranika 2003.*
13. Rogaly, B. (1996). Micro-finance evangelism, 'destitute women', and the hard selling of a new anti-poverty formula. *Development in practice, 6*(2), 100-112.
14. Sahu, R. K., & Tripathy, S. N. (2005). *Self-Help Groups and Women Empowerment*, Anmol Publications Pvt. Ltd., New Delhi.
15. Sinha, F. (2005). Access, use and contribution of microfinance in India: Findings from a national study. *Economic and Political Weekly*, 1714-1719.
16. Tandon, T. (2016). Women empowerment: perspectives and views. *The International Journal of Indian Psychology, 3*(3), 6-12..

11

A Study on Value Chain for Inclusive Growth: The Case of the Bakery Enterprise

Dr. Kaushal Kumar[1] *& Dr. Devendra Singh Bagri*[2]

Abstract

Any country's economic progress and growth are fuelled by microbusinesses and microentrepreneurs. One of the fastest-growing sections of micro businesses is run by women. It raises the amount of money available to women. It fosters independence, self-worth, and self-assurance. Women contribute significantly to national income as microbusiness owners, build solid financial security for their families, and integrate into value chains for inclusive growth. This study identifies a case study and attempts to describe the situation of Sita, a tribal woman microentrepreneur who owns a bakery enterprise in Madhya Pradesh's Annupur District. It is the story of a less educated lady who took up the activity and succeeded in life despite having a strong desire to do it, a willingness to accept chances, and the ability to deal with uncertainty. She serves as both an inspiration and a role model for confidence.

Keywords: *Inclusive growth, entrepreneur, women and bakery*

Introduction

Today, women, who make up roughly half of the Indian population, are seen as the better half of society, but only 10% of all Indian entrepreneurs are women (Mallya, 2011). Changes in the three interconnected dimensions that make up choice—resources, which form the conditions under which choices are made; agency, which is at the center of the process by which choices are made; and accomplishments, which are the results of choices—can be thought of as changes in the ability to exercise choice (Kabeer, 2001). The definition of agency is provided in the World Development Report 2012, which includes having control over resources, making decisions, being free to move about without fear of being attacked, and having a voice and influence in group decision-making processes. The most popular measures of women's empowerment include control over economic and political resources and decision-making, as well as abilities, particularly in the areas of education and health (Desai, 2010). The six components of empowerment denote economic, sociocultural, family/interpersonal, legal, political, and psychological are suggested by Malhotra et al. (2002). Each of these dimensions is intricate and has some subdimensions. When it comes to the idea of inclusive growth, it is widely understood to be a growth that provides an opportunity for all segments of the population, with a special focus on the poor, especially young people and women, who are more prone to be marginalised. In

[1] Assistant Professor, Faculty of Commerce Shri Rawatpura Sarkar University, Raipur, Chhattisgarh

[2] Assistant Professor, Department of Commerce Government Tulsi College Anuppur, Madhya Pradesh

other words, growth is inclusive when it produces and guarantees equal access to economic possibilities together.

Inclusion is defined by the World Bank's Commission on Growth and Development as a notion that includes equity, equality of opportunity, and protection during market and job changes. Here, we emphasize the concept of equal opportunity for firms and individuals in terms of the availability of markets, resources, and an impartial regulatory environment (Deblock & Haji 2008). To increase the incomes of excluded groups, the inclusive growth strategy favours productive employment over direct income redistribution, which puts more of an emphasis on the long term. People can profit from economic growth in the short term through income distribution plans, but inclusive growth enables people to both contribute to and profit from economic growth (Ianchovichina & Lundstrom, 2009; Chakrabarty, 2010). Consequently, "inclusive growth" refers to both the rate and the composition of expansion. Undoubtedly, a rapid pace of growth is required for a significant poverty reduction, but for this growth to be long-term sustainable, it must be inclusive of a large portion of the labour force and broad-based across sectors (Ianchovichina & Lundstrom, 2009). Therefore, it is encouraging to see that women are gaining access to all areas of life and leaving their homes to engage in a wide range of activities. Here, an attempt is made to tell the story of a woman businesswoman in Madhya Pradesh's Annupur District who started her bakery. It describes how insufficiently educated women have shown a significant desire to engage in the activity, she is an inspiration because she is willing to take chances, can deal with uncertainty, and has accomplished something extraordinary in her life. She is also a testament to self-confidence.

Micro Enterprises and Bakery

The 11th Five Year Plan, titled "Towards Faster and More Inclusive Growth," sought to achieve "gender inclusive growth," which would help women who had been left out of the greater rates of economic growth seen in recent years by providing them with more employment and income. The 12th Five-Year Plan has also expanded on the inclusive strategy. Let's now examine the position of women in India in the era of inclusive growth in terms of certain essential elements that guarantee women's empowerment, such as the sex ratio, education, health, economic engagement, participation in decision-making, and the prevalence of violence against women. One of the microenterprise sectors with the fastest growth rates is women-owned companies. It raises the amount of money available to women. Women who run microbusinesses significantly increase the country's GDP while also providing dependable social security networks for their families and communities. A micro firm has a labour force of between 11 and 35 employees and a total cost that includes working capital but excludes the cost of land that is over 1 million but under 40 million, according to Ayodela, 1998. According to Purshotham (2003), a micro-enterprise makes use of local resources and offers some additional options for employment in addition to self-employment. "Any business unit located in rural or semi-urban areas with a capital of not exceeding three lakhs" is referred to as a micro-enterprise. These units are not based on advanced technology, but rather on local resources. According to Chester, & Thanaraj, (2009), "These units may be involved in the production, trading, servicing, finance, and other local activities". It is clear that micro-enterprises fall under the informal economic category and are seen as a bottom-up approach to some issues, including reducing poverty, reducing unemployment, and promoting overall growth. Microbusinesses promote a feeling of freedom. They are regarded as the engines of growth of the Indian economy since they create employment opportunities and stable sources of revenue.

In the context of MSME (Micro, Small, and Medium Enterprises), a bakery is a small-scale business that falls under the category of micro or small enterprise. MSMEs play a crucial role in the economic development of many countries by contributing to employment generation, innovation, and GDP growth. The bakery industry is a part of the food and beverage sector and is primarily involved in the production and sale of baked goods such as bread, cakes, pastries, cookies, muffins, and other related products. Bakeries can vary in size and scope, ranging from small neighborhood bakeries to larger establishments with multiple outlets or franchises. Bakeries are an essential component of the food industry and cater to a widespread consumer base. They often have a strong presence in local communities and contribute to the supply chain of various retail outlets, restaurants, and cafes. Bakeries, being labor-intensive businesses, provide employment opportunities to a significant number of people, particularly in the production and sales departments. Additionally, they also support farmers and suppliers by sourcing ingredients from local or regional markets (Jerome et al. 2019).

Bakery goods have become a highly consumed item due to their nutritional value and affordability. Their popularity has been driven by factors such as rapid population growth, increasing foreign influence, a growing female working population, and changing eating habits. This has significantly contributed to the bakery industry's growth. Additionally, the introduction of healthier bakery products has gained rapid popularity (Majid et. al, 2014). The global bakery products market had already achieved an impressive value of nearly USD 507.38 billion in the year 2020. Projections indicate that the industry will continue to grow steadily, with an expected Compound Annual Growth Rate (CAGR) of 2.5% between 2021 and 2026. By 2026, it is estimated that the global bakery products market will reach a value of approximately USD 574.05 billion. Among the major players in the global market, the United States takes the lead, holding a significant 20% share. China follows closely, accounting for 7% of the global bakery market share. Both China and Brazil are experiencing rapid growth in the bakery products market, with an impressive approximate growth rate of 10% over the past four years. In the context of Europe, the region currently represents the largest market for bakery products. Germany, in particular, dominates the bread and rolls segment within the European market. Overall, the bakery products industry shows promising growth prospects on a global scale, with different regions contributing to its expansion in various ways (Food Marketing & Technology magazine, 2023).

In India, the bakery industry holds a prominent position within the country's processed food sector. Bread and biscuits constitute a major portion of baked goods, accounting for more than one-third of total bakery production. The country benefits from a comparative advantage in manufacturing due to abundant supplies of primary ingredients, making it the third-largest biscuit manufacturing nation after the United States and China. The Indian bakery segment can be divided into three main categories: bread, biscuits, and cakes. While the organized bakery sector produces approximately 1.3 million tonnes of bakery products, the remaining output is contributed by small-scale local manufacturers operating in the unorganized sector. Despite the presence of automatic and semi-automatic bread and biscuit manufacturing units in India, many people still prefer purchasing fresh bakery products from local bakeries. Various biscuit variants are popular in India, including glucose biscuits, Marie, cream biscuits, crackers, digestive biscuits, cookies, and milk biscuits. In the Indian biscuit market, the branded and organized sector holds a share of 60 percent, while the unbranded and unorganized sector holds 40 percent. Moreover, Indian bakery products, particularly biscuits, are in high demand in developing countries. The bakery industry in India has proven to be a profitable venture, supported by compelling facts and figures. In 2018, the industry already achieved a significant value of US $7.22 billion, and it is expected to grow even further, with market projections indicating it will surpass US $12 billion by 2024. This growth potential makes it an attractive investment opportunity and with advancements in technology, some bakeries have integrated modern baking equipment and automated processes to improve efficiency and maintain consistent product quality. The bakery industry in India can be broadly classified into two categories: organized and unorganized. The organized segment consists of more than 2,000 bakeries that are either fully organized or semi-organized. In contrast, the unorganized segment comprises a vast number of approximately 1,000,000 smaller bakeries. The industry faces challenges related to operational efficiency, primarily due to the lack of advanced technology and a shortage of skilled workers. However, organized bakeries in India are adopting social media marketing and engagement strategies to target specific audiences and cost-effectively promote their products. On the other hand, local bakery-cafes, with limited resources compared to international chains, rely more on word-of-mouth recommendations rather than extensive social media marketing. They emphasize the artisanal aspect of their products, focusing on quality over quantity. Larger Indian chains like Barista and Mad Over Donuts, on the other hand, prioritize creating larger quantities of products with strong branding and a sense of trust associated with their brand. Despite the challenges and obstacles faced by the industry, there has been a surge in entrepreneurial endeavors within the bakery industry in India. New technological innovations have allowed individuals to monetize their baking efforts, leading to a booming home baking market. In recent years, there has been a growing demand for healthier baked goods, organic products, gluten-free options, and plant-based alternatives. Overall, the bakery industry in India is evolving and adapting to the changing market dynamics, with both organized and unorganized players finding their unique approaches to succeed in this competitive landscape and starting a bakery is a now popular choice for entrepreneurs due to its relatively low entry barriers and market demand. Many small-scale bakers bring innovation to their products by experimenting with recipes and introducing new flavors and designs, which can attract a loyal customer base (Food Marketing & Technology magazine, 2023; Kumar et al. 2020).

Case Study

The body of research on the rise of female entrepreneurship in developing nations is expanding (Schoar, 2009; Ardagna and Lusardi, 2008; Minniti, 2010; Kobeissi, 2010). In particular, Ghani et al.'s (2012 and 2013) attention is drawn to the growth of women's entrepreneurship in India. Duflo (2012) examined the condition of women in the unorganized sector and discovered that they were more likely to be exploited than males since they were paid less for equal types of work and the same number of hours put in. Equal access to commercial possibilities is not granted to women. Stuart A. Queen defines a case study as "the study of a single circumstance, persons, groups, or institutions as complicated wholes to determine types and process". According to Golich, 2000 "a case study is a story; it provides the concrete narrative information of genuine, or at least realistic, events and it has a plot, explanation, characters, and at times even dialogue." The case study approach enables researchers to preserve the comprehensive and significant aspects of real-world occurrences, including individual life cycles, small-group behaviour, managerial and organisational processes, neighborhood change, academic performance, global relations, and the development of industries. The case study research approach is described as an empirical investigation that examines a contemporary phenomenon in its actual setting by the researcher (Yin 2003). It is a type of qualitative descriptive research that focuses intently on one person or a small group of participants, reaching conclusions just about them and only in that particular situation. Case studies seek to offer a comprehensive picture of a scenario or occurrence, which is made possible by looking at how all the elements interact. A thorough description of the entity is part of the procedure. Interpreting the significance of demographic and descriptive data, such as cultural mores, socially ingrained attitudes, and motivations, is another aspect of thick description. A case study's objective is to present fresh factors and inquiries for further investigation. Therefore, a case study is the gathering and presenting of in-depth data about a specific participant or group of people, frequently including the subjects' accounts.

Methodology

The case study approach has been used. The basis for description and analysis is the interaction with the respondent and the locations visited. The responses were captured and noted down in the checklist to better, more appropriately collect and analyse the data.

Example of "Bakery" 35-year-old Hindu woman named Mrs. Sita. Three kids share her nuclear family unit where she resides. Her secondary education is complete. She is a member of the schedule tribe. She is the proprietor of a bakery in a city. Her motivation for opening her bakery came from her 20 years of experience working for another individual in Kishore Bakery. She's had her bakery for six years. The entire business is run out of a rented space that serves as both a bakery and a residence. Her children's education is largely funded by the school administration. She left the previous unit with five subordinates who now report to her. The machinery required a Rs 2,00,000 initial expenditure. She has a business loan of Rs 30,000 from the Annupur-based microfinance organisation Murda Shishu Loan. She pays the loan's interest of Rs 1300 per week. Her daughters write the tales in the late hours of the night. She, therefore, has little trouble keeping straightforward accounts. At the time of sale, no bills or vouchers are issued. There is no legitimate book of accounts kept. In addition to funding her children's education, she uses the majority of her profit to grow the firm. She also received a Rs 10,000 gold loan from Murda Shishu Loan for which she is responsible for paying interest separately. Money rotation is done in emergency and urgent situations to pay back loans from money lenders with higher interest rates. Weekly cash purchases are generally made. The main monthly expenses are paying interest, funding children's education, maintaining machinery, etc. She has six days a week of work. Regarding daily working hours, flexibility is maintained. She delivers completed goods three times every day at 8:30 am, 11:00 am, and 3:30 pm. There isn't a system of inventory in use. The selling point is where she works. She has no marketing issues because she consistently receives orders from ten schools, some colleges, and stores. Since the clients accept deliveries directly, there is no need to employ salespeople. It has a fixed price system. She values her devoted clientele. She claims, "I can keep my customer due to the quality and flavor I uphold. Cash transactions are accepted. She places a high value on prompt delivery and client satisfaction (quality and flavor). The items cover Annupur town specifically as well as the Annupur district generally. She provides about 1500 pubs, 100 bans, and breads every day. She often earns a net profit of about Rs 15,000 per week. Since deliveries happen every day, no storage space is necessary. She does not believe that her product needs to be advertised because she is so confident in its quality and flavor. She is subordinate to three employees. One employee receives a daily salary of Rs 100, while the other two receive daily salaries of Rs 50 each. She typically decides on price setting and other matters after consulting the staff. A 3000-rupee incentive is provided to the three employees each year. When one of them is ill or unavailable for some reason, they all attempt to manage and divide the workload. There is a sense of collaboration rather than a master-servant relationship. Her dream for her business is growth. Due to her strong will, commitment, and other qualities, she has little trouble realizing her dreams. She is certain that she can keep her current clients through the end. After opening the enterprises, she developed and accumulated several assets, including a rented home, a refrigerator, business equipment, a television, gold, furniture, etc. Although the respondent is aware of the numerous legal security plans accessible to such business owners, she is unaware of their specifics and has not taken advantage of them. Unexpected institution closures are one of the difficulties she encounters. Since it is still a household activity, she has no competition. She makes it plain that if she opened her shop in the main area, she would face fierce competition. Financial hardship is yet another significant obstacle.

Invention

She gladly acknowledges that Murda Shishu Loan, a prominent microfinance institution operating across the entire nation with its strongest presence in Annupur, was instrumental in helping her reach this level. She felt that Murda Shishu Loan's intervention was helpful, timely, and supportive of keeping her projects going. She has a favorable attitude toward the weekly interest payment.

The following are some implications of this value chain for inclusive growth:

1. Change from "Feeling of nobody" to "Feeling of somebody": In every aspect of life, feeling like a nobody or undesired is on the rise. However, this success story shows how a person can alter their thinking if they have a strong desire to succeed.
2. Asset creation and growth: The person can develop their potential in society and produce and grow assets for the family. Due to this action, assets in the shape of gold, cots, machines, TVs, refrigerators, and vehicles have been acquired.
3. Increasing and gaining recognition: As the most vulnerable group in society, women are becoming more and more visible as a result of the creation of businesses. They can make their fair share of contributions to the development of the family and society at large. They also turn into hubs for development, expansion, and vision.
4. Financially involved: The respondent has been economically included as a result of her realization of the necessity and significance of saving for the future of the family and the business.

5. Quality consciousness offers enjoyment and hope: Since she has to keep the consumers, the individual is undoubtedly quality conscious. She is also extremely conscious that the crucial elements of any business should be quality and on-time delivery.
6. Increased sense of self-worth: Regardless of academic level, social background, gender, etc., the example clearly shows that a person obtains a sense of acceptance in society. If there is a sense of resolve and success, the person also feels empowered. Conviction and dedication have improved one's perception of their value. The respondent's confidence has increased as a result of Murda Shishu Loan assistance.
7. Good understanding of target audience: It is apparent that the respondent has a good understanding of her target audience, which helps her move forward without any problems.
8. Becoming an entrepreneur affects a person's overall growth and development, not only their financial well-being. This instance additionally shows how, with enough willpower and persistence, one can mold one's life through hardships.
9. Requires formal training and upgrading: While experience is one of the most significant motivators, ongoing and frequent updating and training of abilities and talents are required. Given that she is a woman, the reply should update her knowledge and abilities. But until a company steps up to give such training with a stipend, the respondent will not be able to attend.
10. Making the most of current abilities to survive: The reply has amply utilised her talent, skill, experience, etc.
11. Strong backer: The instance illustrates the necessity of having a strong backer in one's life. Her prior experience and the financial support from Murda Shishu Loan, friends, and money lenders act as two significant supporters in this scenario.
12. Difficult times never last: The example is loaded with significance. It demonstrates that everyone experiences hardships. However, if one has a high level of self-assurance, tenacity, and commitment, it is possible to do something important and beneficial in life. When there is a good attitude towards everything that comes your way, any kind of hardship ends. Such a respondent's attitude and approach guarantee a genuine and fair sense for bettering and sustaining growth.

One of the methods used in the case study approach for analyzing the case is SWOT (Strength, Weakness, Opportunity, and Threat) analysis. Given the foregoing, the case's SWOT can be summed up as follows:

Strength

1. The highest degree of self-assurance
2. Commitment and self-worth
3. Job Creator
4. Dependable personnel who are dedicated
5. Loyal clients
6. Prompt delivery
7. Taking possession
8. Raised her wealth
9. Steady and long-term gains
10. The capacity to make decisions

11. Building confidence
12. Both monetary and social security

Weakness

1. Fewer opportunities to improve abilities and talents
2. Limited space and fewer mechanisms for technological advancement
3. Being a Women
4. Without having a home or business of one's own
5. Lack of technological expertise Inadequate financial resources

Opportunity

1. Potential for future growth
2. Good, dependable, and consistent clients
3. Expanding customer base preparing to open a shop of one's own
4. Better exposure to society
5. Increased network activity and connections
6. Stable consumer demand for goods
7. Government initiatives that provide support

Threat

1. The future rivalry will be fierce
2. Technological progress
3. Inflation and Globalisation
4. The power went out
5. Political environment
6. Customer loyalty uncertainty brought on by competition and globalisation
7. Apprehension of political meddling
8. Lack of workers

The following issues occur about starting, operating, and maintaining the business to balance its strengths and weaknesses against its opportunities and threats.

1. Can such a small business compete effectively on a national level?
2. Can it still pursue its goals and endure in the contemporary, globalised corporate environment?
3. What would it take to inspire microbusiness owners to turn their shortcomings into strengths and their threats into opportunities?
4. Achieve microbusiness owners, particularly women microbusiness owners, achieve this?
5. How can we make sure that the government is supporting these microbusiness owners so they can succeed in this cutthroat society?

Conclusion

In India, as per the Puranas and scriptures of Hinduism, the women resembled Goddess Lakshmi and when a girl takes birth is considered auspicious, referring to it as "Lakshmi Aagmana". Without women contributing to the creation of growth and sharing in its rewards, economic growth is elusive. Without an increase in the number of women participating in productive activities, growth cannot be sustained. In contrast, women ought to gain from advancement through equal pay, improved access to education and healthcare, control over resources, and involvement in decision-making. A farmer was once passing a giant stone in the center of the road while strolling through a tiny village. Who could be so irresponsible as to leave an enormous stone on the road, the farmer moaned? Why is it not being removed? He left in discontent. A milkman experienced the same incident the following day. Even he left the stone alone, complaining as he walked. The stone was then discovered by a student one day. He decided to throw it aside out of concern that someone may trip over it and damage himself. He used a lot of force on his own and eventually succeeded in removing the stone that covered the walkway. When he returned, he saw a piece of paper next to the stone. He picked up the document and read it. "You are the true wealth of the nation," was written on the inside. Without a shadow of a doubt, it can be asserted that the true wealth of the planet, country, and society is with the micro-entrepreneurs, not the bystanders in the narrative above, but rather the students. The methods for eradicating poverty and the issue of unemployment are micro-entrepreneurs and micro enterprises, engines for growth and development. The respondent has been listed among the nation's inspirations because of their level of motivation, self-assurance, willpower, and drive to accomplish something in life. This instance serves as an example of how a woman can seize an opening, exhibit her innate drive and latent leadership, and become active and noticeable in society. She is a testament to self-assurance and a glimmer of optimism for the next generation. The level of empowerment that women experience varies with their age, socioeconomic status, caste (in India), religion, and country of residence because they are not a homogeneous population. Sometimes very persistent, these influences require steadfast attempts to overcome. Therefore, there is a huge need for more research on the effects of women's entrepreneurship on various groups of women in India. There is a consensus that Muslim women and women from Scheduled Castes/Scheduled Tribes are more disadvantaged and experience severe marginalisation. If the data allow, it is necessary to study and analyze how women in various groups are becoming more entrepreneurial as well as how this has affected the advancement of development indicators.

References

1. Ardagna, S., & Lusardi, A. (2008). *Explaining international differences in entrepreneurship: The role of individual characteristics and regulatory constraints* (No. w14012). National Bureau of Economic Research.
2. Ayodela, H. A. (1998). Sustainability of Micro, Small and Medium Enterprises in Nigeria. *Small Enterprises Development, Management & Extension Journal, 25*(4), 27-40.
3. Chakrabarty, K. C. (2010). Inclusive growth–role of financial sector. *Address at the National Finance Conclave.*
4. Chester, J. R., & Thanaraj, X. A. (2009). Micro Enterprises-An Indian Scenario.
5. Deblock, C., & Haji, R. (2008). Commission on Growth and Development, The Growth Report. Strategies for Sustained Growth and Inclusive Development, Washington, The International Bank for Reconstruction and Development/The World Bank, 2008. *CEIM: Montreal, mai.*
6. Desai, M. A. (2010). Hope in hard times: Women's empowerment and human development. *UNDP-HDRO Occasional Papers,* (2010/14).
7. Duflo, E. (2012). Women empowerment and economic development. *Journal of Economic literature, 50*(4), 1051-1079.
8. EJerome, R., Singh, S. K., & Dwivedi, M. (2019). Process analytical technology for bakery industry: A review. *Journal of Food Process Engineering* , 1-21.
9. Food Marketing & Technology magazine, I. (2023). Retrieved from Food Marketing Technology : https://fmtmagazine.in/bakery-industry-in-india/
10. Ghani, E., Kerr, W. R. & O'Connell, S. D. (2012). What Explains Big Gender Disparities in India? Local Industrial Structures and Female Entrepreneurship. World Bank Policy Research Working Paper, (6228).
11. Ghani, E., Kerr, W. R. & O'Connell, S. D. (2013). Female Business Ownership and Informal Sector Persistence. World Bank Policy Research Working Paper, (6612).

12. Golich, V. L. (2000). The ABCs of case teaching. *International Studies Perspectives, 1*(1), 11-29.
13. Ianchovichina, E., & Lundstrom, S. (2009). Inclusive growth analytics: Framework and application. *World Bank Policy Research Working Paper,* (4851).
14. Kabeer, N. (2021). Gender equality, inclusive growth, and labour markets. *Women's Economic Empowerment: Insights from Africa and South Asia,* 13-48.
15. Kaur, J. (2013). Women Empowerment: challenges & prospects. *EXCEL International Journal of Multidisciplinary Management Studies, 3*(9), 50-54.
16. Khokhar, A. S., & Singh, D. B. (2016). Role of women entrepreneurship in inclusive growth. *South Asia, 11*(9.6), 18-3.
17. Kumar, S., Abdulla, & Singh, C. P. (2020). Productivity growth in India's bakery manufacturing industry. *Journal of Agribusiness in Developing and Emerging Economies.*
18. Majid, I., Kumar, V., & Nayik, G. A. (2014). *Bakery industry in India - Innovations, trends and challenges.* Retrieved from https://www.researchgate.net/profile/Ishrat-Majid/publication/279535583_Bakery_industry_in_India_-_Innovations_trends_and_challenges/links/55964e1f08ae5d8f39312bce/Bakery-industry-in-India-Innovations-trends-and-challenges.pdf
19. Mallya, L. S. (2011). Successful Entrepreneurs of Indian Origin: A Case Study. *Theis submitted by for the Award of the Degree of Doctor of Philosophy. Dr. MGR Educational and Research Institute University, Chennai.*
20. Minniti, M., & Naude, W. (2010). What do we know about the patterns and determinants of female entrepreneurship across countries?. *The European Journal of Development Research,* 22, 277-293.
21. Purshotham, P., (2003). Micro enterprise opportunities in food industry, *SEDME, 30*(2), 36.
22. Schoar, A. (2010). The divide between subsistence and transformational entrepreneurship. *Innovation Policy and the Economy, 10*(1), 57-81.
23. Yin, R. K. (2003). Designing case studies. *Qualitative Research Methods, 5*(14), 359-386.

12

Financial Literacy among the SHGs Women in India

Dr. Ravi Singh[1]*, Dr. Ksh Ranjan Singh*[2] *& Chanambam Chingkheinganba Meetei*[3]

Abstract

Women's empowerment is one of the largest issues facing our nation, and it can only be accomplished by empowering women via education, financial freedom, and independence. Knowing how money functions in a typical situation is what is meant by financial literacy. It especially relates to the collection of skills and knowledge that empowers an individual to use all of his or her financial assets to make intelligent and reasonable opinions. In India, males often earn the majority of the family's income while women typically spend the majority of it. Although women's access to financial services has expanded significantly quicker over the past ten years, their ability to take advantage of this access is still frequently constrained by the disadvantages associated with being a woman. Although many women are skilled at creating budgets and controlling household spending, they sometimes shy away from making important financial decisions as they believe their spouses, fathers, brothers, etc., have a better financial understanding. Every woman has to have at least a basic understanding of finances so that she may make her own decisions and contribute to the overall well-being and prosperity of her family. A financially independent woman can be a tremendous source of economic development because women have a huge capacity to contribute to the economy's growth. This study aimed to provide an overview of women's financial literacy in emerging nations like India.

Keywords: *Financial illiterate, women, empowerment, and economy growth*

Introduction

Emerging and developed economies alike are placing a lot of emphasis these days on how financially literate their populations are. Any country's progress is significantly influenced by its financial system. Financial ignorance implies significant costs. People who are unaware of how interest rate compounding works end up incurring greater debt, paying higher transaction fees, and getting higher rates of interest on loans. To determine the level of financial literacy among working Indian women, Arora (2016) did a study titled Assessment of Financial Literacy. Only 444 of the 700 working women in Rajasthan's metropolitan areas who participated in the survey answered. Three criteria—financial knowledge, financial behaviour, and financial attitude—were used to measure the degree of financial literacy, and it was discovered that women still have a low level of general knowledge of financial planning tools and strategies. According to the

1 Assistant Professor, Department of Commerce Government Chandra Vijay College, Dindori, Madhya Pradesh

2 Assistant Professor, Department of Commerce Manipur University Canchipur Imphal, Manipur

3 Research Scholar, Department of Commerce Manipur University Canchipur Imphal, Manipur

study's findings, women perform better in terms of financial conduct and attitude than they do in terms of financial knowledge. Financial Literacy is the concept of understanding financial trends and how to implement them in real life, such as personal finance, budgeting, and savings. Acquiring financial literacy can help people avoid bad financial decisions and achieve financial stability independently. Learning how to budget, keep track of costs, pay off debt, and plan for retirement are all examples of basic financial abilities. It's about understanding how money works, establishing and accomplishing financial objectives, becoming aware of unethical financial behaviour, and assisting with day-to-day financial issues. More and more financial products are gaining attention, including (Lusardi, 2019) alternative financial services such as payday loans, pawnshops, and rental businesses that impose very high-interest rates. At the same time, in a changing economic climate, people are increasingly responsible for their financial plans and investments and the use of their resources throughout their lives (Youth Financial Literacy Foundation, n.d.). You can better appreciate the worth of money thanks to the advantages of financial literacy. Understanding the worth of money helps us handle our finances by emphasizing the necessity of budgeting, saving, and refraining from pointless expenditures. Our ability to invest and create wealth is made possible by having financial literacy, which keeps us from turning into debt slaves. They typically inform us of the various possibilities for gaining wealth available to us, helping us avoid poor financial choices. Financially literate people are less susceptible to gambling and Ponzi scheme temptations because they are aware of the worth of money as well as how difficult it can be to earn it.

For ages of time, the world has been dominated by men who run the society and women blindly follow them. But women are the basis of mankind and by making them literate, the entire family becomes literate. In earlier days, women were treated inferior to men as they were supposed to take care of the household chores, be a perfect homemaker and raise the family only. Women in modern society these days too are on a majority basis under the influence of parents until marriage and switch over to being under the control of their husbands after marriage. Still, some women are given the right and freedom to express their likes and dislikes and aspire to become someone eminent that society recognizes as an individual. Now, determined women continue to strive to hold a prestigious position amid anti-social elements like dowry, domestic violence, sex-selective abortion, and so on, though the percentage is very minimal.

The biggest and greatest challenge for our country is making women feel empowered at home and in society by giving them the status of honour and respect through education and making them feel more independent than dependent. To encourage and empower women, the government has taken various steps by establishing self-help groups such as Swayamsidha Program to provide them accessibility to become aware of certain welfare programmes and also enhance their skills. When compared to men, women are much more talented in financial planning, budgeting and managing household expenses. But when it comes to a larger part of decision-making concerning investment and handling larger finances, they tend to take a back step as the men in the house generally take the upper hand and they also believe that their husband, father, or brother can do a better job compared to them. Since, they are kept at the back bench in such aspects, in times of divorce, widowhood, etc they face the struggle to handle the sudden situation. Gaining basic knowledge in financial literacy is essential for women which will enable them to make choices in decisions related to savings and investments and help them lead a happy life with their entire family. The purpose of this paper is to conceptually picture the present state of financial literacy among women in India and to identify the challenges or hurdles that curtail them from becoming financially able and channelise feasible solutions to overcome those challenges. Hence, this paper certainly creates a basic perception of financial literacy among women in India.

Scenario of Financial Literacy among Women in India

Financial services are essential for a nation's economic growth. Numerous nationalised banks, microfinance organisations, and other formal organisations are focusing their efforts on extending financial inclusion to rural populations (Akshita, 2016). Financial literacy is a country's asset that defines the economic status of the country. India is a multicultural and multilingual country with a population of 1.40 billion in 2022, with 27.6% of the population potentially one of the top financial literacy countries in the world (India's Growing Financial Literacy, 2022). Being the largest country in the world with a diverse population, its literacy rate on the whole scores 79% when compared to the countries worldwide according to UNESCO. This explicitly narrates that the majority of the Indians can read and write but have less access to education. According to the NSS 75th Round (July 2017–June 2018), 46.2% of men and 41.2% of women between the ages of 3 to 35 are enrolled in school. In the age group 3 to 35 years, 16.6 % of females are never enrolled while 11.0 % of males are not enrolled. (Kempaller, 2022). Due to a lack of basic education, the numerical abilities among women are poor which restricts them from analysing financial information properly causing poor financial planning which ultimately affects their saving & investment decisions and the well-being of the family as a whole (Singh & Kumar, 2017). It is, therefore, highly perceived that men in India are more literate than women and it is essentially vital to make them financially more able and literate.

The threat of financial inclusion continues to exist, as nearly two billion people still do not have a bank account. According to Demirguc-Kunt et al. (2018), this indicates that over 70% of individuals globally have access to basic financial tools like a savings account, a debit card, and the like. Financial knowledge is essential when discussing financial inclusion, though (Grohmann et al., 2018). Institutions including schools, universities, governments, researchers, and society are all interested in the topic of varied groups and several differentiating characteristics (Cabeza-Garca et al., 2019). Inclusive finance and personal traits, particularly gender, are essential for achieving inclusive growth (Soumare et al., 2016). When it comes to financial inclusion, demand and supply are the two indicators of banking services and are viewed as the same thing as a whole (Sethy, 2015). According to the philosophy of inclusive finance, risk transfers should be a part of financial inclusion as well (Honohan, 2005). According to Berentsen and Markheim (Berentsen & Markheim, 2020), peer-to-peer lending is influenced by borrowing rates as well as financial inclusion. Education is crucial for financial inclusion since it enables access to formal financial services, while a lack of it forces people to use informal financial services (Camara & David, 2015). Financially savvy women make sensible use of their resources by making a major contribution to the income and well-being of their families and participating actively in decision-making (Swamy, 2016).

In India, there are barriers faced by women in the name of society and culture as we are in the times where women seek opportunities on par with men, aspiring to have big dreams in life and create a better place for themselves and the families around them. But women leaving home for work are viewed as an irresponsible person who doesn't care about the family and home. To add more, their earnings go to the spouse and they are forbidden the right to enjoy their earnings according to their choice. These barricades have brought down the value of women in partaking in financial inclusions even though they have acquired the least awareness of it and struggling to prove themselves concerning it. Thousands of men and women globally are employed by MSME's in the Indian economy. Even though there are more than 50 million male entrepreneurs in India, just 13.76 percent of them are female. However, only 8 million women are thought to be business owners (Important MSME Schemes for Promoting Women Entrepreneurs, 2021). According to the report made in FY21, the number of MSMEs led by women has shown an improvement of 7% since FY11. The point is, is this 7% a fair growth for 10 years? Much financial fraudulence has been reported due to being financially illiterate. The major cause is a lack of knowledge about what to share. When to share? Why to share? Whom to share? People tend not to realize the consequences of financial illiteracy, they tend to lose a lot of money, and such behaviours have psychological implications.

Challenges of Financial Literacy

In India, nearly 62% of women are financially illiterate when compared to men 38%, which easily means that women are less educated in handling finances than men. Studies also disclose the status of not having bank accounts or having any access to bank services (Aanchal, 2021). Women in India are raised in an environment where they are taught to believe that matters concerning financial decisions and investment are men's space of tasks. Surveys opine that close to 33% of women make investment decisions individually than 64% of men do so (Gupta, 2022). (India's Growing Financial Literacy, 2022) Educating women with financial literacy will gradually reduce the risk rate of personal finance.

The major reason is a lack of adequate knowledge, and women are not used to financial handling, They are not involved in financial practices so they tend to get deceived easily. Even though India is one of the developing countries, there are many regions where women are considered as weaker sex and not provided with an adequate education. In many households' women are considered to be harmonized for household work and inadmissible in financial handling, this is the major reason why housewives are not aware of financial literacy. They are provided with limited access to financial literacy classes and education which leaves them unprepared. The majority of Women follow indigenous methods of financial planning and they are not aware of modern methods of budgeting and personal financial planning and execution and the new financial instruments available in the modern financial markets. (Maiya, 2020), as they repudiate their own opinion on financial aspects and are subjected to follow the financial tasks accomplished by their neighbors without discounting the needful aspects. The prime reasons for slow growth for women-led MSMEs are unconscious biases, challenges in accessing finance and building their network, lack of safety in public spaces, sometimes not getting enough support from family, lack of child-care options, often lack of confidence in their skills in business and so on (Soni, 2021)

The government initiatives provided are not properly utilized and the time taken to provide initiatives in rural areas is much less than that of an urban area which led to a lag in understanding the new financial trend i.e. when an urban population opted to adopt a new financial technology and initiative, rural population pertained to adapt the antiquated financial technology. The literacy rate of India in 2021 is 74.04%. The Male literacy rate is 82.14% and the female literacy rate is 65.46% according to Census 2021 (Literacy Rate of India 2021, 2021). The female literacy rate is far low when compared to the male literacy rate due to these women who are inerudite face hassle in understanding financial trends, using automated teller machines and cash deposit machines, filling bank challans, in reading procedures that are posted for awareness. Despite vetting the financial facts women tend to indiscriminately believe the phenomenon stated by unscrupulous mediums such as loan sharks, extortioners, and Shylocks. Due to this, they are bankrupted and also suffer from deprivations. Since many women are unfamiliar with nominal wage standards, they are consequentially made to work three times more and are underpaid when compared to men.

Measures To Overcome Challenges

1. Women must be recognized by their families and society. This will certainly pave the way for them to become more confident and not hesitate to make decisions concerning finance.
2. Society must develop a broader way of thinking enabling women to become empowered and self-dependent rather than dependent on a male family member.
3. Financial literacy should be added to the school curriculum for better effectiveness.
4. Proper education should be given to all age groups people
5. Women should be counted in financial handling as the same as men, there be should no gender gaps.
6. Entertainment media plays a crucial role since it has colossal coverage over people when compared to any other medium. People are more attracted to visual demos rather than paper pamphlets
7. Self-education is mandatory for analyzing cash flows in day-to-day life, effective management of money, avoiding unnecessary debts, and financial phishing.
8. Women mainly lack in confidence to take over financial handling in every household. This situation should be changed and they should be confident enough to handle personal finances.
9. The major reason women were not involving themselves in financial operations was that they were scared of the process and hesitated to invest, to overcome this financial organizations should provide them proper monetary security so that they believe in the process and investment.
10. Financial literacy depends heavily on how one manages one's money and how efficiently financial resources are used for the growth and well-being of oneself, the business, and the whole family. The initiatives taken by the government persist in creating a drift in the financial literacy level of women. Therefore, more women-specific financial literacy programs are needed to be introduced.
11. Financial inclusion needs to be universal so that women can learn about financial functions and not face difficulties in financial processes such as credit and debit services, savings services, insurance, and pension schemes.

Conclusion

Financial knowledge among women is extremely low. It enables individuals to understand what is necessary to lead a balanced, moral, sustainable, and responsible lifestyle. It directly affects the general well-being of society and individuals. Financially literate women will be better equipped to use financial products and services and make more sensible financial decisions. Women still rely on male family members to make financial decisions, even though it is excellent to see that they are now on an equal footing with men in all spheres of endeavor. Financial literacy for women is essential in our nation, where unemployment and poverty are the two biggest issues. By giving women the chance to contribute to economic progress, we can fuel the growth engine. Women in emerging economies need to become financially literate, even though women in industrialized nations have shown to be, on average, better financial planners. There is still a need for more awareness programmes, and these can consist of workshops, seminars, and financial management programmes at multiple levels to get more financial knowledge about the banking services and benefits that one can attend, even though various initiatives have been taken by various organisations to increase financial literacy. As India is a developing country every citizen has to be aware of financial literacy and know the means and how their money is spent in their day-to-day activities. Numerous studies show that India has a low level of financial literacy, particularly among women, the elderly, and young people who struggle to understand basic financial concepts. It is concluded that inescapable effort is needed to attain stability in financial literacy among women, the financial growth of women not only benefits the government but also their economic value, not only women but even men should also be aware of financial standards to reduce phishing rates in India.

References

1. Aanchal Gupta, P. D. (2021). *Here's To Embracing Financial Literacy In 2021*. Retrieved from FII Media Private Limited: https://feminisminindia.com/2021/01/20/financial-literacy-women-in-finance/#:~:text=Or%20so%20we%20hope!,limited%20access%20to%20banking%20service
2. Ali, A., Rahman, M. S. A., & Bakar, A. (2015). Financial satisfaction and the influence of financial literacy in Malaysia. *Social Indicators Research, 120*, 137-156.
3. Arifin, S. R. M. (2018). Ethical considerations in qualitative study. *International Journal of Care Scholars, 1*(2), 30-33.
4. Arora, A. (2016). Assessment of financial literacy among working Indian women. *Business Analyst, 36*(2), 219-237.
5. Berentsen, A., & Markheim, M. (2021). Peer-to-peer lending and financial inclusion with altruistic investors. *International Review of Finance, 21*(4), 1407-1418.
6. Cabeza-Garcia, L., Del Brio, E. B., & Oscanoa-Victorio, M. L. (2019). Female financial inclusion and its impacts on inclusive economic development. In *Women's Studies International Forum 77*, 102300. Pergamon.
7. Camara, N., & David, T., (2015). Factors that matter for financial inclusion: Evidence from Peru, Aestimatio, *9*, 8– 29, DOI: 10.5605/ieb.10.1
8. Castellanos-Alvarenga, L. M., Denegri-Coria, M., & Sepulveda-Aravena, J. (2022). Relationship between Subjective Financial Knowledge and Financial Well-Being: The Mediating Role of the Financial Executive Function. *Revista de Cercetare si Interventie Sociala, 78*.
9. Cull, R., Demirguç-Kunt, A., & Morduch, J. (2018). The microfinance business model: Enduring subsidy and modest profit. *The World Bank Economic Review, 32*(2), 221-244.
10. Dansby, S. R. (2000). *Foundations of Financial Literacy* (11 ed.). The Goodheart-Willcox Company, Inc. doi: ISBN 978-1-64925-019-3.

11. Financial Literacy Material (2007). *FAME Booklet.* Retrieved from Reserve Bank of India: https://www.rbi.org.in/FinancialEducation/fame.aspx
12. Grohmann, A., Kluhs, T., & Menkhoff, L. (2018). Does financial literacy improve financial inclusion? Cross country evidence. *World Development, 111*, 84-96.
13. Gupta, P. R. (2022). *Having a financial plan is more critical for women than men.* Retrieved from Live mint: https://www.livemint.com/money/personal-finance/-having-a-financial-plan-is-more-critical-for-women-than-men-11602470743033.html
14. Honohan, P. (2005). Measuring microfinance access: Building on existing cross-country data. *Available at SSRN 753568.*
15. *India's Growing Financial Literacy* (2022a). Retrieved from India Brand Equity Foundation: https://www.ibef.org/blogs/india-s-growing-financial-literacy
16. *India's Growing Financial Literacy.* (2022b). Retrieved from India Brand Equity Foundation: https://www.ibef.org/blogs/india-s-growing-financial-literacy
17. Isa, A. H. (2021). Abdul Hamid Isa: The Andragogy-Based Learning Model to Increase Functional Literacy Learning Motivation. *ARTIKEL, 1*(6746).
18. Jayanthi, M. (2019). Determinants of rural household financial literacy: Evidence from south india. *Statistical Journal of the IAOS, 35*(2), 1-6. doi:10.3233/SJI-180438
19. Jha, J. (2020). *Financial Literacy and its importance.* Retrieved from the Hans India: https://www.thehansindia.com/business/financial-literacy-why-it-is-important-700499
20. Kempaller, D. S. (2022). Women Empowerment in India: A Sociological Study. *IJARIIE, 8*(2), 955- 961.
21. Literacy Rate of India (2021). Retrieved from Census of India 2021: https://censusofindia2021.com/literacy-rate-of-india-2021
22. Lown, J. M., & Ju, I. S. (1992). A model of credit use and financial satisfaction. *Financial Counseling and Planning, 3*(1), 105-124.
23. Lusardi, A. (2019). *Financial Literacy and the need for financial education: evidence and implications.* Retrieved from *Swiss Journal of Economics and Statistics*: https://doi.org/10.1186/s41937-019-0027-5.
24. Maiya, U. (2020). Financial Literacy among rural women: A study with reference to kundapur taluk. *Journal of Interdisciplinary Cycle Research, 12*(3).
25. McGurran, B. (2022). *Personal Finance.* Retrieved from experion: https://www.experian.com/blogs/ask-experian/what-is-financial-literacy-and-why-is-it-important
26. *MSME* (2021). *Schemes For Empowering Women Entrepreneurs.* Retrieved from Team MSMEx: https://www.msmex.in/learn/important-schemes-for-women-entrepreneurs
27. Naik, B. T. (2012). Survey of financial services extended to farmers in rural areas: Facts and myths a ground level case study of Sheloshi village in Gagan Bawada Taluka in Kolhapur district. *IBMRD's Journal of Management & Research, 1*(1), 61-63.
28. Program, U. N. (2012). *Financial Literacy as a tool for financial inclusion and client protection.* (UNDP, Ed.) New delhi, India: EII Gee. Retrieved from https://www.undp.org/content/dam/india/docs/poverty/financial-literacy-as-a-tool-for-financial-inclusion-and-client.pdf
29. Sandra Braunstein, C. W. (2002). Financial Literacy: An Overview of Practice, Research, and Policy. *88*, 1-13. doi:10.17016/bulletin.2002.88-11
30. Sethy, S. K. (2015). Developing a financial inclusion index and inclusive growth in India: Issues and challenges. *The Indian Economic Journal, 63*(2), 283-311.

31. Singh, C., & Kumar, R. (2017). Financial Literacy among Women - Indian Scenario. *Universal Journal of Accounting and Finance*, 46-53. doi:DOI: 10.13189/ujaf.2017.050202
32. Soni, S. (2021). *Women's Entrepreneurship Day: Why only 20% of India's over 6 crore MSMEs are led by women?* Retrieved May 29, 2022, from Financial Express: https://www.financialexpress.com/industry/sme/msme-eodb-womens-entrepreneurship-day-why-only-20-of-indias-over-6-crore-msmes-are-led-by-women/2372108
33. Soumare, I., Tchana Tchana, F., & Kengne, T. M. (2016). Analysis of the determinants of financial inclusion in Central and West Africa. *Transnational Corporations Review, 8*(4), 231-249.
34. Swamy, V. (2014). Financial inclusion, gender dimension, and economic impact on poor households. *World development, 56*, 1-15.
35. Youth Financial Literacy Foundation: https://www.yflfoundation.org/blog/rqngrk-ko34859ezmheafu09retwkch-batzk-c9zh3

13

The Impact of Empowering Women's Self-Help Groups to Rural Development in West Bengal

Abhishek Mishra

Abstract

In India, rural poverty is a growing issue that is getting worse very quickly. In India, there are not many ways to end rural poverty. The secret to maintaining employment is self-employment. When it comes to job stability, Self-help group (SHG) members who work for themselves function better than those who work for pay. Two initial interviews of the same set of SHG members within the North 24 Parganas region of West Bengal were done in 2019 for this study and came to some of these conclusions. The focus of the study was on the variables affecting the various measures of women's empowerment among the participants in 26 fully developed all-female SHGs. Additionally, it identified the socioeconomic demographic variables affecting the likelihood that two group members will be empowered. The study concluded that training significantly affects several facets of empowerment and that individuals in the trained group have higher employment rates in addition to higher empowerment rates.

Keywords: *Employment, SHGs, Women Empowerment and decision making*

Introduction

According to Bali and Wallentin (2012), women's empowerment is a process that calls for prerequisites or "resources" that can facilitate "processes" that increase women's agency or capacity for decision-making, which in turn determines "outcomes" that directly affect their welfare. In the 1995 Declaration, it was stressed that women should be empowered by "removing all the obstacles to women's active participation in all spheres of public and private life through a full and equal share in economic, social, cultural, and political decision-making." There are currently almost 300 million poor people in India, and more crucially, a large portion of them reside in rural areas, according to the nation's Eleventh National Development Plan (Chambers, 1997). As a result, about 35% of India's rural population continues to live in poverty. The country's rural areas are home to a particularly high level of poverty among women, scheduled castes, tribes, and other groups. Rajasthan, Madhya Pradesh, Uttar Pradesh, Bihar, Orissa, Chattisgarh, and Karnataka are the states with the highest rates of rural poverty in India. Lack of access to financial resources and productive assets is a significant contributor to poverty among rural residents of India, both as individuals and as communities. Additionally, poor rural residents frequently have high levels of illiteracy, subpar health care, and relatively restricted access to social services Aiyar Swaminathan (2008). Giving rural women financial assistance or loans enables them to become more independent socially and

Assistant Professor, Department of Business Administration University of Burdwan, West Bengal economically, which in turn benefits the entire community. Discrimination against women based on their gender occurs practically everywhere and in every field. Government initiatives (such as loan schemes) and common males in particular in rural India had ignored women's ability to manage money Radheshyam (2008). In India today, self-help groups constitute a fresh form of financial intermediation. This combines access to cheap financial services with a process of self-management and development for the women who are SHG members. According to Manjunatha (2013), NGOs or—in an increasing number of cases—government organisations create and support SHGs.

Self-help groups are one of the most essential components in the participatory method for the economic empowerment of women. It is a vital institution that improves the well-being of women in many different ways. The major objective of SHG is to serve as a platform where its members may assist and give one another space. SHGs are made up of people who are extremely poor and without access to formal financial institutions. It helps its members to grow in their capacity for collaboration and teamwork Kondal, (2014). Women have the chance to receive credit that banks tend to be willing to grant and boost their savings through SHGs. SHGs can also serve as a platform for the community through which women can participate in village affairs and run for office at the local level to address social issues (Babu, 2002). community members and members of society at large. They gather for the objective of using mutual and self-help to resolve their shared issues. The "Self Help Group" (SHG) plan is more appealing and requires less work. It is a tool to end poverty, boost women's businesses, and provide financial support for them in India. Geethanjali & Prabhakar, (2013). The status of women as partners in the democratic, such as economic, social, and cultural spheres of life as those involved, decision-makers, and benefits is improved via self-help organisations. Rural women now have a great lot more confidence to succeed in their daily lives thanks to SHGs, according to Shireesha (2019). Independence in the social, political, and economic arenas is a common definition of empowerment in academic circles. Thangamani and Muthuselvi (2013) claim that women's empowerment is a changing, diverse, passionately debated, and difficult subject. The benefits of empowerment include increased information and resource availability, increased decision-making autonomy, increased capacity for life planning, increased control over outside forces influencing one's actions, and freedom from social standards, religious beliefs, and practices.

Review of Literature

According to Das (2012), SHGs serve as a financial mediator to promote women's emancipation. The paper displays the actual experiences and observations of Dhapukuri development block and Nago SHG beneficiaries. The study shows that the microfinance program's SHG-bank linkage has a significant impact on the participants' economic situation, capacity for making decisions, knowledge, and sense of worth. The paper by Sarumathi and Mohan (2011) tries to concentrate on the function of NGOs in women's financial empowerment. According to a study, NGOs play a critical role in creating a network of micro-businesses in rural areas and helping women entrepreneurs. In this article, Naganagound S.P. (2011) makes an effort to evaluate the success of the Karnataka state's Street Shakti program's microfinance component at the district level. The Stree Shakti programme aimed to empower rural women and develop their capacity in terms of finance, society, and politics.

Bruton, Khavul, and Chavez (2011) the authors of this study introduce the subject of microfinancing to a larger group of management researchers and highlight potential areas for further investigation. The study highlights how dangerous and expensive it is for conventional financial institutions to provide lending facilities to the poor. They don't know much about a certain person's creditworthiness or dependability. It suggests microfinance as a substitute for conventional financial institutions for capital lending to the poor. Access to financial services can significantly improve the economic productivity and social well-being of poor women and their households, but Kabeer (2005) very correctly noted that this does not consequently empower women in the same way that other interventions like political representation and education look for to achieve the radical structural change that true empowerment involves. To establish the various elements of hidden women's empowerment for SHG members, Swain and Wallentin (2009) implemented household survey data about the SHG programme of the National Bank for Agriculture and Rural Development (NABARD) from five states of India. In their study on the effect of SHG lending on the profitability of branches, Srinivasan and Jerinabi (2006) looked at eight branches wherein SHG financing made up over five percent of their loan portfolio. The topic under consideration was an instance study titled "Environment of Women through NGOs: The SEWA Bank Experience". According to Chauhan (2018) the study, the bank (SEWA Self Employed Women's Association) had been offering banking services to the underprivileged, illiterate, and self-employed women and turned it into a successful business. In four Maharashtra districts that were supported by the Maharashtra Rural Credit Project (MRCP), Patil (2014) researched SHGs. According to the survey, 69% of the groups were between 11 and 20 members in size, and 50% of them were illiterate. In selected areas of Tamil Nadu, Lalitha and Nagarjan (2002) conducted critical research on the operation of self-help groups (SHGs). The survey was conducted to track the initiatives done by NGOs to support SHGs. A study on "Micro Credit Penetration Through Self Help Groups: Clues from Growth of SHG Bank Linkage Model in India" done by Venkatesh (2011). The study draws its conclusions after taking into account the promising results that SHGs have achieved using the Bank Linkage Model. An effort has been made to analyse the social impact of microfinance on SHG members in Manipur by Deshpande and Pathan (2009). The study's primary goal is to assess the social effects of microfinance programmes on SHG members by way of their sense of self-worth, capacity for making decisions, and social awareness.

Objectives of the Study

The following objectives comprise the basis of the study:

1. To study the association between SHGs and the socioeconomic growth of rural communities in the state of West Bengal.
2. To research the self-help group strategy for empowering women by giving them access to financial resources.
3. To make suitable recommendations for increasing SHG performance in enhancing rural residents' socioeconomic circumstances.

Methodology

The study's secondary data sources include current literature, data from websites, and publications from the federal and state governments, especially those obtained from the Institutional Finance Department and the State Level Bankers Committee in Bangalore, together with materials from other sources such books, periodicals, newspapers, reports, articles, conference papers, and seminar contents produced by academic institutions. Alongside public sources, the research is based on interviews with a wide range of individuals, including both official and non-official members of the Lead Bank Office and Zilla Panchayath in the selected district.

Determinants of Employment Status and Empowerment Level

Women's empowerment levels and current work positions are related. The likelihood that a group member will be employed and empowered is jointly decided, and some shared socioeconomic demographic determinants have an impact on both. The unemployment rate of 55% of the group members—who were all employed during the first round of the survey—will be better-understood thanks to this research. To achieve this, we employ a variable called "count," the descriptive statistics of which are represented by the number of affirmative responses a representative group member provided to the questions mentioned in Table 1.

Table 1. Descriptive Statistics of the Variable Count

Count	Results
Mean	5.930541
Median	6
Mode	6
Minimum	0
Maximum	9
Percentiles	25 5
	50 6
	75 7

Source: Data collected from primary field survey

The median value in Table 1 is 6, which indicates that, on average, about 50% of the group members responded positively to six questions. By employing a bivariate probit model, our goal was to pinpoint the collection of factors that influence the joint probability of having power and being employed. For this reason, we developed an integer variable called "empowered" that takes on a value of unit if the variable's "count" regarding a group member is more than 6, which is the median value. The "empowered" variables include people who had given more affirmative answers to empowerment-related questions than the average person. The bivariate probit regression is then used to identify the socio eco-demographic elements that affect a group member's combined likelihood of empowerment and employment along with how each explanatory factor affects a woman's employment and empowerment. In the section under "Dimensions of Empowerment," it was discovered that training, religion, and landholding were significant drivers of different aspects of women's empowerment. These factors were taken into account in the regression analysis as explanatory variables. Group size, a factor that is related to groups, was included to measure how it affected job status and empowerment. The regression study additionally took into account the effects of two of the group members' prior occupational categories—self-employed and animal husbandry—on their current job status, using labour in 2005 as the reference category.

Table 2 presents the association between the loan-use pattern and the variable empowered

	Borrowers	Non-borrowers	Family Expenses	Other Family Business	Own Business	Total
Empowered	0	32	80	38	23	173
	1	12	18	25	40	95
Total		44	98	63	63	268

Source: As reported during the survey

Even though more than 84 percent of the borrowers had gotten loans from the organisation, only 28% of those borrowers (a subset of those who were employed group members) utilized the loans for their businesses in 2009. Approximately 68% of the group members who lacked power over their loans had no control over the money and used it to cover household expenses, their husband's working capital needs, or other family companies. The results of this investigation are consistent with those of Goetz and Gupta (1996) and Siraj (2012), who also showed that group members use their loans to support their families. Table 2 shows that, compared to group members who lack empowerment, 42.1 percent of empowered group members had used their loans to expand their enterprises. As a result, empowered women are better able to manage their debt. The women who had received training used their loans mostly (approximately 54 percent) for marketing their enterprises, a cross-tabulation of loan-use patterns and training dummies revealed that people who received no training instead gave the funds to different family members. By combining these outcomes and the findings of bivariate probit regression, we concluded that a trained group member had a greater probability of being employed in the future and so becoming empowered. She would also be the beneficiary of her loan and utilise the money to grow her own business. Training SHG participants is crucial for increasing women's agency.

Major Findings and Suggestions

The following conclusions have been reached based on the analysis and debate in the research of the performance evaluation of women SHGs and rural development in the state of West Bengal:

1. More significantly, the bank linkage program's decentralisation was far more obvious in the majority of the districts. The members and their federations actively participated in group formation, beneficiary selection, loan utilisation monitoring, and loan repayment.
2. Self-Help Groups offer a means of reducing poverty, which enhances the capacity of its members on numerous levels. It is based on collaborative decision-making, which gives members a sense of ownership. The goal of presenting an alternative strategy for sustainable development is substantially different from how many other poverty alleviation/human development projects evolve with a top-down decision-making system and isolation from the people most affected by these decisions.
3. The state of West Bengal has 163161 SHGs that are connected to Rs. 5504 million in bank credit.
4. The SHG approach promotes empowerment, and this bottom-up strategy for rural development has given low-income households a significant amount of positive economic and non-economic externalities.

5. The family's income expanded quickly, leading to the acquisition of household assets and a comparably improved standard of living. Before joining the group, women in the study region had just a radio and a buffalo; after joining the group, they were able to purchase a tape recorder, bicycle, fan, sewing machine, and other items. After joining the club, expenses for accommodation, nutritious food, and health care have gone up. They all agree that being a part of the group has increased their awareness of the value of children's education, health, banks, and their roles in society. They also agree that their confidence in being able to live better lives has increased.
6. SHGs can combat poverty and can be a crucial tool for eradicating it.
7. The study demonstrates that an intervention through SHG-based microfinance results in an increase in income and assets as well as a decrease in the level of poverty.
8. The fact that borrowing has a positive overall impact on income—beneficial for all borrowers, but notably the poorest borrowers—shows how far-reaching the bank linking programme is. There are, however, many issues. Even if poverty is being reduced, the empowerment approach is inadequate. Given that they are women's organisations, a longer-term failure of the plan may result from a lesser level of empowerment.
9. It was found that the majority of female borrowers, particularly those from economically disadvantaged socioeconomic groups, were unaware of the terms and conditions of bank loans, including the interest rate, repayment schedule, and size of instalments. However, it is extremely intriguing to observe that the majority of the women who belong to SHGs are aware of how to open a savings account.
10. The study's key finding is that the bank connection initiative has significantly influenced the recipients' ability to engage in economic activity in the state of West Bengal. During the reference period, bank locations have proliferated dramatically, and advancements for women's development have grown astronomically.

Suggestion & Recommendation

1. Government agencies should make the necessary efforts to organise SHGs for women as much as feasible in rural and slum areas to uplift womenfolk, particularly in extremely underdeveloped states and Union territories.
2. The state and federal governments should collaborate to promote the idea of SHGs without political agendas or self-serving goals while keeping the welfare of women in mind.
3. Banks and other financial institutions should try to promote SHG among women, especially in underprivileged areas like scheduled caste and scheduled tribe's marginalised groups, etc. with an open mind and service objectives.
4. To give the SHG a stable source of income, a group must be firmly encouraged to take part in economic activities and income-generating initiatives. SHG might be urged to establish cooperative societies to advance the community.
5. To aid SHGs that promote women's employment Mass media, such as newspapers, TV, radio, and other sources, can play an important role in increasing awareness of the advantages of SHGs among women and the general public at large by publicising success stories of SHGs, examples of NGO and government efforts, and additional details about SHGs.
6. Women's associations should step up and join projects for the advancement of women.

Conclusion

It has been shown very successful in reducing poverty in rural India by primarily providing economic help to the rural population, especially to rural women. Giving rural women financial assistance or loans enables them to become more independent socially and economically, which in turn benefits the entire community. In light of this, the current study is designed to look at the connection between Self Help Groups and the socioeconomic growth of rural populations in general and of women in West Bengal state in particular, as well as provide suitable steps for maximizing the impact of SHG functioning to enhance the socioeconomic conditions for rural residents. SHG is an effective tool for empowering women. SHGs began taking a significant part in rural development. It is a voluntary organisation in a certain village. Those who live in poverty banded together under one cause. They contribute a small amount to savings, and with the money saved up, group members are offered credit for beginning new businesses at a very low-interest rate. Therefore, a nation must be established to support women's SHGs. Self-help takes many different forms in traditional rural civilizations. Such plans are necessary for undertaking tasks like housing and farming operations that must be accomplished within a certain amount of time. People also exchange the tools needed for agricultural productivity.

References

1. Aiyar Swaminathan, S. A. (2008). Roads will lead to rural prosperity. *SWAMINOMICS, column in Sunday Times of India, 3.*
2. Azim, S. (2013). Women Empowerment through Self Help Groups. *Southern Economist, 52*(6), 28.
3. Babu, S. (2002). Empowering women through self-help microcredit programmes. *International Journal of Multidisciplinary Researches*, 30.
4. Bali Swain, R., & Wallentin, F. Y. (2012). Factors empowering women in Indian self-help group programs. *International review of applied economics, 26*(4), 425-444.
5. Banerjee, T., & Ghosh, C. (2012). What factors play a role in empowering women? A study of SHG members from India. *Gender, Technology and Development, 16*(3), 329-355.
6. Bruton, G. D., Khavul, S., & Chavez, H. (2011). Microlending in emerging economies: Building a new line of inquiry from the ground up. *Journal of International Business Studies, 42*, 718-739.
7. Chambers, R. (1997). *Whose reality counts 25*. London: Intermediate technology publications.
8. Chauhan, A. (2018). *An analysis of socio-economic impact of women empowerment through microfinance schemes with special reference to Udaipur cluster* (Doctoral dissertation, Ph. D. Thesis, Business Administration/Management (Faculty of Commerce & Management) to the University of Kota).
9. Das, S. K. (2012). Ground realities of self-help group-bank linkage programme: An empirical analysis. *International Journal of Research in social sciences, 2*(2), 464-479.
10. Declaration, B. (1995). Beijing declaration and platform for action fourth world conference on women. *Paragraph, 112*, 859-865.
11. Deshpande, M. G., & Pathan, F. M. (2009). Micro Finance for Poverty Alleviation some Reflections By. *Adarsh Journal of Management Research, 2*(1), 69-73.
12. Geethanjali, R., & Prabhakar, K. (2013). Economic development of women through self-help groups in YSR district, Andhra Pradesh, India. *Studies on Home and Community Science, 7*(1), 25-34.
13. Goetz, A. M., & Gupta, R. S. (1996). Who takes the credit? Gender, power, and control over loan use in rural credit programs in Bangladesh. *World development, 24*(1), 45-63.
14. Jain, R., Kushawaha, R. K., & Srivastava, A. K. (2003). Socio-Economic impact through self-help groups. *Yojana-Delhi-, 47*, 11-13.

15. Jain, S. (2000). Empowerment of women through NGOs: The SEWA bank experience. *NGOs and socio-economic development opportunities*, 112-122.
16. Jerinabi, U. (2006). *Micro credit management by women's self-help groups*. Discovery Publishing House.
17. Kabeer, N. (2005). Is microfinance a'magic bullet'for women's empowerment? Analysis of findings from South Asia. *Economic and Political weekly*, 4709-4718.
18. Kondal, K. (2014). Women empowerment through self-help groups in Andhra Pradesh, India. *International Research Journal of Social Sciences*, 3(1), 13-16.
19. Lalitha, N., & Nagarajan, B. S. (2002). Functioning of the SHGs in Selected Districts of Tamil Nadu. *Self-Help Groups in Rural development, New Delhi: Dominant Published and Distributors.*
20. Manjunatha, S. (2013). A sociological study on the influence of social networking sites on the interpersonal relationships of college students in Bangalore and Mysore cities of India. *International. Research Journal of Social Sciences*, 2(6), 12-19.
21. Manjunatha, S. (2013). The Role of Women Self–Help Groups in Rural Development of Karnataka State, India. *International Research Journal of Social Sciences*, 2(9), 23-25.
22. Manjunatha, S. (2013). The usage of social networking sites among the college students in India. *International Research Journal of Social Sciences*, 2(5), 15-21.
23. Naganagoud, S. P. (2011). Micro finance & women empowerment: A study of stree shakti programmes in Bellary district of Karnataka. *Public Policy and Administration Research*, 1(2), 11-18.
24. Patil, V. A. (2014). Women Empowerment through Self Help Group with special reference to Shirol Taluka. *10. Marketers shifting from the Herd to the Swarm Fizz or Fizzle?*, 13(2), 7.
25. Radheshyam, J. (2008). Farmer suicides in West Maharashtra too. *Times of India, 7th February, 2008.*
26. Sarumathi, S., & Mohan, K. (2011). Role of Micro Finance in Women's Empowerment (An Empirical study in Pondicherry region rural SHG's). *Journal of Management and Science*, 1(1).
27. Shireesha, E. (2019). Empowerment of women through Self-help groups. *International Journal of Scientific Development and Research (IJSDR)*, 4(12), 13-16.
28. Siraj, M. (2012). Do microfinance programs benefit women in developing countries?. *Advancing Women in Leadership Journal*, 32, 24-35.
29. Suneetha, V., & Ramanamma, M. V. (2018). A study on the Role of Self-help Groups in Economic Empowerment of Women. *International Journal of Research in Social Sciences*, 8(9), 270-283.
30. Swain, R. B., & Wallentin, F. Y. (2009). Does microfinance empower women? Evidence from self-help groups in India. *International review of applied economics*, 23(5), 541-556.
31. Thangamani, S., & Muthuselvi, S. (2013). A study on women empowerment through self-help groups with special reference to Mettupalayam Taluk in Coimbatore District. *Journal of Business and Management*, 8(6), 17-24.
32. Ud Din, I., Barman, I., & Wani, R. A. (2019). Role of Self-help Group In Rural Development In India. *Think India Journal*, 22(4), 1423-1430.
33. Venkatesh, P. (2011). Micro Credit Penetration Through Self Help Groups: Clues from growth of SHG Bank Linkage Model in India. *Indian Streams Research Journal*, 1, 6-11.
34. Yunus, M. (2007). Credit for the poor: Poverty as distant history. *Harvard International Review*, 29(3), 20..

14

Strategic Management: A Tool for Growth and Development in Indian MSME

Dr. Bharat Nirwal[1], Sonam Sunil Dhanava[2] & Ravindra Bhikaji Bhise[3]

Abstract

Indian Micro, Small, Medium, and Micro firms are crucial to the growth of a nation's economy. It generates one million jobs annually, accounts for roughly 45% of industrial output, and 35% of exports, employs 42 million people, and produces more than 8,000 high-quality goods for both Indian and global markets. This specific study aims to comprehend the challenges MSMEs encounter while implementing strategic management as a strategy for long-term competitive advantage. Significant research has demonstrated that strategic management improves MSMEs' performance. However, the majority of Indian MSMEs do not implement strategic management, and the causes behind this are little understood. This specific study aims to assess strategic planning as a management tool for MSMEs, to assist them in gaining a sustained competitive advantage. The main goal of this study is to evaluate the value of strategic management concepts, and practices as they are applied to MSMEs, and to offer recommendations on how to employ strategic management to avoid severe crises and company failures, which frequently occur in Indian MSMEs. The conclusion is that MSMEs are particularly in need of strategic management. Threats and crises can be avoided, and MSMEs can eventually gain a competitive edge if strategic management is properly used at different phases of operation.

Keywords: *MSME, strategic management, challenges and competitive advantage*

Introduction

MSMEs are regarded as a significant industry sector in India, and the government is encouraging this sector to expand through many programmes and programmes under the Make In India, Stand Up India, Startup India, etc. umbrellas. The hazards facing MSMEs have increased as a result of escalating competition and insufficient resources. Strategic management is crucial in these difficult times. The majority of MSMEs place little emphasis on strategic management, yet this is even though strategic management practices aid SMEs in establishing and achieving long-term organisational goals (Honga et al., 2001). Companies need to establish specific strategies if they want to expand and remain competitive in this market. Strategic management is becoming more and more important as a result of rapid globalization, changing business environments, information technology advancements, rapid changes in customer preferences, changes in the demand-to-supply ratio, rising outsourcing activities, and the breakdown of value chain

1 Assistant Professor, Department of Commerce Late Nitin College Pathri, Parbhani, Maharashtra

2 Research Scholar, Shikshak Sanchalit Shikshan Sanstha's, Arts College & Commerce & Science College, Wada, Palghar, Maharashtra

3 Research Scholar, Shikshak Sanchalit Shikshan Sanstha's, Arts College & Commerce & Science College, Wada, Palghar, Maharashtra

systems. The Indian economy is expanding quickly. The MSMEs in India in particular are helping the country thrive. It generates one million jobs annually, accounts for roughly 45% of industrial output, and 35% of exports, employs 42 million people, and produces more than 8,000 high-quality goods for both Indian and global markets. A strategy is thought of as a thorough plan for a company to succeed. Managers use strategy to get things done. Although there is a correlation between strategic management practices and organisational success in small business companies, most of these businesses pay less attention to developing efficient strategies to boost performance. The Indian market is expanding quickly, and the country's industries are excelling in some fields including manufacturing, precision engineering, food processing, pharmaceuticals, textiles and apparel, retail, information technology, agriculture, and services. SMEs are increasingly able to expand their commercial operations in their main industries. Due to the evolving nature of competition, MSMEs are now exposed to more prospects for growth. MSMEs face significant obstacles and more opportunities in the global economy. This essay challenges the conventional method for comprehending the significance of strategic management and offers recommendations for using strategic management to avoid corporate failure. It is suggested to implement strategic management in stages to address the issue of MSMEs while taking into account the local situation in India.

What is MSME?

The following is a new definition of a micro, small, and medium enterprise under the MSME Act of 2006:

The following parameters were used to categorize MSMEs in the manufacturing sector based on their investment in plant and equipment:

1. Micro Enterprises: Less than Rs. 25 lakh
2. Small Businesses: Between Rs. 25 lakh and Rs. 5 crore
3. Medium-sized businesses: 5 to 10 crore rupees

The following criteria were in the investment range for MSMEs in the service sector:

1. Micro Enterprises: Less than Rs. 10 lakh
2. Small Businesses: Between Rs. 10 lakh and Rs. 2 crore
3. Medium-sized businesses: 2 to 5 crore rupees

MSMEs & Indian Economy

MSMEs, or micro, small, and medium enterprises, are widely acknowledged as major drivers of economic expansion. MSMEs are India's second-largest employer after the agricultural sector. They produce approximately 6000 different items, making up almost 40% of all industrial production, 95% of all industrial units, and 34% of all exports. According to estimates, the MSME industry requires only Rs. 72,000 to create one job, compared to Rs. 5.5 lakh for the huge organized sector. The importance of MSMEs becomes significant amid the current global recession, where some huge sectors are on the point of collapsing. According to estimates, the MSME sector must expand at a rate of 12% to meet the goal of 10% growth by 2011. The growth of MSMEs in India, however, is found to be considerably behind that of our South East Asian neighbours, like Thailand, Malaysia, Japan, China, and others. This sector struggles to grow because of some significant obstacles.

Research Methodology

The study, of Strategic Management A Tool for Growth of Micro Small and Medium Enterprises, purpose of this study is to examine and evaluate the implications of the strategic management concept as a competitive tool for MSMEs to achieve long-term growth. Information was gathered for this purpose from a variety of sources, including books, magazines, research papers, and research articles. Senior business consultants were also interviewed informally. For this, many research articles are reviewed.

Scope of the Study

Changes are happening quickly in the 21st century, and every organization is seeking ways to improve its performance. Organizations transformed as a result of this strategic management idea in terms of consistency, growth, profitability, and sustainability. There is a lot of room to study strategic management to comprehend, accept, and use it within the company to realize the idea of synergy. Due to globalization and rising levels of competition across all industries, MSMEs find it difficult to formulate effective strategies by comprehending both internal and external environmental factors. Compared to larger organizations, the majority of SMEs have straightforward systems and processes that enable flexibility, quick feedback, a short decision-making chain, and a greater understanding of and faster reaction to client needs. Despite these benefits, SMEs are under enormous pressure to maintain their competitiveness in both home and international markets. A real effort is made to advance this idea of strategic management. The study's time constraints and use of non-statistical methodologies for data analysis and interpretation raise the possibility that the results may not be generalizable to the entire market.

Significance of MSME

MSMEs are regarded as the driving force behind economic progress because they:

I. Create job opportunities.

II. Support regional and local development by hastening rural industrialization by tying it to a more developed metropolitan sector.

1. The growth of MSMEs contributes to a just and equitable distribution of wealth through regional economic activity dispersion.
2. Assists in encouraging self-help, and entrepreneurial culture by bringing skills and capital together through various loan and skill enhancement initiatives. Contributes to export earnings.
3. As being indigenous is essential for sustainability and self-sufficiency, it aids in coping with economic fluctuations and maintaining a fair growth rate.
4. Transforms domestic raw materials into semifinished products that are then transferred to large-scale companies with the resources, know-how, and machinery needed to transform them into finished commodities.
5. Give rural residents a chance to earn money and develop personally as they can work from home. This facilitates a just and equal distribution of income by generating possibilities for employment that are open to all Americans without discrimination. since global corporations and major conglomerates have begun to source from nations with robust.
6. SME sectors attract direct foreign investment. For large companies that operate in international markets, the production of semi-finished items is particularly cost-effective due to the low cost of labor.
7. The SMEs serve as catalysts for achieving the growth goals of developing nations.

Major Challenges for MSME

1. A lack of professionalism manifested in MSMEs' poor management. They don't have the right plans, policies, or strategic judgment. Small owner-managed businesses frequently lack strategic thinking.

2. Compared to larger businesses, the majority of SMEs have straightforward systems and processes that allow for mobility, direct feedback, short decision-making chains, and a better grasp of and quicker response to client needs.
3. MSMEs must comprehend both internal and external aspects to design effective strategies due to globalization and the rising level of competition in all industries. Despite these positive characteristics, SMEs are under significant pressure to keep up with competition in both domestic and foreign markets.
4. Consumer needs, technical advancements, and competitive paradigms are all constantly changing the nature of global rivalry. As a result of these changes, businesses are being forced to compete simultaneously in a variety of areas, including product creation, manufacturing, distribution, communication, and marketing. It is one of the biggest issues facing MSMEs in India today.
5. Managing finances and making the most use of resources are additional challenges. Though credit to MSMEs falls under the priority sector lending category, the percentage share of credit to MSMEs is declining as the priority sector lending is expanded to include quickly expanding areas like home loans and education loans. Only 14.2% of registered MSMEs and 3.09% of unregistered MSMEs received financing from banks in the Third All-India SSI Census (2001-2002).
6. Lack of technological innovation and understanding of market expectations is one of the main issues facing MSMEs. This is especially true for the textile industry. Since the majority of household appliances still use outdated technology, production costs are still expensive and the quality of the final product falls short of market expectations. Due to increased competition from imports brought on by the liberalization and opening up of the economy, MSMEs must upgrade their technology to produce goods of higher quality at lower costs.
7. India is renowned for having high-caliber human resources in science and technology, but because there has been relatively little technological advancement in the small business sector, its manufacturing costs are substantially greater than those of other developing countries in Asia.
8. Indian MSMEs lack the marketing know-how required to market their products. It results from a lack of knowledge of marketing strategies and planning. The majority of MSMEs are unable to make the required design and technical developments to satisfy market expectations because they lack the funding to support market research. Because of this ignorance, middlemen can take advantage of and abuse the poor weavers and artisans by paying them meager prices for their products and services.

Strategic Management and MSME

The process of developing an organization's goals, implementing them, and managing decisions that are made to accomplish those goals in the current and future environments is known as strategic management. In other words, according to Dauda, Akingbade & Akinlabi (2010), strategic management entails using a company's internal strengths and weaknesses to maximize its external opportunities and reduce its external dangers and difficulties. According to Uwa (2021), strategic management is the process by which managers determine the long-term direction of an organization, set specific performance goals, develop strategies to reach these goals in light of all relevant internal and external circumstances and commit to putting the chosen action plans into action. Schoemaker (1993) asserts that the main objective of strategic management is to consider a company's overarching goal, or to ask, "What is our business?" To influence outcomes tomorrow, goals are set, strategies are created, and activities are made now. To do this, it is vital to compare the objectives and needs of the present with the needs of the future while taking into account the available and potential material and human resources. According to the research on the subject, strategic management focuses on selecting a strategy and planning how that approach will be implemented. Three components can be considered to be a part of it: The stage of strategic choice involves formulating potential courses of action, evaluating them, and selecting one of them. The strategic implementation stage, deals with planning how the selected strategy can be put into action (McIvor, 2000).

Using strategic management to implement sustainable growth By generating significant employment, eliminating regional disparities, and serving as a breeding ground for entrepreneurs, the MSME sector has a vital role to play in India's emerging economy. Despite their valuable contributions, SMEs, according to Jocumsen (2004), are hampered by high failure rates and subpar performance levels. According to the SIDBI annual report, 14.47% of MSMEs are deemed sick and 21.6% of MSMEs have closed. According to Giriraj Singh, Minister of State for MSME (2015), India has 5.37 lakh ill MSME units, with Karnataka placing fourth with 38,277 sick units based on preliminary data from the RBI. For a growing nation like India, this is quite concerning and raises curiosity about the cause of failure. 90% of Indian start-up businesses fail within five years, according to a study conducted by the IBM Institute for Business Value in partnership with Oxford Economics. Why do tiny companies falter?

Does the use of strategic management enhance the performance of MSME? The strategic management idea is excellent for enhancing business performance. Since the concept of strategic management was introduced during a difficult economic downturn and in a setting that was changing quickly, a significant percentage of empirical studies on the subject over the years have concentrated on identifying the group of business strategies that are believed to help organisations prosper financially. Early studies conducted by management academics concluded that applying strategic management does not typically result in higher profitability (Szewczak & Snodgrass, (Eds.) 2003). However, a considerable number of recent studies contend that a profitable strategic management system can be implemented. Recent research demonstrates the direct connection between strategic management and the performance of companies. It may be concluded from one of this research by Hongal, & Charantimath (2014) that firms with strategic planning methods more closely approaching strategic management theory were found to demonstrate higher long-term financial performance both relative to their industry and in absolute terms.

The following reasons strategic management is beneficial:

1. It offers greater direction to the entire organisation on the vision, which is the key component of "what it is we are trying to do."
2. It increases managers' and organisational members' sensitivity to emerging opportunities and perilous trends.
3. It supports the success of an organisation by assisting in overcoming risks and uncertainties.
4. Strategy improves the standard of commercial judgments.
5. Fostering a managerial style that is more proactive.
6. Assisting in organizational unity.

7. The rates' ongoing increase. relative market share growth.
8. Earnings growth and earnings per share growth.
9. Adding new items and product lines is still ongoing.
10. The number of the company's customers keeps growing.
11. There are no disproportionate seasonal or cyclical changes.

Encouraging the development of a dynamic business plan that will guarantee the company's continued success. Strategic management can therefore have an effect, as we can deduce. According to Nwadike, Abuba, & Wokoma (2017), using the strategic management style, where managers from all levels of an organization collaborate on planning and implementation, has significant behavioral ramifications. According to Hornberger (2021), one way that strategic management can make a difference is by creating a business model that is continually changing and will lead to sustainable success for the organization.

It should be emphasized that strategic management has grown in importance for managers in recent years and that managers may more easily offer their organization a feeling of purpose by clearly articulating the mission of their organization. Additionally, organizations that engage in strategic management are better competent than others to forecast the future. The small firm strategic management process: In small businesses, formal business planning is frequently a process where owner-managers make an effort to carefully assess their industry environment and create a structure and direction for future actions. A purpose statement, an analysis of the company's current status, and the creation of growth projections are frequently done in the first stage (Mazzarol, Reboud, & Soutar, 2009), subsequently, strategies and goals are created. A monitoring-evaluation process is constructed, and these components are documented for internal and external stakeholders (Mazzarol, 2001). According to Bryce and Useem (1998), finding the optimal fit between the goal, possibilities, and the firm's skills is sometimes a difficult task, and external consultants are frequently engaged to help. However, the owner-manager is ultimately in charge of the plan's execution, according to Woods and Joyce (2003). Such prospects typically involve a great deal of uncertainty; therefore, an entrepreneur must get funding and direct the team's efforts. The interplay and administration of strategy in harmony with available resources and organizational structure, however, must be covered in a strategic plan for an established and expanding venture (Mazzarol, Clark, & Reboud, 2014). The establishment of the company's strategic intent, involving a distinct vision and mission that can direct operations and bring together key stakeholders, notably employees, is going to be the most crucial area of attention for strategy (Kakabadse & Kakabadse, 2005).

Conclusion

The performance of MSMEs is impacted by strategic management. The application of strategic management also has a favorable impact on organisational profitability. It is advised that the proper strategic planners, strategic situations, strategic analysis, and strategic decisions be in place. Only in stages is the implementation feasible. The management needs to reconsider the usage of strategic management positively. The value judgment, drive, and talent of a company's senior managers, as well as the strategic implementation within the constraints of the volatile environment's ambiguity and unpredictability, are what determine a firm or strategy's ultimate success. Environmental and capabilities analysis, strategic formulation, strategic execution, strategic assessment and control, and capacity utilization are just a few of the areas in which strategic management challenges are crucial. Small-scale businesses are thought to require the application of strategic management practices, and MSMEs should think about strategic management policies to enhance organizational performance and address global concerns. This study indicates that MSMEs should institutionalize strategic management as it appears to be a required strategy for coping with a dynamic, fiercely competitive, and uncertain business environment after seeing the role of MSMEs in the expansion and growth of the economy. To improve performance and get a competitive edge in the global market, MSMEs should use a strategic entrepreneur strategy rather than the conventional approach. MSMEs should apply formal strategies like strategic management to improve productivity, quality, cost reduction, and innovation as well as to raise the skill of the labor force to match global criteria to avert major illness and harness the power of the sector.

References

1. Bryce, D. J., & Useem, M. (1998). The impact of corporate outsourcing on company value. *European Management Journal, 16*(6), 635-643.
2. Dauda, Y. A., Akingbade, W. A., & Akinlabi, H. B. (2010). Strategic management practice and corporate performance of selected small business enterprises in Lagos metropolis. *International Journal of Business and Management, 5*(11), 97.
3. Hongal, P., & Charantimath, P. (2014). Strategic management-A tool for growth of Micro Small and Medium Enterprises [MSME] a study. *International Journal of Innovative Research in Engineering & Management (IJIREM), 1*(2), 5-9.
4. Hongal, Pushpa, Poornima, C., Gururaj G. & Phatak (2019). Strategic Management in Indian MSMEs-A Literature Review. *International Journal of Management, IT and Engineering* 7(11) 152-181.
5. Hornberger, R. C. (2021). *Encouraging Employee Buy-In for Cybersecurity Monitoring Programs: A Social Influence Perspective* (Doctoral dissertation, University of Maryland University College).
6. Jocumsen, G. (2004). How do small business managers make strategic marketing decisions? A model of process. *European Journal of Marketing, 38*(5/6), 659-674.
7. Kakabadse, A., & Kakabadse, N. (2005). Outsourcing: current and future trends. *Thunderbird international business review, 47*(2), 183-204.
8. Mazzarol, T. (2001). Do Formal Business Plans Really Matter?–An Exploratory Study of Small Business Owners in Australia. *Small Enterprise Research, 9*(1), 32-45.
9. Mazzarol, T., Clark, D. N., & Reboud, S. (2014). Strategy in action: Case studies of strategy, planning and innovation in Australian SMEs. *Small Enterprise Research, 21*(1), 54-71.
10. Mazzarol, T., Reboud, S., & Soutar, G. N. (2009). Strategic planning in growth-oriented small firms. *International Journal of Entrepreneurial Behavior & Research, 15*(4), 320-345.
11. McIvor, R. (2000). A practical framework for understanding the outsourcing process. *Supply Chain Management: An International Journal, 5*(1), 22-36.
12. Nwadike, G., Solomon, A. & Wokoma, D. A. (2017). Enhancing Management Strategies for Profitability of Corporate Organisations in Nigeria. *Equatorial Journal of Finance and Management Sciences, 2*(2), 17-33.
13. Schoemaker, P. J. (1993). Strategic decisions in organizations: rational and behavioural views. *Journal of Management Studies, 30*(1), 107-129.
14. Szewczak, E., & Snodgrass, C. (Eds.). (2003). *Managing the human side of information technology: Challenges and solutions*. IGI Global.
15. Uwa, K. L. (2021). Multivariate Analysis of the Factors that Influence Strategic Management Practices among Commercial Banks in Nigeria. *European Journal of Business and Innovation Research.*
16. Woods, A., & Joyce, P. (2003). Owner-managers and the practice of strategic management. *International Small Business Journal, 21*(2), 181-195.

15

The Role of Social Security Arrangement of Employees in Microfinance

Dr. Baby Dhurvey[1] *& Kalpana Kanwar*[2]

Abstract

By helping the weak to obtain credit, build wealth, and stay out of poverty traps, microfinance offers social security for the most vulnerable. Several World Bank task supervisors and project planners are motivated to include microfinance features in social funds and various other multisectoral initiatives as it has come to be recognized as a valuable tool to improve livelihoods and lower the vulnerability of the poor. As a result, there will be an increasing need for knowledge about effective methods for project planning and execution. Vulnerabilities, loss of income due to various contingencies, low wages and little or no social security arrangements form significant aspects concerning workers' employment in microfinance. Even if the nation has made considerable advancements in different spheres, the dream of extending social security benefits to workers remains a distant dream. The recent pandemic also exposed the gaps in social security arrangements all across the globe. Much needs to be done to extend social security arrangements to children, female workers, domestic workers, and old-age workers in the sector. The present paper attempts to highlight the impact of ensuring social security on the workforce employed in microfinance.

Keywords: *Social Security, impact, microfinance and informal sector*

Introduction

A broad financial system's contributions to the creation of an efficient social protection plan have recently received increased notice. The UN approach extends the role of social protection to securing basic needs as a pre-condition for human and social development (Yai, 2010). Similar to access to clean water, fundamental healthcare, and early education, being entitled to financial services allows people to profit from a market-based economy. Social security remains one of the major strengths for people living in a state of destitution and poverty. It is regarded as a labour right and the claims are made out of the income received against the contributions of the labour (Das, Das & Mohanty, 2012). In a developing and welfare State like India, social security, both in theory and practice, has evolved significantly incorporating not only social insurance and income protection but has come up with the inclusion of security of basic social rights like food, health care, health, livelihood, education and so on (Bloom et al, 2010). The schemes offered under social security are lifelines to industrial workers. Although the unorganised sector employs a substantial share of the working population, the social security arrangements in the sector remain a cause of serious concern. Unlike the organised sector where the social security arrangements have got legal

1 Assistant Professor, Department of Commerce Govt. Adarsh College Umaria, Madhya Pradesh

2 Assistant Professor, Department of Commerce Govt. Evpg College, Korba, Chhattisgarh

backing, the Indian unorganised sector has largely remained out of the regulatory framework for a considerable period (Kannan, 2010). The picture concerning social security arrangements is found to be dim in the unorganized sector. The workers perform their jobs under extremely precarious conditions and labour rights violations are frequent in the sector. The current consensus among those involved in the development, including both governments and non-government organisations, is that microfinance presents important prospects for a broad-based financial system, poverty reduction, economic regeneration, and development initiatives. Low-income people in developing nations have been given access to a variety of product lines in the microfinance sector, including loans, savings accounts, and insurance. The growth of the micro-finance industry is a response to the claim that low-income groups cannot access financial services because they cannot afford related expenses. The State has also adopted an apathetic approach toward addressing the issues inherent within the sector (Baruah, 2016).

Review of Literature

Social security offers assurance to people employed with some basic income during times of contingencies (Aaron, 2011). Several definitions of social security have been offered by different scholars who, while framing the definition, kept into consideration the national context and histories of their times. It was the International Labour Organisation (ILO) that primarily defined Social Security as the guarding mechanism offered and undertaken by society and the government for the welfare of the economically and socially distressed people and protect the earning competence of such people due to some sort of contingency like sickness, invalidity, old age, death, etc. The protection also includes subsidies offered to families with children (Jhabvala, 1998). However, the definition given by the International Labour Organisation suffered from certain limitations which later on were compensated by several other interpretations given by researchers and academicians over a while. The definition given by ILO was criticized on the ground that most of these definitions have been framed depending on the experiences faced by the developed countries only and exclude the experiences of the unorganised sector (Farooqui, 2020). Social security measures can broadly be divided into two different domains: social assurance and social assistance. One is contributory and the other one is non-contributory. Based on the policies and intended targets, different schemes are implemented by different governments.

Organizations including banks, nongovernmental organisations (NGOs), nonbank financial institutions (NBFIs), and governments can provide the underprivileged with financial services (loans, savings, money transfer services, and microinsurance) through the use of microfinance. In Africa, during the past two decades, micro-finance schemes emerged as an alternative to ensuring access to financial services for small borrowers (Aryeetey, 2008). Due to the limited success achieved by top-down policies and programmes, as well as the non-sustainability of previous government-backed credit programmes specially designed for the poor (Adjei et al, 2009). The microfinance banks in Nigeria began to perform with formal institutions and isolate themselves from their primary clientele, which created issues with liquidity and other managerial issues. Additionally, in South Africa, concerns were raised about the validity of new financial initiatives that aim to increase access to credit due to the issue surrounding the "go-banking" contractual arrangement between NEDBANK and pick "n" pay. The majority of these issues are brought on by the industry's inadequate regulatory practices. Using social capital contracts, the industry is primarily either uncontrolled or self-regulated.

Microfinance Regulation and Social Security

Particularly in rural areas, the social protection structures are deeply ingrained, informal systems of social protection. In general, laws for microfinance appear to be an effort by the government to protect and help people better manage their risks and deposits while also bolstering the case for development and financial access. The micro-finance regulations seem to follow the social risk management framework that adds the issues of macro-economic stability and financial market development in addition to the social protection measures (Canagarajah & Sethuraman (2001).

Social Protection (SP) has two purposes: one is to help the poor survive in difficult circumstances, and the other is to encourage these consumers to lead better lives. The SP policies differ from place to region and depend on a variety of elements, including the locals' culture and needs. These policies must take into account the short- and long-term effects of SP policies on specific or general customers or programmes. As was previously said, the microfinance industry has experienced rapid growth in recent years. Numerous businesses were drawn to this sector's expansion, which further broadened the reach of the services. However, this change in the microfinance landscape's focus makes the SP issue much more significant. The unorganised or informal sector as an area of research started to attract researchers and policymakers during the 1970s when Keith Hart offered the conceptual overview of 'informal sector' while conducting his study on Ghana. In India, the term 'unorganised sector' prevails in use which is defined as "that part of the workforce who could organise themselves in quest of a common objective because of limitations like (a) employment which is largely casual, (b) ignorance and illiteracy, (c) scattered nature of establishments, (d) supervision strength of the employer operating singly or in combination. Another problem with the unorganised sector is the engagement of the heterogeneous workforce and different patterns of employment (Chaudhary, 2014). Registering or listing of unorganized workers is still one of the critical issues. To get rid of these challenges, an all-inclusive social security arrangement is required to be put well in place.

Methodological Considerations

The present paper attempts to emphasize the impact of social security arrangements in Microfinance. To achieve its objectives, the present paper ascertains a qualitative approach where relevant literature has been explored to highlight the trends and shifts in the social security system in microfinance. The literature explored consisted of the different reports published by different institutions like the International Labour Organisation, Ministry of Labour and Employment, India, along with other sources like scholarly journals, websites, newspaper clips and conference proceedings. The institutional reports published only after the year 2014 have been consulted for discussion purposes.

Discussion

The high degree of informality of the Indian sector remains a cause of concern for policymakers, academicians and researchers since the informal or the unorganised sector comprises around ninety percent of the Indian economy. The Periodic Labour Force Survey (PLFS) held in the year 2017-2018 highlighted that sixty-eight percent of the workers engaged in the Indian unorganised sectors perform agricultural tasks like animal husbandry, agri-food, fishing rearing, and other ancillary activities. The male workers in the unorganised economy contribute to more than seventy-one percent of the total workforce, and the women workers correspond to more than fifty-four percent. The workforce employed in the sector faces relentless irregularities when it comes to offering social security benefits like provident funds, medical insurance, etc. (Mehrotra, 2020). After the outbreak of the global COVID-19 pandemic in the year 2020, the lacunas and limitations in social security coverage by different countries have been exposed (Khan, 2022). The situation has been more serious in India considering the high concentration of unorganised labour in the economy. Interestingly, the policy response towards the social security policy responses has also been encouraging after the global pandemic and the Government of India is making sincere efforts to address the problem of extending social security benefits to the ailing sector in different forms. Let us see them in some detail.

Trends in Pension Coverage

Pension schemes form an important part of statutory employee benefits in the organised sector. To provide pension coverage to the unorganised workers drawing wages up to fifteen thousand, the government introduced pension plans during the year 2018-19 which are slowly gaining acceptance among the workers employed in the sector. By the end of April 2022, 46,63,847 enrolments were made on the portal requesting to avail pension benefits. The number of workers registering on the portal was 39,82,760 by the end of the year 2019, 44,76,901 by the end of the year 2020, and 45,94,050 by the end of the year 2021. The statistics can be presented in the following table:

Table: 1

Year	Number of enrolments	Rise in enrolments
2022	46,63,847	69797
2021	45,94,050	117149
2020	44,76,901	494141
2019	39,82,760	--

Sources: Press Information Bureau, New Delhi

It can be observed that the number of enrolments fell during the year 2020-21 due to the global pandemic as millions of people lost their jobs and other sources of livelihood. However, the trend has again picked up which shows that the social security arrangement concerning the pension benefit is gradually raising acceptance. The reason for slow enrolment can also be attributed to the lack of awareness among the target population. The initiative requires more publicity drives across the corners of the country to make it more successful. Similarly, there were 1.6 million subscribers under the National Pension Scheme (NPS) belonging to the unorganized sector workers during the year 2021. It was 0.78 million during the year 2014. The government also launched the Atal Pension Yojana in the year 2015 to cover the workers engaged in the unorganised sector. Below are some statistics.

Table: 2. Enrolments under APY during the period from 2019-20 to 2021-22 (up to 31st October, 2021)

2019-20	2020-21	2021-22	Total
68,83,373	79,14,142	47,24,189	1,95,21,704

Sources: Press Information Bureau, New Delhi

The rise in the enrolments has been very encouraging and significant which suggests that the revival of pension arrangements is witnessing acceptance among the workers of the unorganised sector. Pension arrangement in the name of NPS for Traders, Shopkeepers and Self-Employed Persons aims to offer pension benefits to people who are self-employed and have businesses. The coverage of social security arrangements is becoming more exhaustive and extensive. The very objective of making India a pensioned society may appear to be a distant dream but not impossible if further enthusiastic efforts are exerted in this direction.

Trends in Health Security Coverage

Commendable achievements have been made in this direction in the last few years. The workers in the uorganised sector have to perform their jobs under conditions which often are very vulnerable and cannot at all be considered to be decent. This makes their health conditions exposed to sickness, disease and often to death. The Indian government, intending to achieve SDG Goal 3 by 2030 by extending universal health coverage (UHC) and health and well-being to all, launched the ambitious Ayushman Bharat Pradhan Mantri Jan Arogya Yojana in the year 2018. The scheme has been acknowledged to be the world's largest healthcare arrangement specially meant for the workers and their families belonging to the unorganised sector. This has also resulted in the growing awareness of the workers towards health concerns. The employers have also shown keen interest in the implementation of the scheme. Through the scheme, the government also targeted to address the maternity-related concerns of the female workers employed in the sector. The arrangement aims to extend health coverage to eligible labourers employed in the Indian unorganised sector. As per one estimate, around 17.90 crore individuals will be issued with smart cards by the end of the financial year 2022. This number itself highlights the immense success of the arrangement. Thus, a shift towards providing health security coverage has been witnessed in recent years. The government seems to be more alarmed by the health concerns of the workers employed in the sector.

Trends in Labour Reforms

The Second National Labour Commission appointed in the year 2002 recommended an umbrella-type legislative framework for the workers in the unorganised segment since legislations concerning labour vastly remain neglected in the sector. At the same time, the Act did not make mention of how the funds will be arranged for extending these social security schemes to the concerned target population. To address the shortcomings, the Government proposed the Code on Social Security, 2020 aiming to extend social security to workers in the informal sector. The Act also aims to come up with social security arrangements meant for the workers who are employed in the gig and platform economy which now form an important and substantial part of the Indian economy. The Act also extends the coverage of the Employees' State Insurance and Employees' Provident Fund for such enterprises employing less than ten workers. The Act is proposed to apply to establishments that perform hazardous or life-threatening occupations irrespective of the number of workers engaged. The proposal of this Act pinpoints the strong State intervention towards providing protection and security of the lives of the unorganised workers. Also, in a bid to reap the advantages of different social security arrangements, registration of the workers in employment in the sector on the Shram Suvidha Portal is made binding. The approach may be a novel one but it has its own set of limitations owing to the little education level of the workers employed in the sector. But this highlights another significant trend which is the digitization of the data related to the informal workers in India. All these efforts are offering encouraging results for the safety of the workers. Moving towards digitization will make the sector more formalized resulting in the identification of the beneficiaries and reaching out to them.

Regarding social security arrangements in the Indian unorganized sector, the following are some of the trends and shifts that can be highlighted:

- Social security arrangements are making the workers in the unorganized sector financially sound.
- A shift in the role of government towards the workers in the sector can be identified. The State agencies have become more assertive in implementing social security schemes in the sector. Thus, the interventionist role of the State can be highlighted in the present scenario.
- The social security arrangements are becoming more comprehensive and now are extended to cover life, health, insurance, pension, employment, children, and women engaged in the sector.
- There is a shift towards digitization of the data which is slowly making the sector move towards being formalized. If this purpose can be achieved several concerns prevalent in the sector can be resolved easily since there will be genuine facts and figures to devise policies for the workers at risk in the sector. For skill enhancement and employment purposes, the data has been linked with the MSME sector, Skill Development and National Career Portal. This will offer multiple benefits to the workers who can now all-round development of their working lives along with employment opportunities.
- Honest attention has also been paid to meeting the needs of the women and children belonging to the unorganized sector. Interestingly, due to the sincere approach adopted by the government to enroll female workers in the unorganised sector around fifty-four percent of women have been registered in the e-shram portal. The government has accepted the trend of the 'feminisation of the sector' and taken honest steps to resolve the inconsistencies related to women and children in this sector.
- In recent developments, workers representing the agricultural sector have also been paid attention. Through the credit schemes, the target of formalization is being achieved.
- Reforms in labour laws have been made to redefine and identify the target people in the unorganised sector and special arrangements for funds have been made for the betterment of social security arrangements in the sector. Legislative compliances are being imposed to make social safety arrangements a mandate for such workers in the sector.
- An approach to address the issue of disguised employment in the sector can also be observed. When we say disguised employment, we mainly refer to the engagement of female workers. Women workers mainly remain occupied with agricultural activities or are employed as domestic workers. Both sectors have little data to access resulting in nonrecognition of the rights of such workers. Registration on the portal is making the workforce more visible.
- The social security arrangements are becoming technology-driven which will revolutionise the future of social security arrangements in India.

Conclusion and Implications

All the trends and developments highlighted in the above sub-sections are indicative of the fact that social security coverage becoming more holistic and comprehensive within the unorganized sector of India. Earlier, the employment practices and prevalent inconsistencies of the unorganised economy were rarely monitored by the government. Naturally, this resulted in a lack of data on the workers employed in the sector making it difficult for the government to come up with plans for social security arrangements in this sector. To address this issue, the government has very much focussed on the need for creating a national database of such workers which will assist the government to target its policies efficiently. With such a database coming into existence, policies related to minimum wage (as mentioned in the Code on Wages Act), direct transfer of benefits, etc. will be addressed. The focus is on the integration of technology with the social security structure of the country. Due to the high-level concentration of irregular workers like street vendors, rickshaw pullers, casual labourers etc. in the sector, there exists the problem of identification of the real beneficiaries. As a result, suitable policies could not be drafted for such workers for a very long period. Recently, the government has come up with social security arrangements for the workers who are self-employed, or are vendors, craftsmen, women, artisans, labourers etc. The government is trying to make the social security arrangements more inclusive in the sector. However, more efforts towards the direction of ensuring social security coverage for female workers in the sector are required. It has been researched and universally accepted that the participation and contribution of women in the sector are higher as compared to male workers. Some supportive arrangements concerning child care (like Universal Child Care), making the enrolment process for health security more accessible and easier etc. need to be extended without fail. Health and nutritional arrangements are vital to the success of social security arrangements. Small task forces with the help and assistance and support of academic institutions and NGOs can be formed to track the development of social security arrangements and lacunas in the sector. Mission Vatsalya is a welcome step in this direction. The scheme intends to safeguard the childhood and life of each child in the country. To make the social security arrangements more comprehensive, the Government of India launched schemes for female workers representing the unorganised sector. Schemes like Mission Shakti, Mission Poshan and Mission Vatsalya facilitate the mission of women empowerment in the sector. These arrangements endeavours to make the women economically and socially empowered along with infusing the spirit of self-reliance. The schemes extend care and protection to them and their children during testing times.

Budget remains one of the main concerns when it comes to arranging social security coverage for the unorganised sector workers. We have witnessed a decline in government spending on the schemes, particularly in the unorganised sector. For example, there was silence on the part of the government in its budgetary announcements in the years 2021 and 2022. Though there are statutory provisions for preparing a social security fund under the newly introduced legislative framework of the Code on Social Security, the provisions are yet to see the light of the day. However, the authorities are more considerate towards making the social security arrangements more contributory by minimizing the contributory share of the different stakeholders. Plans are also underway to increase the role and liabilities of the State governments toward extending social security arrangements to the target population. To deal with the issue of health post-pandemic, specific budgetary allocations were made to address the health challenges, in general, and specific, of both the organised and the unorganised sectors. But at the same time, there are huge gaps in terms of gender budgeting in India. Since female labour force participation (FLFP) is very low and contributes to around ninety-five percent of the female working population actively working in this sector, they find it extremely difficult to access the benefits of social security arrangements. The efforts of the female workforce in agricultural and unpaid work need to be recognised and registered to make these schemes reach them and reduce the gender divide.

References

1. Aaron, H. J. (2011). Social Security reconsidered. *National Tax Journal, 64*(2), 385-414.
2. Adjei, J., Arun, T., & Hossain, F. (2009). Asset building and poverty reduction in Ghana: The case of microfinance. *African review of money, finance, and banking, 33*(3), 265.
3. Aryeetey, E. (2008). From informal finance to formal finance in Sub-Saharan Africa: Lessons from linkage efforts. *AERC/IMF African Finance for the 21st Century Unpublished Manuscript.*
4. Baruah, V. (2016). *Addicts, peddlers, reformers: a social history of opium in Assam, 1826–1947* (Doctoral dissertation, Cardiff University).
5. Bloom, D. E., Mahal, A., Rosenberg, L., & Sevilla, J. (2010). Economic security arrangements in the context of population ageing in India. *International Social Security Review, 63*(3-4), 59-89.
6. Canagarajah, S., & Sethuraman, S. V. (2001). Social protection and the informal sector in developing countries: Challenges and opportunities. *World Bank.*
7. Chaudhary, R., & Verick, S. (2014). *Female labour force participation in India and beyond* (pp. 1-32). New Delhi: ILO.
8. Das, K., Das, B. K., & Mohanty, S. (2012). Social security in informal sector: A Myth. *Odisha Review, 9*, 60-69.
9. Farooqui, M. B. M. H., & Pandey, S. (2020). Social security for informal workers in India. *CPR ISBN, Available at: Brief_SocialSecurity_InformalWorkers_21Nov2020. pdf.*
10. Jhabvala, R. (1998). Social security for unorganised sector. *Economic and Political weekly*, L7-L11.
11. Kanan, K. P. (2010). *The Challenge of Universal Coverage for the Working Poor in India* (No. 2). Working Paper.
12. Khan, M. A. (2022). Mega Risks, Social Protection, and Sustainability. In *Cities and Mega Risks: COVID-19 and Climate Change* (pp. 229-258). Cham: Springer International Publishing.
13. Mehrotra, S. J., & Kaveri, V. S. (2020). Business Contingency Plan for MSMEs under COVID-19 Environment. *Prajnan, 49*(3).
14. Yi, I. (2010). Social protection, social security and social service in a development context: transformative social policy approach. *Journal of International Development Cooperation, 5*(4), 57-84.

16

A Study on the Role of Self-help Groups (SHGs) in Empowering Rural Women in Chennai

Dr. A. Jerena Rachael

Abstract

Self-help groups (SHGs) may serve as centers of resources for empowering women, which has a trickle-down effect on society as a whole. A few of these are gender bias, alcoholism, domestic violence against women and children, maltreatment, and social exclusion. The decision to stay socially, economically, and socially destitute or to organize themselves to end their privations may ultimately be left up to them. Self-help groups were designed with the idea of utilizing their potential as a strong tool for rural women's empowerment and the reduction of rural poverty. It should be made clear that empowering women as a whole was not the primary objective. The objectives eventually filtered down into the overall development of the family, community, and society, which was started by and for women. To objectively assess the role of SHG membership on rural women, the present study was specifically conducted in this context. A study was done to determine the extent to which the members' participation in SHGs helped them achieve different levels of empowerment. Evaluations of personal, social, economic, and financial empowerment were made.

Keywords: *Self-help groups, microcredit, social security, and women's empowerment*

Introduction

In almost all developing nations, including India, self-help groups (SHGs) are increasingly important for empowering poor women, and Chennai is no exception in terms of the contribution made by women's groups, also known as women's collectives, to the freedom and empowerment of low-income women. The NGOs have been working on the socio-economic development of the underprivileged sectors of society for the past four to five decades and initially organised Credit Unions. Since the advent of the early 1990s, when the SHG system came into being. As a result of initiatives from NABARD and directives from the Reserve Bank of India (RBI), the majority of these Mahila Samajams and credit unions have been converted into SHGs and connected to financial institutions for better credit facilities. The State Government of Chennai began organising the urban poor women into neighborhood groups (NHGs) in the middle of the 1990s. In terms of SHG-Bank connection and financial facilities, NABARD has classified these NHGs as SHGs (Rao, 2009). Women's self-help organisations, created specifically for rural women, can be a potent weapon for reducing rural poverty by empowering women and releasing them from the control of predatory moneylenders. These groups are an effective channel for community involvement in developmental initiatives. As a result, the current study assesses the contribution of self-help groups to raising the socioeconomic position of rural women in Chennai as well as the degree of

Assistant Professor, Department of Management Aarupadai Veedu Institute of Technology, Paiyanoor, Chennai empowerment attained by these women as a result of their involvement in SHGs. A study of the literature shows that studies examining the effects of self-help groups for rural women, particularly in Chennai, are uncommon. The primary goals of the study were to determine the personal, social, economic, and financial empowerment attained by SHG members and to evaluate the relationship between group features and empowerment. Therefore, the goal of the study is to regulate the level of empowerment among SHG members as well as the kind and severity of both group- and individual-related issues that they deal with.

Review of Literature

The simplified literature review on self-help groups that is provided below made it easier to streamline the study's methodology. Self-help Groups in Empowering Women: Case Study of Selected SHGs and NHGs by Anand, published in 2002, SHG members unanimously stated that the thrift component of the group served as an "informal bank at their doorstep." It showed that the absence of incentives for group leaders contributed to their decreasing enthusiasm for leading the group and the progressive decline in the functional efficiency of even the successful groups. The SHGs' efforts to increase the women members' understanding of new economic options, had a very good impact on them. Anju and Malhotra and Schuler (2005) aimed to highlight the most viable methodological techniques for measuring and analysing women's empowerment in their study assessing women's empowerment as a variable in worldwide development. They make an effort to summarise the research on women's empowerment from the domains of economics, sociology, anthropology, and demography, as well as what is known and what is unknown about what generates it, how it affects development and the fight against poverty. They offer some specific recommendations based on their study for where the field is in terms of defining, conceptualizing, and evaluating empowerment, utilizing and improving pre-existing frameworks, gathering information and conducting analyses, and incorporating techniques from relevant literature. The relationship between microcredit provided by SHGs and health is examined in the Mohindra (2003) paper on Women Self-Help Groups in Chennai State, India: A Public Health Perspective. In addition to giving women the chance to engage in financial activities and broaden their social networks, the report notes that SHGs also foster female autonomy and solidarity, which in turn promotes improved health awareness, increased access to healthcare services, and improved family member health decision-making abilities. Meenai (2003) attempted to clarify and simplify the approach to women's empowerment through credit-based self-help groups in his book Empowering Rural Women: An Approach to Empowering Women Through Credit-based Self-Help Groups by offering both the theoretical perspectives and practical guidance and tips to operationalize the same. Credit-based self-help groups were portrayed as an integrated method in which credit served merely as a starting point and a tool for operationalizing other facets of group dynamics and management. Saravanan (2014) noted that women's ignorance, powerlessness, and susceptibility are the main reasons contributing to their disadvantage. She emphasized that changing women's attitudes was the most important thing that needed to be done. The work participation rate of women in India is less than half that of men, according to Rathee (2013) in his edited volume book India: Economic Empowerment of Women. Despite efforts to improve the economic empowerment of women, the majority of the active female population is still restricted to micro, small-scale businesses and the informal sector. In their research article, WSHG: A Vehicle for Women Self-reliance, Authority (2014) highlighted the success of a few women's SHGs in Orissa's Ganjam area. They analyzed the workings of these SHGs and ways to strengthen them by implementing web-based apps for increased information exchange about their results and effectiveness. Women's empowerment is defined by Minimol & Makesh (2012) in their book Women's Empowerment in South Asia as the capacity of women to transform economic and social development when allowed to fully participate in decisions that affect their lives. This is accomplished by offering tools that empower women to become leaders within communities, regions, and countries, as well as through leadership development courses, coaching, consulting, and other means. Ramesh (2006) underlined the significance of women SHGs for women's empowerment through the provision of an easy credit delivery mechanism in his essay Women SHGs in Orissa - a crusade for women empowerment. He discussed the purpose and history of SHG, its growth, its organisational structure, its connections to established financial institutions, and its contribution to the empowerment of women.

Statement of the Problem

Self-help groups (SHGs), often referred to as savings and lending groups, are primarily informal associations whose members combine money and re-lend among the group as needed or on a rotating basis. These groups are motivated to take collective action by a shared sense of need. Many of these organisations were founded around particular industrial pursuits, Members were encouraged to save money, and collective resources were used to cover members' unforeseen needs, such as food. Organisations for women's self-help, developed especially for women in rural areas, can be a potent weapon for reducing rural poverty by empowering women and releasing them from the control of predatory moneylenders. These groups are an effective channel for community involvement in developmental initiatives. This study aims to assess the contribution of self-help groups to raising the socioeconomic position of rural women in Chennai as well as the degree of empowerment attained by these women as a result of their involvement in SHGs. A study of the literature shows that studies examining the effects of self-help groups for rural women, particularly in Chennai, are uncommon. The present study was initiated to critically evaluate this environment especially.

Objectives of the Study

1. To determine the degree of financial, social, economic, and personal empowerment attained by SHG members.
2. To identify the role of SHG members in empowering women.
3. To examine the relationship between group attributes and empowerment.

Methodology of the Study

For the study, an exploratory research design is used. The research was done between June 2021 and June 2022. The participants in the study are women who attend self-help groups in Chennai. The sample respondents were chosen using a judgment sampling method. The ten zones that make up the Chennai District include Tondiarpet, Basin Bridge, Pulianthope, Ayanawaram, Nungampaakam, Kodampakkam, Saidapet, Adayar, Kilpauk, and Ice House. The Universe is made up of all the female members of the SHGs operating in the Chennai District. 15 SHGs were chosen at random by the researcher from each of Chennai District's zones. Four women members were chosen at random from each of the SHGs in each of the randomly chosen zones of the Chennai District, allowing data to be collected both before and after their membership. A sample of 50 competent and focused responders served as pre-test subjects for the questionnaire that was initially developed. Thus, 63, 66, and 71 responders from the three strata made up the final sample size of 200.

Data Sources

This study is restricted to only the SHGs Funded by NGOs, Government and Formal financial institutions functioning in the Chennai district. This study ignored Groups functioning in Chennai District without A sample of 50 responsible and focused responders who served as pre-test subjects for the questionnaire that was initially developed. Thus, 63, 66, and 71 responders from the three strata made up the final sample size of 200. Only SHGs funded by NGOs, the government, and formal financial institutions operating in the Chennai district are included.

Data Collection and Analysis

To collect the primary data, an interview schedule was used. To acquire a better understanding of the actual situation, direct personal discussions and participatory observation with members of different SHGs were also conducted. Mean score and ANOVA were the analysis methods that were used. On a scale of one to five, the mean score was used to determine the levels of the different qualities. The median score ranges from one, which indicates the least degree of opinion [on empowerment, issues, the extent of activities, etc.], to five, which indicates the highest level of opinion.

Common words used in the Study:

Cohesion:

A connection between group members brought about by a strong sense of identification with the group as a whole.

Justice for all:

forming a community founded on the values of solidarity and equality, one that respects and appreciates human rights and acknowledges the worth of every person.

Equality:

Equality is the relationship between a collection of various things, people, actions, or circumstances that are similar in at least one way but not in all ways, i.e., respecting one particular aspect, with differences in other features. It is characterized as a procedure by which individuals acquire more power over their material and intellectual resources. The four components of economic, social, political, and legal empowerment can be used to describe overall empowerment. Development is the progression of one's circumstances, whether personally or collectively.

Limitations of the Study

The study is region-specific, and the use of sampling has a drawback in that the results could not be universally representative. However, this micro research can be viewed as a pilot project that can be repeated in various settings by using comparable tactics and methods. The purpose of the need study is not to evaluate the programme. Evaluation is a considerably bigger undertaking that requires gathering and comparing many sorts of data to a baseline. Despite being a micro study, it is helpful and futuristic because it discusses numerous facets of women's empowerment and the intervention strategies used by the NGOs.

Results

Based on the SHGs' category, the member profile was determined. Investigations were done into the various types of groups was carried out.

Category of SHGs

There are 18 SHGs in total that are included in the study, and 200 members are included as respondents. Five groups built the sample of SHGs, seven of which were financed by different NGOs, with Matsyafed serving as one of the key sponsors, and six from the other category. Others include SHGs related to local movements and communities that were established SNDP [Sree Narayana Dharma Paripalana Yogam], KPMS [Chennai Pulayar Maha Sabha], Churches, Wincentre, etc. are the supporters of the event. The sample of respondents was obtained from 63 NGO respondents funded by Asha Nivas, 65 NGO respondents, and 72 NGO respondents sponsored by others.

SHG Activity Types and Group Characteristics

The group traits that were sought to be identified included mutual trust, cohesion, transparency, interaction, leadership, accountability, cooperation, equality, and member satisfaction. On a scale of one to five (very high to very low), close to 60 to 70 percent of the participants thought that these qualities were present at high levels. Accountability and interdependence among individuals, followed by a sense of equality, represented the highest level of existence. Cohesion and engagement among members appeared to be features that were at least present, along with transparency in operations and accounts. Lack of transparency in business dealings and financial records can be a serious issue that raises suspicions of hostility and dissatisfaction among members because one of the key goals behind SHG activities is extra cash generating. No matter whether or not commercial operations were conducted, group-wise analysis revealed that the NGO-sponsored groups had the lowest levels of transparency. Nearly all groups indicated very low levels of activity in legal, social justice, and dispute resolution endeavors. There were political campaigns and involvement, albeit at low levels. The relevance and usefulness of microcredit facilities and bank connections were extremely ignored and underutilized, according to every significant information that has come to light. The members' low levels of education could be a major issue in this case. The study revealed that participants with higher levels of education had a more realistic understanding of the availability of microcredit and bank linkage services than those with lower levels of education. The use of credit facilities to finance commercial activity was extremely uncommon and infrequent. Even less land was purchased on a leasehold basis for agricultural purposes, although there are numerous opportunities for such activities. Before the members feel capable enough to take on such risks, they likely require additional direction and confidence building. Manufacturing as a whole was likewise quite low. Those who participated in these activities stuck to the usual pickle, soap, dried fish, etc. There were initially numerous cases of reported umbrella and laptop manufacture, for example, but these industries gradually faded out due to worries over cost affordability and marketing challenges. They are unable to compete in the market.

Personal Empowerment of Members

The personal empowerment [generic] traits with the greatest stated level of empowerment were self-respect and mutual regard. All other traits, including self-assurance, independence, and acceptance by family members, also showed significant levels of empowerment. It was clear that the participants felt a sense of accomplishment after participating in several group-related activities. As an example, a rural woman may be required to calculate interest rates weekly to make weekly deposits or borrow personal loans in the group fund. Even while the time required for these computations can consume a significant portion of the meeting time, the members—the treasurer, in particular, feel an overwhelming feeling of accomplishment and joy when they are finished. It must be stated that society has more or less accepted the organised women's movement as a component of the social order. The rest of the family members, especially the male members, do not express much irritation about the difficulties created when group sessions are held on weekends in a member's house.

Table 1: Level of Personal Empowerment

Attribute	Very High	High	Moderate	Low	Very Low	Mean Score
Confidence	8	85	3	2	2	3.97
Independence	6	86	7	1	0	3.96
Self-respect	7	89	4	0	0	4.03
Mutual respect	10	84	6	1	1	4
Family acceptance	11	73	10	3	1	3.9
Relative acceptance	14	66	13	4	1	3.9
Average	9	80	8	2	1	3.96

Sources: Compiled from Primary Data

Social Empowerment of Members

Women from rural areas often participated least in social programmes. Rights and social issues were still not widely known. It is anticipated that the groups would provide a very useful location for women to discuss their challenges, remedies, and goals, not just the formality of meetings and activities. In several instances, it turned out that the group members themselves believed the sessions had failed to give them any social empowerment. For example, many members admitted that although they felt that the effects of these addictions in life are highly noticeable and irreversible, they never brought up topics like dowries, alcoholism, etc. within the group. The capacity for activity planning, interpersonal coordination, group harmony, and public speaking were shown to be areas where the group activities performed at low levels of effectiveness. This proves how badly these organisations and their activities address the issue of social empowerment in their work. Members reported relatively low levels of social programming involvement. Members reportedly participated in multiple groups.

Economic Empowerment of Members

Experts and philosophers have talked extensively about the potential of SHGs to provide members with work prospects, either directly or indirectly. Direct employment can be provided by businesses, while other organisations might open up job chances by offering training in technical or entrepreneurial skills. The groups performed poorly in terms of supplying members with career possibilities or improving their technical or entrepreneurial abilities. Very few participants reported gains in their work prospects and skill sets. One area where a very high level of empowerment had been achieved was health improvement. Primary health centers [PHCs] are essential for meeting society's basic health needs in rural areas. The importance of these centers has grown in the months since the outbreak of Chikun Gunia [a disease identified in rural Chennai coastline districts] and its aftereffects. Rural women typically make up a large portion of those who attend medical outreach programmes and rural awareness campaigns. SHGs frequently assist in the implementation of such schemes. It can be the cause of the alleged empowerment in terms of personal/family wellness.

Table 2: Level of Economic Empowerment

Attribute	Very High	High	Moderate	Low	Very Low	Mean Score
Employment Opportunity	1	6	3	15	75	1.4
Technical skill		1	1	3	95	1.08
Entrepreneurial skill	1	4	2	10	83	1.29
Family Health	14	25	53	5	3	3.53
Living conditions	5	29	60	3	3	3.34
Economic status	5	15	71	4	5	3.11
Social security	1	5	67	23	4	2.76
Average	5	12	38	9	38	2.36

Sources: Compiled from primary data

Members' Financial Empowerment

Almost a third of the members reported modest income level empowerment, which shows that this was almost completely offset by modest savings improvement. Higher levels of expenditure growth are seen to be the only direct cause of diminished saving capacity. Mobile phone use was intense. Many of the participants acknowledged that their mobile phone expenses had significantly increased. The empowerment level in terms of financial management abilities was almost always poor. Personal possessions showed a very modest level of improvement, once again except for mobile phones. It has also been shown that rural women's participation in SHGs has not enabled them to feel financially secure.

Group-related Problems Faced by Members

The occurrence of several group-related issues was assessed. Examples include obstacles to participation, drop-outs, disagreements, and a lack of openness. A few issues affected the group. Conflicts between members and meeting absences were two issues that nearly 15% of members described as being present. Unusual meetings, inaccurate records, records that couldn't be accessed, a lack of internal audits, and the existence of pressure groups were all mentioned in passing.

Association between Empowerment and Group Characteristics

At various levels, groups displayed traits such as cohesion, leadership, and mutual trust. The test was meant to determine whether the members' various levels of empowerment were connected to the traits shown by the group. The test determines whether there is a relationship between the two sets of variables that is positive or negative, as well as its direction, strength, and significance. The positive symbol [+] and the negative symbol [-] are used to indicate positive and negative relations, respectively.

Association between Personal Empowerment and Group Characteristics

Confidence, independence, respect for oneself and others, and acceptability from family and friends are all examples of personal empowerment characteristics that showed a very low link with group member trust. At a 95% level of confidence, the relationship was statistically significant. Cohesion showed weak to low degrees of positive correlation, which was statistically significant, between various empowerment characteristics. The correlation between transparency and self-esteem and confidence was marginal and statistically insignificant. Empowerment demonstrated weak but statistically significant relationships with leadership, responsibility, satisfaction, and cooperation. Self- and mutual respect were moderately correlated with interdependence. Overall, it was discovered that there were only weak/ low/very weak/very weak associations between group traits and personal empowerment [moderate levels included, though rarely so].

Association between Social empowerment and Group Characteristics

As can be observed, the vast majority of the relationships are antagonistic. It is also clear that there are cases of zero ties and that all relationships are either weak or extremely weak. The link proved to be statistically significant in very few instances. Except for responsibility, interdependence, and satisfaction, there was no correlation between organisational skills and mutual trust. All other correlations were negative and none of them reached statistical significance. The only group qualities that had favourable relationships with group cohesiveness were interdependence and responsibility. All relationships with characteristics were negatively impacted by public speaking, with a lack of mutual trust showing to be most important. Except for responsibility, social acceptance was inversely correlated with that trait. Social programme involvement showed positive but unstable connections to accountability and leadership yet no significant relationships with group features. Most group traits were weakly positively correlated with membership in other organisations, although cohesion and transparency were negatively correlated. Economic empowerment indicators have been found to have a very weak or negligible correlation with group characteristics, with very few instances of a statistically significant correlation occurring. It turned out that entrepreneurial abilities and empowerment in terms of employment opportunities were significantly adversely correlated with group characteristics. A positive correlation was found between living conditions, financial situation, and social security. Leadership alone had a negative correlation with health. A statistically significant relationship between social security's low correlation with equality and satisfaction was found.

Association between Group Features and Financial Empowerment

It can be shown that a sizable portion of the association had relatively weak relations overall. There were extremely few instances of statistically significant associations, it was discovered. All associations, except a few, were favorable in its favor. Empowerment in terms of income was positively correlated with cohesion, although none of these correlations were determined to be statistically significant, transparency, accountability, cooperation, and interdependence, and negatively correlated with others and unrelated to equality. All characteristics' factors and empowerment in terms of saving had roughly similar numbers of positive and negative associations. Spending was found to have a statistically significant low link with leadership, responsibility, and trust between individuals. Cohesion, transparency, interaction, leadership, cooperation, interdependence, and equality were found to be significantly associated with financial management skill empowerment. Transparency, accountability, cooperation, and interdependence were all found to be adversely correlated with personal empowerment, albeit none of the correlations were statistically significant. All group qualities were shown to be only very weakly related to improvements in financial security, with relationships to cohesion, equality, and satisfaction being skewed negatively.

Discussion

Table 3: Result of the ANOVA

Statements		Sum of Squares	df	Mean Square	F	Sig.
Personal Empowerment	Between Groups	382.29	4	95.5	3.17	.018
	Within Groups	2258.19	196	30.1		
	Total	2640.48	200			
Economic Empowerment	Between Groups	297.36	4	73.8	2.53	.039
	Within Groups	2134.43	196	23.1		
	Total	2431.79	200			

Sources: Compiled from Primary Data

The table above shows the F test values along with the significance of the impact of SHGs on women. Comparing the F test and significance values, all the ANOVA comparisons favor the acceptance of the null hypothesis. It is to be noted that significance values are below 0.05 for a 5% level of significance in all the variables accepting personal empowerment and economic empowerment degrees of freedom (4, 196), F = 3.17 and significance of 0.18. is F(4,196) = F = 2.53 and significance of .039.

No matter whether or not commercial operations were conducted, group-wise analysis revealed that the NGO-sponsored groups had the lowest levels of transparency. Nearly all groups indicated very low levels of activity in legal, social justice, and dispute resolution endeavors. The personal empowerment [generic] qualities that were reported as having the highest level of empowerment were self-respect and mutual respect. All other traits, including self-assurance, independence, and acceptance by family members, also showed significant levels of empowerment. The ability to organize activities, group cohesion, interactions, and public speaking were shown to be areas where the group activities performed at low levels of effectiveness. This clearly shows how badly these organisations and their activities address the issue of social empowerment. Members reported relatively low levels of social programming involvement. Very few participants reported gains in their work prospects and skill sets. One area where a nearly high level of empowerment was attained was health improvement. Almost three-fourths of the participants reported modest increases in income, but these gains were almost completely offset by modest increases in savings. The increased degree of expenditure growth is considered the only direct cause for the decreased ability to save. Conflicts between members and absenteeism were identified to be the main issues. There were not many cases of dropouts and there was no internal audit. One instance of a SHG that had to be disbanded due to member disagreements, absenteeism, and dropouts was documented. The participants' issues were found to be most frequently related to family obligations. The lack of family support was the next most important factor. Although the male family members were no longer actively opposed to their women's participation in SHGs, they were never actively supportive. Low socioeconomic position, poor motivation, and meager group benefits turned out to be serious issues. The fundamental essence of SHG and its associated activities need to be rethought. It's time to recognise what went wrong, or, failing that, what wasn't quite right. As ameliorative measures, the following are suggested:

1. It is appropriate to regard intellectual empowerment as more important—or at the very least, equally important—than social, economic, or financial

empowerment. Intellectual empowerment is frequently left out of discussions about personal empowerment. The goal is to increase the members' capacity to think and act more effectively, moving them from having dull thinking to having sharp thinking and from having thick actions to having delicate actions.

2. SHG meetings are advised to broaden their reach. Even though holding meetings is currently all but required, the proceedings lack a useful agenda. A meeting's agenda should be predetermined and geared towards promoting intellectual empowerment. Concurrent issues from the social, economic, or political spheres should preferably be discussed.
3. It is also important to take into account the approval of some well-known senior figures as the group's mentors. They can participate in group meetings and regulate and direct the proceedings such that they have a purpose. Additionally, these mentors can educate the group's participants on the subtler and more comprehensive facets of the present conversation subjects. Thus, achieving intellectual empowerment might be made easier.
4. Members, especially younger members, need to be educated on the value of financial security. The younger members' lack of saving behaviours and the group's overall reliance on covert savings strategies raise serious concerns.
5. Rural women's employability is extremely low. The extremely small number of salaried and income-producing members proves it. Some steps can be taken to give members technical/professional training to improve their skills. The local government, professional/technical educational institutes, etc. can be contacted for assistance, however, it may be expensive.
6. The groupings' social activities are observed to be extremely limited. Social activity involvement has to be more actively promoted by groups. SHGs can benefit greatly by taking an active role in society.
7. The commercial activities that the organizations generally engage in are found to be quite limited. The usual marketing and processing operations are carried out. SHGs ought to consider looking at a wider variety of activities.
8. In almost every instance, it was determined that the commercial operations carried out either stopped or stayed the same without leading to any gains in operational efficiency. Existing activities have relatively little potential to generate cash. Skills and training advancements can guarantee increased commercial activity viability and profitability.
9. Members are still reported to struggle with a lack of family support. By itself, the group can coordinate its members' efforts to plan events that will maximize the support of family members.

Conclusion

This study showed that the SHG idea is a more effective instrument for empowering rural women and helping them improve their social and economic status. They are more involved in family decisions. When women use microcredit facilities, they may acquire tools and other resources for their companies and careers. After encouraging women to save money, group loans are provided for specific financial objectives. The majority of poor women first use this money for household expenses to support their family. The women are informed and educated on a variety of topics, including politics, money management, speaking openly in public, and current events. They are prodded and inspired to advance in society. It can be said that their consciousness and knowledge have grown. The study's major findings are in favour of SHGs' stronger contribution to women's empowerment by ensuring their financial security and enabling them to save money for future investments in development. Additionally, it was discovered that the SHGs gave the residents of villages the assurance they needed to be socially and economically independent. It creates loan policies, awareness campaigns, and other initiatives. However, self-help groups have a beneficial effect on Chennai's female empowerment. This study might therefore conclude that the idea of SHGs for rural women's empowerment is still not fully matured in achieving its goal. The success of SHGs in raising rural women's status as a more important group in society can be furthered by further efforts in modifying group characteristics and rearranging group goals.

References

1. Anand, J. S. (2002). *Self-help groups in empowering women: Case study of selected SHGs and NHGs*. Centre for Development Studies.
2. Authority, V. B. (2014). Annual-Report 2013-14 Visva-Bharati, English Version.
3. Malhotra, A., & Schuler, S. R. (2005). Women's empowerment as a variable in international development. *Measuring empowerment: Cross-disciplinary perspectives, 1*(1), 71-88.
4. Meenai, Z. (2003). *Empowering rural women: An approach to empowering women through credit-based self-help groups*. Aakar books.
5. Minimol, M. C., & Makesh, K. G. (2012). Empowering rural women in Kerala: A study on the role of Self-help Groups (SHGs). *International Journal of Sociology and Anthropology, 4*(9), 270.
6. Mohindra, K. S. (2003). A report on women Self-help Groups (SHGs) in Kerala state, India: a public health perspective. *Universite De MontreAl. Mar.*
7. Ramesh, C. P. (2006). Women SHGs in Orissa–a Crusade for Women Empowerment. *Self Help Groups and Women Empowerment, Sahoo RK, Tripathy SN, Anmol Publications Pvt. Ltd., New Delhi*, 44-45.
8. Rao, D. K. (2009). Micro Finance and Support Organisations in the Southern States of India. Nagayya. *Journal of Rural Development, 28*(3), 285-301.
9. Rathee, N. (2013). Economic empowerment of the women: The need of the hour. *International Journal of Education and Management Studies*, 3(4), 515.
10. Saravanan, S. (2014). A Study on Socio-Economic Profile and Problems faced by the Women Self-help Groups in Coimbatore District-Tamil Nadu. *IPE Journal of Management*, 4(1), 151.

17

Entrepreneurship and Growth in MSMEs: A Study in Madhya Pradesh

Manharan Anant[1] *& Remsingh Hatila*[2]

Abstract

Small and medium-sized businesses (SMEs) play a significant role in the Indian economy. The government of India has prioritized growth with equal opportunity and the eradication of poverty since the earliest plan periods. An essential component of how economies are organized is entrepreneurship. This didn't happen all at once in emerging nations. Variations in growth rates are frequently attributed to the extent to which different nations support the entrepreneurial spirit. In addition to highlighting Madhya Pradesh's contribution to the literature on entrepreneurship from the perspective of economic development, this essay also aims to highlight the numerous contributions made to the field. The entire paper is based on a literature review, and it is evident from the literature that entrepreneurship development should be used to promote employment. However, the study concludes that there is an urgent need to focus on MSME, which would result in economic growth for the entire state as well as the country. To this end, the state and central governments and their agencies should support entrepreneurial values and capabilities to combat the current state of unemployment in the nation.

Keywords: *Entrepreneurship, Development, Growth and MSMEs*

Introduction

Small and medium-sized businesses in India vary widely in terms of their size, the variety of products and services they offer, and the levels of technology they employ. MSME could act as entrepreneurship's foundation. They benefit a nation that is just beginning to industrialize by producing goods as well as by acting as a breeding ground for talented entrepreneurs and managers. India has a poor track record when it comes to entrepreneurship. But there's no denying that its reputation is rising. India's standing in the industrialized world has risen in the past. India is currently one of the world's major industrialized countries. through the emergence of startup businesses that foster both social and economic growth, the production of knowledgeable and prosperous entrepreneurs, and the invention of new technological advancements. The only reason this effort has been successful is because of entrepreneurial endeavors. According to Feki (2016), the economy before the 20th century showed the first indications that entrepreneurship became a long-term driver of economic progress.

With a head count ratio (HCR) of more than 30%, states such as Bihar, Madhya Pradesh, Odisha, and Uttar Pradesh possess a high prevalence of poverty. More than 30% of rural residents still live in poverty. In this context, it is commonly recognized that micro and small businesses (SMEs) play a significant role in

[1] Assistant Professor, Department of Commerce Govt. Naveen College Jatga, Korba, Chhattisgarh

[2] Assistant Professor, Department of Commerce Govt. Adarsh College, Umaria, Madhya Pradesh

inclusive growth and the generation of jobs (Bereket, 2010). The main goals for the MSME sectors are to leverage local workers and resources to create employment opportunities at cheap capital costs. The expansion of the MSME sub-sector is being highlighted due to its potential to create employment opportunities as well as its contribution to the state's industrial production. After agriculture, this subsector is the one that generates the most jobs. Most economies around the world have a thriving and expanding sector of micro, small, and medium-sized businesses. Levy and others, 2005) According to Audretsch et al. (2006), developing settings that are conducive to entrepreneurship and growth of micro and small businesses has grown into a top policy objective in practically every nation on the planet. Since it is commonly acknowledged that MSMEs are underrepresented in the global economy, Lester et al. (2007) asserts that there is broad consensus regarding the benefits of developing strategies to increase the impact of MSMEs on global trading. For instance, MSMEs typically provide about 50% of GDP and 60% of total employment in rich economies, but only about 30% of exports and considerably less in developing ones.

Review of Literature

The procedure of the research is ongoing. The literature review appears to be essential since it offers the current study valuable feedback that helps to advance research efforts. Here, some of the key pieces of prior study literature on MSMEs' many aspects are provided. Carree (2010) asserted that small businesses play a crucial role in the generation of jobs. According to him, businesses employing less than 100 people created eight out of ten new jobs in America throughout the 1970s. However, a wealth of data refutes the idea that small businesses are the primary contributors to the creation of new jobs. (Das, 2014). This study examines the microeconomic data that is currently available to determine whether MSMEs help India's economy grow in terms of the total quantity of units, production, jobs, and exports. Synergistic takeovers are more likely to be friendly transactions than disciplinary takeovers, Shoaib 2011 analysis. Deals that go over the management's objectives of the target company are referred to as hostile transactions. According to Frankel (2004) analysis, the existence of profitable insider transactions suggests that "trading on inside information is widespread" and that insiders do transgress security laws. Evidence of excess profits generated by investors in previously acquired enterprises is provided by Sehgal (2012). in the initial disclosure of impending mergers. According to Erdugan's (2012) analysis of SEC-reported transactions, business insiders typically receive minor excess profits. The barometer of general economic, social, and industrial growth is entrepreneurship, which has brought about revolutionary transformations in society. The area and reach of marketing products and services have expanded as a result of an action, as well as the distribution and mobilization of the production-related elements. According to Shattock, (2005). Entrepreneurship is encouraged as a means of achieving the transition from a knowledge society to an innovation economy. According to Nkechi et al (2012), entrepreneurship is increasingly being recognised as a means of generating employment, empowering the unemployed, and fostering economic dynamism in a society that is rapidly going global. Sharma (2013) noted that she focused on encouraging female entrepreneurship. He also emphasizes that men and women are equal participants in all spheres of life, particularly in the development of the economy. According to Prasad's (2006) analysis of the credit flow between commercial banks to MSMEs, the rate of growth of small business credit is failing to keep up with the rate of growth of bank credit as a whole.

Objectives of the Study

The purpose of this study is to examine government strategies for the growth of micro, small, and medium-sized firms in terms of their contribution to entrepreneurship and job creation in the Indian setting. The MSME sector has often been described as the "engine of growth" for emerging countries. This study focuses on a general overview of MSMEs at various stages and examines some recent developments that determine the growth and importance of this sector to the Indian economy. Major federal and state policy changes over the past few years have been made to enhance and expand this business. Among these recent policy improvements, the MSME Development Act of 2006 is possibly the most significant.

Research Methodology

This study has been divided into several categories based on a study of the literature on entrepreneurship and MSMEs that has been published in several journals and research papers, which is most relevant for comprehending the significance of entrepreneurial growth for MSMEs.

Need of the Study

MSMEs have played a significant role in India's industrialization process because they are prevalent in rural and economically underdeveloped areas and have the potential to increase revenue. The issue of entrepreneurial education in micro, small, and medium-sized businesses, particularly in the state of Madhya Pradesh, is being researched. To create jobs and improve the standard of living of the populace, it is vital to speed up the growth of small-scale industries, particularly in a less developed area like the Annupur district.

Relevance of the Study

Micro, small, and medium-sized businesses (MSMEs) are seen as the force behind economic expansion and a catalyst for just development. Compared to large businesses, the MSME sector has a substantially higher labour intensity. MSMEs account for over 90% of all enterprises in most nations, are acknowledged for generating the greatest rates of job growth, and make a sizable contribution to both economic output and export. Compared to the entire industrial sector, the market for micro and small businesses has regularly had stronger growth rates in recent years. The majority of the state's population (87%) resides in rural areas and depends heavily on agriculture (73%) for their livelihood. Due to inadequate financial infrastructure, rural issues are evident. MSMEs are currently playing a significant role in changing the socioeconomic situation of the state's unbanked poor in rural areas by providing them with credit. Numerous job prospects for rural kids are being created by MSMEs in nearby households and micro businesses. In light of this, the current study, which examines the successful impact of MSMEs in enhancing the socioeconomic situation of Madhya Pradesh's rural poor, is significant and fascinating.

The Micro, Small, and Medium Enterprises (MSMEs) of India play a significant role in the expansion of the Indian economy. During the age of industrialization in the provincial area, these MSMEs offer support and employment opportunities while also lowering the disparity in income among the inhabitants. Through initiatives like venture formation, domestic manufacturing, minimum initiative requirements, operational adaptability, and innovation-focused undertakings, among others, MSMEs play a key part in the growth of the Indian economy. Small and medium-sized enterprises (SMEs) are free to compete with big companies that drive economic growth and are present in the economy. There are about 36 million housing units in this region, which employs up to 80 million people. This region produces 6000 commodities, which accounts for 8% of the country's GDP. It accounts for 40% of all fares and 45% of all assembling yield in the country. We must thus acknowledge MSMEs' contribution to generating employment opportunities and endeavor to advance the country as a whole. The Ministry of Micro, Small, and Medium Enterprises of the Government of India is responsible for developing strategies, initiatives, and arrangements for the growth of these MSME firms. The execution of these projects is also guaranteed by the Ministry of MSMEs' devotion to upholding them. MSMEs are essentially improved and advanced by the State Government, with backing from the Central Government.

Entrepreneurship, Innovation, Economic Growth, and MSMEs: A Relationship

MSMEs are acknowledged as the largest employers of rural youth and have a profound impact on both their way of life and other aspects of rural tribal life in Madhya Pradesh. The MSME sector is a significant contributor to India's current export performance. This industry accounts for 40% to 50% of Indian exports. Nearly 35% of exports are direct exports, while 15% are indirect exports. Entrepreneurship and innovation are not mutually exclusive concepts. Both have a connection and correlation. The core of entrepreneurship is innovation. By putting freshly manufactured goods to use in practical ways, it helps the nation's entrepreneurial base grow. Schumpeter asserts that business ownership is a creative endeavor. Essentially, an entrepreneur is an innovator. The size and operation of the MSME determine the extent to which an entrepreneur will participate in technical innovation. Thus, MSMEs can be considered significant development and advancement drivers. The majority of these entrepreneurs are employed by SMEs, whose level of innovation is influenced by the entrepreneur's traits as well as the area and industry in which the business operates. However, the policy plays a significant role in determining innovative behavior. Innovation needs government assistance, which is crucial. This can take a variety of shapes, such as improving the business environment, offering venture funding, utilizing migrant labor, and offering technological and more active state-private sector cooperation. Entrepreneurs may drive policy and institutional change rather than being only influenced by the policy and organisational environment in some cases, especially in unfavorable environments.

The importance of entrepreneurship in strategies for economic growth has grown. This is largely attributable to the fact that entrepreneurs are what propels the economy's expansion and the establishment of new jobs. The economy and society of the nation are significantly impacted by entrepreneurs and their enterprises. Micro, small, and medium-sized enterprises (MSMEs) are more important to entrepreneurship in emerging nations like India. The micro, small, and medium-sized business (MSME) sector is the backbone of the modern economy. This is a turning point in the transition from antiquated to contemporary technologies. Small and medium-sized businesses (MSME) drive faster economic growth. Due to their geographic versatility, MSMEs are highly suited for rapid industrialization in both rural and urban environments. Local entrepreneurs are encouraged to develop, which results in a decentralized system of ownership that avoids economic wealth compared to concentrating on the ownership of certain individuals. They are also incubators located for new businesses, raising a future generation of business leaders and managers. Small and medium-sized enterprises (MSMEs) allow skilled workers and aspiring entrepreneurs to start their businesses on a budget. In addition to other facets of running a business, they take part in small and medium-sized economic operations like the buying and selling of goods and services. Both the general public and other businesses can purchase their products and services. By providing new goods that address local demands and enhance the standard of living for locals, they contribute to economic diversification. Locally accessible raw materials, human capital, and technological resources are utilized. Thus, inclusive socioeconomic success can reduce interpersonal conflicts and stability in the local areas. Nowadays, practically every nation in the world has as one of its top policy goals the development of entrepreneurship and MSME. MSMEs have a significant structural and flexible role in all economies, according to business owners. Small and medium-sized businesses (SMEs) are a key factor in the expansion of both employment and revenue in many emerging nations.

It should come as no surprise that Broughel (2019) proposed a model whereby capital and labour are the key drivers while investigating the root causes of economic growth. Self-employment and small businesses would become even more pointless if knowledge became a significant factor in their development and competitiveness in international markets. There aren't enough qualified workers in the industry in India, which necessitates an increased number of entrepreneurship development programmes nationwide for the expansion of the Indian economy. The country's high economic growth improved company prospects, which in turn increased labour demand and, ultimately, employment growth. The economy of Madhya Pradesh is heavily reliant on industries. Industries are crucial to the state's economic development. The MSME industry in Madhya Pradesh produces nearly 6,000 different items, from low-tech to high-tech ones, in addition to offering a wide range of services. 200.19 lakh working enterprises in rural areas made up In the MSME sector, operating enterprises accounted for 55.34 percent of the total, while urban areas accounted for 44.66% of working enterprises (161.57 lahks). In this industry, 31.79% of the businesses were involved in manufacturing, as opposed to 68.21% in services. in 2014. Private investment has rarely kept up with the state's economic boom, but MP has averaged above 10% growth in the last three years, up to 11.8% in 2013-2014 although the national rate has decreased (Goswami, 2015).

If the following factors are supported, the state's industries could do better:

1. In comparison to other states, the cost of fundamental necessities including land, water, and skilled labour is quite low. Additionally, the state permits industrial units to own power plants that can generate the necessary amount of electricity.
2. The state government is committed to helping the investors and giving them a peaceful environment. High-powered committees and boards have been established by the state government to prevent delays in gaining various permits and approvals.
3. Even though Madhya Pradesh has access to water, power, connection, land, talent, and trust, it still lags behind Gujarat and Kerala.
4. Low levels of industrial potential awareness are a problem, and other forms of connection are bad for the industry.
5. Insufficient industrial development hubs.
6. The main issue these industries face is their inability to compete with big businesses. They are not able to compete with big businesses because they lack access to the economies of large-scale production.
7. The absence of government involvement.

8. The absence of social and familial support for women.
9. The majority of business owners are ignorant of technical advancements, marketing strategies, etc. due to a lack of education.

The Central and State governments are mostly in charge of developing entrepreneurship. The following are some of the government's initiatives to support entrepreneurship:

1. Entrepreneurship and Skill Development Training Programme
2. Cluster Development
3. Credit Facilitation
4. Technology Upgrading
5. Increasing Competitiveness; and
6. Market Assistance
7. The policy places a strong emphasis on giving MSMEs' infrastructure needs top priority.
8. In all industrial areas, industrial parks, industrial corridors, and land banks, a minimum of 20% of the land must be set aside for MSMEs.
9. The State Government would guarantee that government departments and agencies purchase products and services from MSMEs situated inside the state's borders via a rate contract system to strengthen forward linkage.
10. A Construction of an MSMEs-specific industrial park or area.
11. To encourage young educated people to have an entrepreneurial spirit.
12. To improve MSMEs' ability to compete by clustering.
13. Convergence of plans and materials.
14. Commercial banks and other financial institutions are urged to open branches specifically for MSMEs to offer business loans at preferential industrial rates.
15. The District Industrial Centre (DIC) was established at the district level to offer MSMEs essential support services for their expansion and development. At the district level, the District Information Centre (DIC) serves as a promotion organisation for MSMEs and provides the necessary assistance and direction for the establishment of the unit.
16. At the district level, DIC is the organisation responsible for marketing the Pradhan-Mantri Employment Guarantee scheme.
17. The DICs' main goals are to: speed up efforts to foster industrialization across the district; encourage rural industrialization and the growth of rural industries and handicrafts; achieve economic equality across the district's various regions; assist new entrepreneurs in starting businesses; and provide financial assistance and marketing resources to new innovators.

Although the entrepreneurs are unaware of it, these schemes are advantageous to them. The government must take action to promote this programme.

Multiple Initiatives to Encourage Entrepreneurship in Madhya Pradesh:

1. Government should prioritize promoting small businesses. The government must establish a vast network of institutions to aid in the creation and expansion of small businesses across the nation.
2. Policies should concentrate on addressing market, system, and government shortcomings impeding the establishment of new firms, to encourage job creation, innovation, and economic growth. Priorities include initiatives to enhance and strengthen entrepreneurship skills and improve the efficient use of public study and procurement opportunities. Other objectives include facilitating the internationalization of SMEs and entrepreneurship.

3. The government should assist management and staff training in businesses, and forge official linkages between the industry and organisations in charge of fostering exports or attracting foreign direct investment.
4. In these areas, governments are attempting to find and evaluate policies that are pertinent, useful, and efficient.
5. It is necessary to strengthen the analytical underpinnings for informed policy formulation, to promote coordination between governments and regional and global organisations and institutions, and to facilitate benchmarking and the exchange of best practices.
6. International prospects should be sought out by business owners, with an emphasis on market potential and growth.
7. Business owners should make preparations now for the resources they will require after the economy has stabilized.
8. Entrepreneurs should give the investment priority.
9. Professional advisors should stress the importance of prudent financial management during the recovery and warn clients against overtrading.

The advantages offered to MSMEs included protection from late payments and central government initiatives for the improvement and promotion of ill units. Along with the option to purchase commodities given to MSMEs with preferential policies and exit plans, the RBI's progressive policy towards credit advantage also supported the MSME.

Conclusion

Entrepreneurship is required for rapid and sustainable economic development and progress. It generates the talent and expertise required for more growth, less unemployment, and reduced poverty. for the businesses to successfully generate wealth and job possibilities. For students to desire to be entrepreneurs and contribute to the prosperity of the state rather than seeking employment with the government, the government must create an atmosphere that is conducive to investors, build solid government policies, and foster an entrepreneurial mentality in them. The nation's infrastructure needs urgent attention from the government. Making sure folks with innovative ideas have the financial support necessary to make their ideas a reality is crucial. One challenge for government officials is to approach the problem holistically while achieving a balance between industry and agriculture. Industrial clusters must be established to assure shared amenities, thereby eliminating inequities across the locations and facilitating growth in the micro, small, and medium-sized company (MSMEs) sector. Numerous promotion organisations are attempting to establish the industry in Madhya Pradesh with incentives and concessions. With the difficulties come great opportunities for small businesses. Small and micro businesses spend more heavily on the growth of the state. Because these businesses create many more jobs than large-scale businesses do, Madhya Pradesh is emerging as a leader in both economic and entrepreneurial development. MSMEs unquestionably contribute significantly to the use and enhancement of local resources.

References

1. Audretsch, D.B., Max, C.K. & Eric, E.L. (2006). Entrepreneurship and Growth, New York: Oxford University Press.
2. Bereket, T. (2010). *The role of micro and small enterprises in employment creation and income generation: A survey study of Mekelle city, Tigray region, Ethiopia* (Doctoral dissertation, Mekelle University).

3. Broughel, J., & Thierer, A. D. (2019). Technological innovation and economic growth: A brief report on the evidence. *Mercatus Research Paper.*
4. Carree, M. A., & Thurik, A. R. (2010). *The impact of entrepreneurship on economic growth* 557-594. Springer New York.
5. Das, S. K. (2014). Growth and prospect of MSMEs in Odisha: An analytical approach. *Odisha Review*, 102-111.
6. Erdugan, R. (2012). *The effect of economic factors on the performance of the Australian stock market* (Doctoral dissertation, Victoria University).
7. Feki, C., & Mnif, S. (2016). Entrepreneurship, technological innovation, and economic growth: Empirical analysis of panel data. *Journal of the Knowledge Economy*, 7(4), 984-999.
8. Frankel, R., & Li, X. (2004). Characteristics of a firm's information environment and the information asymmetry between insiders and outsiders. *Journal of Accounting and Economics*, 37(2), 229-259.
9. Goswami, P., & Thakur, Y. S. (2015). Growth of entrepreneurship in msme in Madhya Pradesh. *Asia Pacific Journal of Research* 1(28).
10. Lester, L. R., & Leigh, S. (2007). Trading Places–SMEs in the Global Economy. *Ashcroft International Business School, Anglia Ruskin University, Cambridge, UK.*
11. Levy, M., & Powell, P. (2004). *Strategies for growth in SMEs: The Role of information and information sytems.* Elsevier.
12. Nkechi, A., Emeh Ikechukwu, E. J., & Okechukwu, U. F. (2012). Entrepreneurship development and employment generation in Nigeria: Problems and prospects. *Universal Journal of Education and General Studies*, 1(4), 88-102.
13. Prasad, C, S. (2006). Micro, Small and Medium Enterprises Financing in India-Issues and Concerns‖, Cab Calling, 11, 35- 40.
14. Sehgal, S., Banerjee, S., & Deisting, F. (2012). The impact of M&A announcement and financing strategy on stock returns: Evidence from BRICKS markets. *International Journal of Economics and Finance*, 4(11), 76-90.
15. Sharma, P. (2013). Women Entrepreneurship Development in India‖, *Global Journal of Management and Business Studies.* 3(4), 371-376.
16. Shattock, M. (2005). European universities for entrepreneurship: Their role in the Europe of knowledge the theoretical context. *Higher Education Management and Policy*, 17(3), 13.
17. Shoaib, A. (2011). Measuring performance through capital structure: Evidence from banking sector of Pakistan. *African Journal of Business Management*, 5(5), 1871-1879.

18

The Effect of Information Communication Technology (ICT) on MSME

Mairembam Rajeev Singh[1] *& Thingbaijam Malvika Devi*[2]

Abstract

This study tried to examine the economic impacts on businesses of cloud accounting system deployment on Micro, Small, and Medium-Sized Enterprises (MSMEs) and related aspects. The study's items are representative of MSME cloud accounting system providers and the operational accounting procedures they support. This research has examined the various sorts and various associations of Cloud enlisting that can be utilized as the instrument for the authentic turn of events and movement of our reliable life. This considered sensibility will assist any relationship with utilizing Information and Communication Technology (ICT) in an unmatched manner. Pay and use when the need comes will also help the relationship to limit the use of assets for sporadic and less delicate associations for them comparatively as their clients. Regardless of how a wary report is coordinated to set up the idea, a full-length examination may reveal some more bits of a near idea.

Keywords: *MSME, ICT, Cloud Computing and Impact*

Introduction

Understanding what is meant by "ICT" and how the technology links to the information systems and the "core" productive systems used by MSMEs in developing countries is first important to get insight into the significance of ICT use by MSMEs. For analytical purposes, it is also necessary to take into account the variations among businesses, which are indicated in the straightforward, two-part classification presented in the preceding section (livelihood and growth firms). Reasonable business approaches help in conveying benefits by improving key plans, with no antagonistic result on the worldwide or nearby climate. By and large, undertakings dependably experience issues, difficulties and freedoms to suffer over the long haul. The vast majority of the affiliations. This may comparatively generally broaden energy utilization, causing huge regular concerns. During the time spent accomplishing business status, adequacy takes towards the back visitor plan and this can impact the business climate. The ideal and financially watchful reaction to this issue can be refined by Computing, which offers dominance to business and gives a stage to reasonable with expanded benefits, better climate and human assets on the board. By far most of the affiliation's instruments similarly for the most part widen the energy usage, causing a colossal standard concern. During the time spent achieving business status, sufficiency takes toward

1 Research Scholar, Department of Commerce Manipur University, Canchipur Imphal, Manipur

2 Research Scholar, Department of Commerce Manipur University, Canchipur Imphal, Manipur

the back guest plan and this can affect. Different affiliations truly have hindrances in relocating to the Cloud because of its high reliance on the Internet. The study, created from a Cloud Computing point of view has been examined to accomplish the business artfulness and reasonableness on individuals, planet and benefits, as three gigantic parts of authenticity, have been introduced. Mechanical significant assessments have been introduced as the Cloud Computing occasions of beating torment.

Authentic Cloud Development

Feasibility suggested 'Proficient Development' "as the capacity to address the issues of the present while adding to what exactly specific allies to come ages' necessities." The focal standard of 'Achievable Development' is living back to front climate limits and confining the utilization of work environments which impels the debasement of climate assets and the ordinary environment of humankind. Notwithstanding, our place of assembly of functional movement is altogether wider than simply the climate. It surmises our spotlight ought to be pointed on to the medium term, for instance, set aside your money, improve your success and is regularly identically quick and steady. Again, on the off chance that we go for a customer worker application in our office rather than free PCs, it will cost less what's more devour and less force. Last yet not least, on the off chance that we put resources into scattered handling work environments, it will confine the undertaking also as force use. So, improvement is a necessity for a solitary individual to have a relationship with the entire human area, we ought to in like way deal with the way that these exercises don't hamper the needs of people later on to come. Passed on preparing is a creating model permitting re-evaluating of all IT needs through Internet office. It permits quick application improvement and testing for little affiliations that can't manage the cost of huge hypotheses on IT framework. NIST depicts Cloud taking care of as follows: "Scattered preparing is a model for empowering obliging, on-request network consent to a commonplace pool of configurable enlisting assets (networks, workers, putting away, applications, and associations), (National Institute of Standards and Technology Gaithersburg, 2011) that can be quickly provisioned and passed on with immaterial association exertion or master affiliation correspondence. This Cloud model advances accessibility and is made out of five fundamental qualities, three help models, and four sending models."

Association Oriented

Coordination collectively: is the capacity to pass on a flat-out mix joining semantic intercession, stream control, mix plan, etc Essentially, mix as-a-association combines the vast majority of the highlights and cutoff points found inside standard undertaking application blend (EAI) progression yet passed. Security-collectively, as you may have hypothesized, is the capacity to pass on center security benefits in a roundabout way ludicrous. While the run of the run-of-the-mill security associations is clear, more present-day associations, for example, the character of the square are opening. Cloud is executed utilizing Service-Oriented Architecture entirety of the limits/parts are open crazy as a help. Regardless of whether it is changing, stage, or design everything can be gotten to as a help. Assets or example figures, hoarding, and affiliation limit needed to be viably and moved i.e., increment or lessening at runtime relying on client basics.

Economy of Scale

According to Duncombe & Heeks (2002) and Heeks (1999), information and communication technology (ICT) is an electronic method for gathering, processing, storing, and transmitting information. Digital information, such as that found in computer software and sent via communication networks like the Internet, is the foundation of ICT. Other 'non-digital' pre-existing media are, however, significantly more pervasive in the developing world as a whole (Kenny, 2002). These comprise data stored as electromagnetic waves, such as those used in radio, television, and analog (pre-digital) communications networks. Also included are paper-based technologies that rely on information that is stored as the written word, such as those found in books, manuals, and newspapers, as well as information that is transmitted orally and stored in the human mind, or what can be referred to as "indigenous knowledge" (Davenport & Prusak, 1998). In Cloud figuring, clients pay for associations on a compensation for each utilization (or pay even more similarly as costs arise) premise. This brand name watches out for the utility section of appropriated handling. That construes, Cloud associations are offered as "metered" associations where suppliers have a bookkeeping model for surveying the utilization of the associations, which helps being made of various evaluating bookkeeping model partners in the control and improvement of asset use. To offer fundamentally reliable kinds of help, Clouds show autonomic leads by administering themselves if there should arise an occurrence of disappointments or the show defilement.

Segments of Cloud Computing

This stack clarification is an appropriated enrolling Cutoff aggregately (in any case called plate space on demand), as you may expect, is the ability to utilize gathering that genuinely exists at a disposed of site yet is slyly a close-by taking care of resource for any application that requires accumulating. This is the roughest section of passed-on planning and is a fragment or model that is used by most of the other dissipated enrolling parts. Database by and large: engages to utilize the relationship of a remotely worked with enlightening collection, offering it to various customers and having it reliably work like the instructive combination was close by utilize instructive combination progress that would commonly cost a massive number of dollars in stuff and programming, are as follows;

1. Data-as-a-association is the capacity to devour data, by implication worked with, through a specific interface like an API. Models meld stock worth data, address underwriting, and credit determining. Cycle collectively: is eliminated asset that can coordinate different assets, like associations and information, either worked with inside an equivalent flowed preparing asset or by implication, to make business measures. You can consider a business association as a
2. Stage collectively is a finished stage, including application movement, interface improvement, information base turn of events, gathering, testing, etc, went on through a distantly worked with the stage to endorsers. Considering the standard time-sharing model, current stage-as-a-master networks empower.
3. The board/association collectively is any on-request association that empowers to coordinate at any rate one cloud association. These are conventionally immediate things such as geology, asset use, virtualization, and uptime for the bosses. Association frameworks are opening up moreover, offering, for example, the capacity to support portrayed systems on information and associations. The capacity to test region or cloud-passed-on frameworks utilizing testing programming and associations that are by implication worked with. It ought to be seen in Web territories, and inner endeavor frameworks, and they needn't mess with a stuff or programming impression inside the undertaking.

4. Foundation collectively really laborer farm collectively, or the capacity to distantly get to taking care of assets. Essentially, you rent a veritable worker that is yours to do with as you will and, for the most part, is your specialist farm, or conceivably some piece of a laborer farm. The capability with this procedure versus more standard passed-on handling.

Innovativeness Being Used Plans Drew in by the Cloud Computing

1. Work things can "follow the sun" When and alliance is utilizing any data distantly. In this manner, the affiliation empowers more basic efficiency and capacity by permitting clients all through the planet to participate in experiences and access their data. when specialists are working from various pieces dependably pick their work and data whenever and from any place as demonstrated by their time receptiveness.
2. Commitments can "follow the moon" When we utilize the work environments of any foundations, it makes a massive extent of warmth and gobbles up confirmed storing up and assessment of the data domains utilization. The experts' particularly by and large brilliant quality ones, make essential extent of warmth and require monstrous extents of energy to keep their equipment cool. Having obligations to "follow the moon" (i.e., relocate to specialist farms where it is by and around evening time and overall cooler regions) proposes lessened energy uses and usage.
3. Commitments can "keep the law". Before long go to its authentic parts. The ease of moving information online awards obligations to be found where the administrative and genuine scene is for the most part appropriate for the essential work. This unfathomable spots a raised significance on strategy producers in nations expecting to choose the advantages and benefits related to passed-on figuring.

Why Coursed Figuring is the Unprecedented Segment to Continue in the Future?

Time and Money

Inappropriate handling of the clients does see the value in the upsides of bound together framework and updates data constantly. Business affiliations need to get to the delicate information convenient to acquire benefits in business. So, they are getting this chance and outfit the capacity of the cloud. For instance, clinical analyses that were vital for a long time of in-house figuring moved to spread frameworks, essentially reducing enrolling.

Individuals and Collaboration

Two or three years sooner, working from home consistently surmised getting back enormous loads of paperwork and chatting with different social affairs individuals through phone lines and talking about the issues. This was not a competent method for veritable neighborhoods these days. Essentially, there was now an essential for social affairs to get together and demand errands and yields. With the start of the cloud, working from home advanced to online support between dissipated social affairs (More, 2013). It isn't, presently difficult to work with individuals orchestrated in various zones, occasionally various nations, during available time or even external open time. Social events eventually contain individuals appropriated across gigantic geographic zones and effectively make choices on any issue. As investigated, the limit of various kinds of cloud to resuscitate data persistently, offering sorts of help or foundation empower the subject matter experts or bosses to address gives right away. Nowadays taking an interest no longer strategies getting together in the social affair room or going for standard telephonic discussions.

Dislodging Hardware

Right when affiliations use scattered figuring, they are used to move data and information designs to the cloud, which sets aside money similarly as lessens squandered assets or the affiliations. Relationships as of now don't have to buy stuff and frameworks that need establishment and upkeep. Precisely when affiliations use on-request cloud associations like Amazon Cloud, affiliations decline the expense of buying introducing frameworks. In-house specialist farms are usually set up to oversee top hours, for example, during thing appearance of online retail locations. The extra assets dispersed for demand hours are not routinely utilized in bit-by-bit tasks. Data headway. Cloud master focuses in addition can improve their frameworks to reduce squandering. They besides have the limit of updating their designs as demonstrated by association requests. This is all things considered very exorbitant for the relationship to do and accomplishes squandered assets. Less in-house machines derive affiliations could divert assets towards improving different bits of business works out. In like manner, it assists them with going for feasible improvement without hampering the needs of the future.

The Cloud and Sustainable Development in Developing Nations

1. Sustainable improvement is an issue that generally from a financial perspective, the beneficial assets are lacking while as the human necessities are unlimited there is a need for perceiving procedures for using typical and capital assets in the friendly event enough the unfathomable essentials of the current and people later on which require a deliberate exertion of general countries while guaranteeing the climate. Scattered preparation is one of the ICT models that extraordinarily impact upon real movement into the degree distribution by accessories such governments, learning foundations, business endeavors, customers not completely given nonappearance of information about it and the preliminary of the pleasing framework.
2. With the cloud, the assets that were used by and large programming, equipment, additional rooms, and figuring are concentrated and got to whenever from specialist farms. Thinking about this establishment, this article hypothetically portrays cloud and portrays its advantages and difficulties before completing an enamoring end indistinguishable from traditionalist progress in provincial countries.
3. ICTs are affixed to money-related perspectives, society movements and climate assurance. As both ordinary and capital assets necessities are vast, there is an essential for generally to recognize a deliberate exertion for a stunning new turn of events and usage of ICTs for a useful new turn of events. ICTs empower assets to be settled, get the opportunity to, be put away and adequately used today and later on, while getting the climate.
4. ICTs incorporate movements, for example, the web which if all around are monetarily reasonable and socially embraced for the public position help of the general area. The web and its joined degrees of progress are applicable for the making of work and things, displaying works out, and dispersal of data on how different individuals like culture, religion, demeanor and information can live separately as a, generally speaking, serene additions of an ensured climate. This study looks at is web in giving assets like programming, figuring, equipment and cutoff in a virtualized, business attempts, buyers, society, direction and examination affiliations in any case without difficulties for the sensible turn of events.

Types of Cloud Capabilities

One of the passed-on figuring limits that outfits clients with business-express cutoff points, for example, email or client the bosses. In SaaS, affiliations and engineers can utilize the business-unequivocal cutoff points made by outsiders in the cloud. A few events of SaaS suppliers are:

Google Apps: gives electronic office instruments, for example, email, schedule, and records the bosses give up a gigantic plan of electronic applications, by and large for immense business use. This kind of appropriated enlisting limit is suggested as a limit that gives essentially a computational framework open over the web (measure cycles or cutoff). IaaS licenses affiliations and fashioners to develop their IT foundation on the request premise. A few instances of IaaS suppliers are:

Go Grid: gives clients acceptance to viably adaptable enrolling and cutoff assets, likewise as given subject matter experts. IBM Computing on Demand gives clients acceptance to altogether configurable workers despite respect for added associations like information put away.

1. Benchmarking the tasks, for example, proactively seeing administrative changes, perceiving and reacting to client needs and arising contenders checking and reacting to the developments in the provider or right-hand affiliations, and so forth All affiliations that have made strides in the as of late referred to tasks.
2. Microsoft Live Mesh gives clients acceptance to an orbited record structure; facilitated at single-use rack space Cloud allows clients to be constantly flexible in taking care of and limited assets, also as unapproachable cloud applications and devices. The third sort of passed-on handling limit (PaaS) improvement stage award clients to use their source so settled relationship to make and host vocations of a more noteworthy expansion exclusive have the choice to oversee.
3. Conceivable business keeps an eye on the issue of the current age without influencing the deftness of things to come age to address their issues the pivotal supplement is on individuals, planet and benefit. The quickly changing conditions client needs ought to be tended to rapidly, to make strides and be before the contenders (individuals). These activities ought to be done sensibly and effectively. With less human exertion and promptly with the assistance of ICT (advantage). More essentially, these business tasks and strategies ought to deal with, generally speaking, ecological issues and should keep up with the logical and large new turn of events (planet). Worthiness recommends the Green duplicity, yet requests for a general consideration that social, typical and monetary feasibility are steadfastly similar to the drive to progression in all procedures (Hutchins, 2010).

The Use of Technologies

The ability of ICT to provide disadvantaged women and men with access to better information and communications represents its potential to help reduce poverty. ICT may remove barriers to information access and communication, empowering businesses and the underprivileged in general. ICT generally enables lower transaction costs, better supply chain and market communications, and better knowledge about new prospects. ICTs can, more specifically, Increase the usage of accessible communications (email, fax, mobile phones) to provide consistent access to markets (local, regional, and international). Enhance communication with suppliers and transportation connections to and from markets (through databases of businesses, products, and suppliers). Making informed decisions, especially regarding the cost of raw materials and completed items, enables businesses to negotiate better pricing with traders. Disseminate details on non-financial business development services that are accessible locally and globally (such as marketing, business skills, and training programs).

The IT assets can be helpfully provisioned and scaled with the assistance of Cloud Computing. In on-premise development, the relationship of the IT foundation will dependably be an excess. This is overwhelmingly done to acclimate to the unexpected rise in the obligation which is unpredictable. Keeping away from a change of IT limits dependent upon need and the wrong presumption for the IT needs could be the safeguard this. The association utilizing Cloud can no ifs, ands, or buts stay away from this over-provisioning as the significant office can be utilized in pay-according to utilize the style. Over-provisioning is extravagant if there should arise an occurrence of Cloud endeavors.

Scattered preparation offers extensive access, through different access gadgets from any place whenever premises. Globalization in business grows the scope of business across the globe. Individuals who are moving need to interface with their business works out. The things utilized in business should be stacked on the PCs and should be stimulated on each resuscitating in the base office. The business orders collected over telephones ought to be restored appropriately to screen the business development. Cloud gives a stage and contraption-free arrangement association following should be possible utilizing the general phones. This takes the business to a huger level, what's more, giving fantastic quality contraptions to their delegates rouses them to pass on their lethargic breaking point.

The utilization of the on-premise workers is low. They may also run at a 5-10 percent normal use rate. The submitted nature of the expert to an individual association credits to this low use. In any case, through the virtualization structure, the Cloud connects with different clients to get to the subject matter expert. Various applications can also be worked with in the interim on a similar worker in separation. This radically develops the usage to 70 percent. Despite the way that high use accomplishes more energy use, it is counteracted by serving a wide degree of clients with practically identical energy use.

Certainly, even the standard BIs have high disappointment rates and tremendous accomplished expenses, which can be diminished vehemently with the ending up blurring Computing and SaaS. BI gadgets, which were excessive for SMEs can get moderate whenever utilized from Cloud. As per Adrienne Hall, General Manager, Microsoft Trustworthy Computing.

Individuals Business Development

1. Individuals are the spine of any business and society. Unprecedented pioneers and laborers dependably have the most sway in the achievement and reasonableness of any business. By and by, people should be kept up with the most recent headway instruments to contribute their best. Cloud will be dependably picked as the best choice for IT execution in business taking into account its augmentation in each circle of every strategy and association. A touch of the significant benefits of getting Cloud for business has effectively been examined in the past area. The compensation per-utilize model of the Cloud draws in individuals, as their lifetime interest in IT foundation is generally decreased. These SaaS applications are for the most part enlistment-based and the clients can get to the applications through the web program or weak customer over the Internet. As demonstrated by

Gartner, SaaS applications offer no hint of dropping down. Gartner also expands that general spending on SaaS will move to 17.9 percent this year and stay solid through 2015 when it is reviewed to reach $22.1 billion.

2. There's an arrangement that security is a cutoff to Cloud gathering, yet when affiliations embrace and put resources into Cloud associations, they discover the advantages far outperform past concerns.' Time and cash spent in overseeing security before utilizing Cloud associations is being re-contributed by SMEs to encourage their business and be more certified. The new review in like way shows that in India 61% of SMEs that use Cloud associations had the choice to utilize more staff in places that advantage game plans or business headway; 63% put resources into even more thing movement or progress and 62 percent experienced improved deftness in having the decision to increase and diminish IT limit when required (SME Times, May 2012). A touch of the wide regions under which the Cloud offers benefits to businesses for better human assets the pioneers are comfort, information the board, web support and learning.

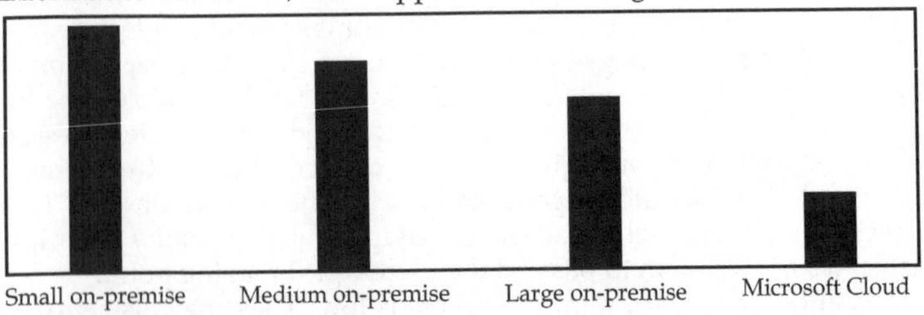

Fig. 1: Cloud Development Graph in Different Frameworks

Spread enlisting holds the confirmation of not just giving connecting with and strong expense save resources at the undertaking level, yet can comparatively basically add to the more prominent social goals of energy capacity, regular attestation and practical new turn of events. Despite the way that Cloud suppliers are taking most breaking point thoughts about the climate, the clients ought to utilize the Cloud benefits proficiently. Affiliations should avoid utilizing the associations of Cloud suppliers who truly use database products rather than innocuous to the biological system power assets in their specialist farms. The carbon impression decrease subtleties ought to be surely alluded to in the help level blueprints and clients should show their anxiety towards this. Unmistakably the Cloud execution will reduce the petrol subordinate outcome when separated from on-premise activities, and in this way ought to be advanced by the public position and industry Cloud. The Cloud climate should support explicit guidelines relating to restriction, security, protection, energy productivity, accessibility and undaunted quality. The standards ought to correspondingly deal with the public force approaches and rules according to the topographical necessities.

Conclusion

The expansion utilization of spread figuring in business improvement disturbing cloud computing through MSME in cloud server base new start-up commodity result structure Information and correspondence advancement has led to the development of conversation at whatever point coursed handling is truly green. From some evaluation it is gauged that the characteristic impression from laborer properties will out and out form some spot in the extent in this article, we isolated the advantages offered by Cloud enrolling by contemplating its uncommon definitions and benefits, the associations it accommodates end clients, and its arrangement model. At that point, we examined the segments of Clouds that add to oil subordinate outcomes and the highlights of a broad point of view. It is crucial to underline that when thinking about ICTs for enterprise development, the vast majority of MSMEs in developing countries simply use them as a way to exchange information Enterprises (and support agencies) may utilise a variety of tools for communications and information management, including newer, digital ICT. Therefore, the main concern for enterprise development practitioners and policy is whether and how the information accessible to MSMEs is sufficient for their needs. Another important concern is how market failures contribute to the low quality and quantity of information available to MSMEs and how ICTs can be used to address this.

References

1. Barr, A.M. (1998) Enterprise performance and functional diversity of social capital, Working Paper Series/98-1, Centre for the Study of African Economies, University of Oxford, June 1998.
2. Bateman, A., & Wood, M. (2009). Cloud computing. *Bioinformatics, 25*(12), 1475-1475. Retrieved from https://doi.org/10.1093/bioinformatics/btp274
3. Beil, J., Egan, B., Fidelman, M., Kaplan, J., Scott, K., & Tierney, J. (2011). Trends Report: Cloud Computing. *Focus Research.*
4. Bianzino, A. P., Chaudet, C., Rossi, D., & Rougier, J. L. (2010). A survey of green networking research. *IEEE Communications Surveys & Tutorials, 14*(1), 3-20. Retrieved from https://doi.org/10.1109/SURV.2011.113010.00106
5. Bibi, S., Katsaros, D., & Bozanis, P. (2012). Business application acquisition: On-premise or SaaS-based solutions?. *IEEE Software, 29*(3), 86-93. Retrieved from https://doi.org/10.1109/MS.2011.119
6. Biswas, B. (2015). Sustainable Development through Cloud Computing. *America International Journal of Research in Humanities, Arts and Social Sciences,* 241-248. Retrieved from http://www.accenture.com
7. Brorson, T., & Larsson, G. (2011). Environmental management: how to implement an environmental management system in a company or other organisation. *Sustainable improvement.*
8. Buyya, R., Yeo, C. S., & Venugopal, S. (2008). Market-oriented cloud computing: Vision, hype, and reality for delivering it services as computing utilities. In *2008 10th IEEE International Conference on High Performance Computing and Communications,* 5-13. Retrieved from https://doi.org/10.1109/HPCC.2008.172
9. Czernicki, B. (2011). Silverlight 4 business intelligence software. *Apress,* 1-535.
10. Davenport, T. & Prusak, L. (1998). Working knowledge: how organisations manage what they know, Harvard Business School Press.
11. Davenport, T. (2005). The importance of knowledge workers in a global economy. *Blog Entry.*
12. Duncombe, R.A. & Heeks, R.B. (2002). Enterprise across the digital divide: information systems and rural micro-enterprise in Botswana, *Journal of International Development, 14*(1), 61-74.
13. Foster, I., Zhao, Y., Raicu, I., & Lu, S. (2008). Cloud computing and grid computing 360-degree compared. *Grid Computing Environments Workshop, Ieee,*1-10. Retrieved from https://doi.org/10.1109/GCE.2008.4738445
14. http://cloudscorecard.bsa.org/2013/assets/PDFs/BSA_GlobalCloudScorecard2013.pdf, Accessed on 5/07/2023
15. http://www.sd-commission.org.uk/, Accessed on 5/07/2023
16. https://www.profitbricks.com/dedicated-server-vs-cloud, Accessed on 7/07/2023.
17. Irina Guseva. (2010). Top Technology Predictions for 2010 and Beyond. *Twitter.*

Retrieved from http://www.cmswire.com/cms/enterprise-20/gartner-top-technology-predictions-for-2010-and-beyond-006390.php

18. Kalange Pooja, R. (2013). Applications of green cloud computing in energy efficiency and environmental sustainability. *IOSR Journal of Computer Engineering (IOSR-JCE)*, 25-33.
19. Kaushik, R. T., Cherkasova, L., Campbell, R., & Nahrstedt, K. (2010). Lightning: self-adaptive, energy-conserving, multi-zoned, commodity green cloud storage system. In *Proceedings of the 19th ACM International Symposium on High Performance Distributed Computing*, 332-335. Retrieved from https://doi.org/10.1145/1851476.1851523
20. Kenny, C. (2002). Information and communication technologies for direct poverty reduction: costs and benefits, *Development Policy Review*, *20*(2), 41-157.
21. Khang, A., & Sivaraman, A. K. (2023). Big data, cloud computing and IoT: tools and applications/edited. *Journal on Future Revolution in Computer Science and Communication Engineering*, 4(4), 599-602. Retrieved from http://dx.doi.org/10.1201/9781003298335
22. Kumar, V., & Vidhyalakshmi, P. (2012). Cloud computing for business sustainability. *Asia-Pacific Journal of Management Research and Innovation*, *8*(4), 461-474. Retrieved from https://doi.org/10.1177/2319510X13481905
23. Linthicum, D. S. (2009). Cloud computing and SOA convergence in your enterprise: a step-by-step guide. *Pearson Education*.
24. Mell, P. & Endurance, T. (2009), The NIST Definition of Cloud Computing. *National Institute of Standards and Technology*, 1-3.
25. Soror, A. A., Minhas, U. F., Aboulnaga, A., Salem, K., Kokosielis, P., & Kamath, S. (2008). Automatic virtual machine configuration for database workloads. *ACM Transactions on Database Systems (TODS)*, *35*(1), 1-47. Retrieved from https://doi.org/10.1145/1670243.1670250
26. Stewart, E., & Kennedy, J. (2009). The sustainability potential of cloud computing: Smarter Design. *Environmental Leader: Environment and Energy Management News*. Retrieved from http://www.environmentalleader/

19

Suta's Case Study: Push and Pull factors Encouraging Women Entrepreneurs

Dr. Sneha Singh Munda

Abstract

This paper is all about Women's empowerment, achieved through the growth of female entrepreneurs. As well as their contribution to the social reformation of the weaker section of society by using the tool of entrepreneurship. Women constitute more than half of the labor force, and the economic responsibilities they play are integral to the development framework. The female entrepreneur can offer innovative remedies to issues that are currently plaguing a variety of industries. The core characteristic of a lady is nurturing; therefore, they are dedicated to empowering not just themselves but the entire society as well. As a result, female entrepreneurs frequently support talents whose professions are on the verge of ending owing to a lack of funds, revenue, and promotion. Women entrepreneurs are embracing these fading industries which automatically empower the weaker section of the society. Here in this paper, we are solely focusing on two dedicated women entrepreneurs Sujata and Tanya Biswas, and their remarkable journey of "Su-Ta" with the help of a Case study of "Suta".

Keywords: Empowerment, Women Entrepreneurs, Suta's, Push and Pull factors

Introduction

India has a long tradition of considering women to be representations of the deities Buddhi, Shakti, and Prosperity, such as Saraswati, Durga, and Lakshmi. Hence, a woman is born with an innate capacity to multiply anything. Kautilya is well-known as the founder of Indian economics, but women naturally excel at management. Being a homemaker, she manages everything on the restricted household budget while making sure that every family member's needs are met. Although she doesn't have a C.A. degree or a diploma in financial management, she is a perfect homemaker. According to William Golding, the British, Novelist, Playwright & Poet, "I think women are foolish to pretend they are equal to men. The fact is that they are far superior and always have been. Whatever you give a woman, she will make greater. If you give her sperm, she will give you a baby. If you give her a house, she will give you home. If you give her groceries, she will give you a meal. If you smile at her, she gives her heart. She multiplies and enlarges what is given to her. So, if you give her any crap, be ready to receive a ton of shit". We might infer from this that the Indian woman has always been great at handling pressure-filled circumstances. The Push and Pull factors determine the women's priority. All the qualities a woman needs to run a successful business are already there in her.

Assistant Professor, Department of Psychology Indira Gandhi National Tribal University, Amarkantak, Madhya Pradesh

Literature Review

Since ancient times, women have held a prominent position in Indian society. However, once the country gained independence, their financial and scholastic standing declined, and they once more worked for years to forge their own identities in various fields. The paradox of the status and position contradictions in today's society is that, although we praise the lady on the one hand, we do not consider women's participation in major life decisions.

Therefore, Indian women suffered for a very long time with a lack of educational, social, political, and economic freedom. The domain of men never permitted her any independence in a patriarchal culture. Women were intended to be inferior in a variety of spheres of life and limited to domestic duties, marriage, childbirth, and child-rearing.

According to Voda and Florea (2019), some personality qualities and difficulties restrict women from starting businesses as often as males do. Despite making up over fifty percent of the world's population, women own substantially fewer enterprises than males do (World Bank Enterprise Surveys, 2012). Due to persistent societal, legal, and institutional hurdles that prevent women from reaching their full potential, this gap is considerably wider in emerging countries. There are clear disparities between male and female entrepreneurs, especially in some parts of the world (World Bank, 2012).

As time went on, certain social reformers realized the significance of achieving equality as well as equity for women in society. Emancipation of women entered the picture. It was found that women who craved their autonomy stood out from the group of women who considered patriarchal society's laws and order as an essential sine qua non for existence. Holland (1997) showed that a key factor influencing career choice is personality.

Zhao & Seibert (2006) showed that the individual pursuit of self-employment is explained by differences between the personality structures of entrepreneurs. Women who stood for empowerment were different from others because of certain distinguishing features.

A study was carried out by Jha (2012), Ushakiranet al. (2012), and Memon (2012) in Assam's Lakhimpur, Jorhat, and Kamrup women entrepreneurs, to determine what exceptional qualities inspired certain women from the North-East to enter the domain of men. Hence, they found that factors like high self-esteem, self-confidence, and a desire to become self-sufficient, prior experience, urge to do something to provide employment opportunities to others, as well as encouragement from family to take action influenced them to start an enterprise that is why most of the respondents entered in the areas of weaving, food processing, and preservation. Moreover, it is very interesting to note that a sense of autonomy, freedom to make their own decision, and A sense of independent decision making in their life and career is the motivational factor behind this urge support to pursue entrepreneurship. Due to the tug-of-war forces that pushed women to establish independent occupations and stand on their own feet, respondents picked these professions. It also evolved as a consequence of their realization of the urgent need for employment in Assam, which motivated them to establish a business to offer other young women, better economic survival. The significant push and pull elements encourage them to pursue weaving businesses so they can share their skills and abilities with others and make the best possible use of what they already have to help society as a whole.

The primary driving forces for women to start their businesses are push and pull considerations. Push factors are the unfavorable events or situations that lead a woman to launch her own business-like unemployment, excessive downtime at a prior job, unreasonably high expectations from the previous company, the expectation in the family that the woman will care for the family, the need for flexible working hours, and other factors (Leyton-Roman et al., 2021).

Instead, pull considerations are good reasons to decide whether to pursue an entrepreneurial enterprise. These are the intrinsic motivations that drive women to become business owners. These are brought on by the idea of independence, being your boss, decision-making autonomy, and a sense of self-achievement, as well as wanting to be creative, hold positions of power, and earn sizable sums of money (Troise and Tani, 2020).

In the majority of developing nations, women start businesses out of a desire to raise their financial standing, feel more accomplished, or elevate their social standing (Leyton-Román et al., 2021). Social variables such as achieving high social status, becoming a role model to others, and becoming a leader were discovered to be significant motivators for women entrepreneurs.

Jha (2012) supports these findings. Dhaliwal (2000) revealed that women business owners define success as generating income, managing their families, or understanding economic ideals. That is, individuals become conscious that they have achieved a certain level of success once they realize that they are earning money and supporting their families.

Women entrepreneurs typically focus on having influence over their destiny, building stronger relationships with their customers, and creating important things (Gautam, 2016). Sarwoko and Nurfarida (2021) stated that an entrepreneur must possess an internal locus of control, motivation to attain goals, a moderate amount of risk-taking propensity, inventiveness, the ability to withstand stress, as well as greater levels of self-efficacy (Kusumawijaya and Astuti, 2021).

Entrepreneurial success is mostly attributed to the traits of innovation and superior interpersonal, psychological, and technical skills which are mostly found in a lady because they possess the innate quality of managing, acting strong in time of crisis, handling stress keeping herself calm (Li et al., 2018; Tshiaba et al., 2021).

Social networks are essential for helping people become psychologically committed and motivated so that they can thrive in their business endeavors (Jiatong et al., 2021). These considerations lead to the conclusion that specific personality features can help women entrepreneurs succeed in business. Women entrepreneurs are also driven and committed, which keeps them concentrated on achievement.

The analysis of human behavior in the existent literature has given gender variations concerning the Big Five personality traits considerable attention. According to Schmitt et al. (2008), these disparities can appear to be explained by inherent biology and social culture. However, investigations have produced contradictory results, although a pattern can be seen. Gender variations in the Big Five personality traits were recently the subject of a systematic review.

To explain this, Soto et al. (2011) feel that considerable social and psychological struggles experienced throughout adolescence, such as awareness of unfavorable gender expectations, stereotypes, body image concerns, and negative self-perceptions, are the cause of high levels of neuroticism, anxiety, and depression in females.

According to Weisberg et al. (2011), women are more likely than men to acquire attractive traits because they exhibit higher levels of enthusiasm, friendliness, and compassion, which are indications of sociability and positive emotionality. They are more trustworthy than men in this regard. Vecchione et al. (2012) suggested in other studies that women tend to be agreeable because of their outstanding interpersonal skills, empathetic thinking, and sociability.

According to Dimitriadis et al. (2018), women are less resistant to new experiences than men. They claimed that women are more sensitive to aesthetics sense. Similarly, to this, creativity has been proven to significantly enhance females' intentions to start their businesses compared to males.

Ahl (2006) concludes that different pull and push factors may drive women and men entrepreneurs. A study of female entrepreneurs showed that the main drivers for women entrepreneurs were independence, achievement, and satisfaction, economic necessity (Hisrich, 1984). This finding is consistent with other studies that show that pull factors are often the dominant drivers of women entrepreneurs in developed nations (Sarri &Trihopoulou, 2005; Wang, Walker, & Redmond, 2006).

Whereas Sociocultural responsibilities attached to women also affect their decision to choose entrepreneurship. According to Kephart and Schumacher (2005), Socio-cultural variables like the need to balance work-family and familial obligations, and the "family-embeddedness" perspective all play a role. The "motherhood" role (Brush, de Bruin, & Friederike, 2009) encouraged women entrepreneurs to launch their businesses.

So to become the "Jack of All traits" A woman needs her own pace to fulfill all the responsibilities, expectations, and duties related to her. That's why they love to be entrepreneurs.

According to Thebaud (2016), women entrepreneurs' decisions to launch their enterprises are heavily influenced by the need for greater flexibility in juggling job obligations with family duties. Women may be forced to choose self-employment over a work opportunity due to the requirement for greater flexibility.

This study was produced to observe the prevalence of such features and motivate elements that are pushing and pulling Indian women to enter the field of entrepreneurship after reviewing a huge body of literature. In this paper, we are concentrating on the "Suta" case study, a saree business founded by two fearless and intrepid women. This paper is all about their company's step-by-step development and incredible journey.

This paper concentrates on the case study of a company called "Suta" which was inspired by the love and memories of two outstanding siblings, Sujata and Tanya Biswas, in their early years. In essence, Suta was about a six-yard representation of an Indian woman's identity—her Cotton Saree. A six-yard piece of dignity, carried by most Indian women, a saree symbolizes her pride, dignity, individuality, respect, strength, and weakness. This six-yard fabric depicts a picture of an Indian woman on a globe. Indians view sarees as more than just a piece of clothing and as a symbol of respect for their grandmothers, mothers, and sisters. Many of our fondest childhood memories involve our mother. Indian mothers use the corners of their sarees for a variety of purposes. Sometimes a poor mother will make an umbrella out of the pallu to protect her children from the sun and rain, a handkerchief to wipe their tears and sweat, and a towel to dry them off after bathing or to clean their mouths after feeding. Maa's saree corner acts as a bandage when her little one gets bruises, and her anchal serves as a curtain while she feeds her child.

The saree is an integral part of our culture and is worn at every stage of life. Girls enjoy dressing up like their mothers in sarees when they are little. With their first salary, Indian youngsters choose to buy sarees for their mothers. Sarees are the most sacred attire to wear at weddings. A mother gives her daughter her wedding saree, and a daughter gives her daughter her daughter as a legacy. So, for Indians, a saree is not just a dress but also an emblem of love, emotion, and devotion.

India is a country with many diverse states, yet the majority of Indian culture still includes this six-yard drape. It appears in a variety of colors, draping styles, materials, concepts, and patterns, but Indian women perceive it to be their initial affection. Sujata and Tanya are therefore no longer an exception and have been fascinated by the saree's magical powers.

Who are these Sujata and Tanya Biswas. The two siblings grew up in Kharagpur, and spent their childhood playing hide and seek and running from the trails of sarees where their grandmother used to dry her sarees,". The softest, most aromatic fabric touched the faces and skin as the young girls rushed around them. Even after they had grown older and had assimilated into the corporate grind, this reminisce persisted.

Sujata received her engineering degree from CET Bhubaneswar and her MBA from IIFT Delhi. She has about eight years of experience working across the Essar group, Jindal group, and IIT Bombay. Taniya, an engineer who graduated from IIM Lucknow, worked for IBM and the Tata Group for almost three years.

The sisters had huge dreams, so the two decided to quit their corporate professions and start this beautiful handloom journey. As a result of their mutual passion and the memories they hold for textiles and pleasant recollections of their youth, created "Suta" as a result of their hard work and aspiration.

Even though none of them is from the clothing industry, their intrinsic feminine souls drove them to fantasize about "Suta". They had no previous experience in garment manufacturing, but they decided to give it an attempt because they were raised watching their grandmothers and mothers wearing the dignity of a six-yard. Suta sells hand-woven sarees from India's charming villages.

The journey of Suta started with hometown visits where Sujata encountered many traditional weavers, with whom she often conversed. They frequently vented about their miserable working conditions and low pay. Though she was in awe of their incredible talents, she later learned that many of their financial sources of support were in doubt. These interactions left a lasting impression on her and spurred her to seek to better the lives of these marginalized populations.

Faleye (1999) stated that women's development is not only about reducing poverty by increasing productivity but also about women's liberation and empowerment. True development means the development in the three categories of a woman. These are (1) Individual; (2) Social; and (3) Economic Development (Rodney, 1972).

So with the keen thought of, individual, social, and economic development, Suta's journey started officially in 2016. However, the siblings' passion for drapes dates back to their early years. "We played hide-and-seek as kids on the lawn. The sisters consider themselves to be the ideal two Cerebral hemispheres of the brain in the creation of this Mumbai-based saree company. Their love for textiles and art forms, and a strong will to empower very talented and deserving artisans, made them quit and take a big step toward their dream.

"Su from Sujata and Ta from Tanya soon added, the word Suta, which means thread and is a combination of their names Su(jata) and Ta(niya), "The magic of thread, drew them like a magnet and is the best way to describe how they came together. The fairytale-like coincidence of the syllables in our names delighted us. It seemed to be fated to be, they continue. Suta, always realized its social and moral responsibility towards Society. Suta has not gained overnight success due to some magic but it has gained success because of the praises and blessings it got from the poor and talented weavers.

Suta was laid with the Ideology of not searching for a job, being the creator of Jobs. The foundation has blossomed into a microeconomy in the neighboring villages of Shantipur and Dhaniakhali. Sujata and Taniya's immediately recruited the whole neighborhood of weavers into their business and this act mostly supported the women weavers involved in the weaving.

Suta has expanded tremendously since it was founded by two young women who caught the entrepreneurial bug, growing to a team of 20 in Mumbai and 50 weavers across the nation. Its gorgeous handloom sarees, which come in jamdani weave, malmal, malkesh, banarasi, and handwoven variations, are being exported to markets abroad as well as across the nation. Now the weavers, "are incredibly proud of what they doing in creating every single piece of the “Suta” saree, and now they have a stable income and help in raising their living standards. Now they are sending their kids to the school to get good education but yet they are thinking about bringing their next generation into the same business rather than losing their ancestral craft."

Obstacles faced by Suta: The sisters experimented with various ideas after quitting their comfortable jobs as corporate employees and even tried their hand at product photoshoots before understanding that their real potential lay in the actual things rather than the pictures. Sujata explained that they had made a few outfits and publicized them, but instead of requests for shoots, they got inquiries about the merchandise. The next step was an immediate shift of direction and a search throughout rural India's hidden treasures for the perfect fabric and skilled weavers. The search, stated by Sujata and Taniya, headed them to remote villages in Madhya Pradesh, Meghalaya, Varanasi, the city that gave the world the Banarasi saree, Maniabandha in Odisha, the Kutch district of Gujarat, and West Bengal, where they currently have two offices in the towns of Shantipur in the Nadia district and Dhaniakhali.

While Sujata and Tanya have worked hard to make the Suta a well-known brand, they haven't forgotten the integral part that the weavers, artists, and other team members had in establishing the Suta beyond its rivals. The founders always applaud the tireless efforts of their team members. The weavers were traditionally acknowledged for Suta's enormous success. We might easily understand what they are talking about by taking a quick look at the Suta Bombay page. Instead of following the standard shopping path, their social media marketing includes uploading images of the artists together with colorful stories. Suta aims to discuss saree storytelling, associated with a personal story, piece of facts, or the draper's story in each post. The saree is featured prominently in some of these photograph posts.

Suta has added a vision, mission, and goal in the lives of many women weavers, and some of the women weavers became the important supporting pillar of the family. Suta Boosted Women's Empowerment through Entrepreneurship- According to Lavoice (2000), Autonomy was the most preferable aspect in any professional field and entrepreneurship or self-employment is a tool for empowering women. Autonomy was highly regarded as a means of achieving individual liberty. This degree of independence offers the following opportunities:

1. The ability to make their decisions: decision making denotes the selection that serves as the empowerment;
2. Capable of performing the desired task; suggests employment in non-traditional domains gaining access to stronger networks, which directly results in empowerment.
3. Achieve financial security: Financial security is a significant contributing factor in women's empowerment.

Patiently and continuously, Sujata and Taniya took care of every work to minimize expenditures they had built their company organically, step by step, before focusing on chasing massive figures. When there were only two of them, They did everything on their own, from maintaining the office to transporting a saree. Even for vendor meetings, they used trains rather than hiring a cab, they recollect. Being modest starting small, and knowing one's value for what it is all contribute to greatness.

Suta faced Up and Down's in 2017, it was the lowest point of Suta's journey. As "Suta" launched in 2016 to spread the awareness about brand in 2017 they displayed their most exclusive designs and sarees at the Mumbai exhibition The Lil Flea and it caught fire. The sight of the precious merchandise on fire shocked both of them at that time Sujata had been five months pregnant.

Although they had fallen, they weren't hurt. Sujata claimed that holding the mud- or fire-stained sarees "felt like holding your wounded child in your arms." Sujata and Taniya are only one and a half years apart in age leaning toward one another in times of trouble. They have continued to contribute their special talents to the company, assisting in its continuous growth. They stated, that they are at a revenue of 5.5 crore this year and they are working hard to double the top line throughout the following year. Suta is more than simply work for us, as Taniya described, it serves an important part in their lives. It has completely intermingled with their personal lives. So for these two ladies, their work is their passion. They Worship their Work.

Significance of the Study

Suta not only dispels the misconception that business is not a woman's cup of tea, but also contributes to the establishment of a woman entrepreneur's distinct identity. Two women defy the conventional wisdom that a person who has specialized in one field cannot succeed in another. They refute the idea that success as an entrepreneur requires a particular family or professional background and that people from different backgrounds can't make it. Break the misconception that business fundamentals are meant to be inherited not to be learned. Both of the women disproved this because they lacked a background in business and mastered the fundamentals of the textile industry via their tenacious perseverance. They exhibited their true inner toughness by traveling from the Bay of Bengal to the Rann of Kutch purely in search of works of art. On a worldwide scale, they are attempting to give our Indian culture new hues and an identity. They are doing right with their creation by promoting the names and fame of the skilled but underprivileged weavers in addition to expanding their saree empire and acknowledging their social duty. On their magazine pages, they specifically address the weavers' stories. so that a wearer also feels a sense of individuality and worth. As well as time to time they are capturing the love and passion of Suta clients. This personal touch makes making products of Suta different from other saree brands. These ladies are not working but in a real sense, they are living their dream. Every saree is carefully chosen because their business is not about the numbers on the balance sheet but rather about the feelings.

Conclusion

So, after going through the study, we can conclude that the growth and development of Suta are not only important for founder members but also for families and women artists associated with the firm. Suta is helping in the economic development of women and the perception of self-worth. The women's future has brightened by increased self-confidence brought on by the development of their businesses. The most significant changes result from an increase in income, which not only improves a person's life but also raises her level of living, bringing about financial stability for the family. The income growth also benefits the family as a whole, giving everyone access to a better standard of living, including improved access to education for the kids and better family health. Gaining status in society women's contribution to family income has changed women's status in the family and society gradually. Now they are consulted by the men to participate in the important decisions of their life.

Suta is spreading the awareness that women can grow their businesses, by modernizing the workplace, introducing new technology to boost output, hiring more people, and increasing their purchasing power will improve their social and economic standing. For new equipment, tools, and accessories, and to enhance their capital structure government also offers some initiatives to resolve the weaver's issues. The government has started a Mudra scheme for any Indian citizen who has a business plan for an activity that generates non-farm income, such as manufacturing, processing, trading, or the service sector, and whose credit need is up to 10 lacks, can go to a bank, MFI, or NBFC to apply for MUDRA loans under PMMY. PMSBY (Pradhan Mantri Suraksha Bima Yojana) for weavers between the ages of 18 and 50. The scheme's benefits will total Rs. 2 lakh, and they will be paid out in the event of the beneficiary's death or permanent disability. We can promote Indian weavers in our way - Although it's all about Suta, Suta is all about two strong ladies who are working for the well-being of the weavers located in the nook of an Indian hamlet. So it's the responsibility of every Indian citizen to help the Indian traditional weavers to grow. Methods to help Indian handloom Weavers are- Buying products manufactured by Indian weavers, acquiring from retailers who source exclusively from neighborhood weavers, taking part in campaigns to support weavers, Communicating about Indian textiles, Sharing with your friends and on social media, Participating in fundraising events for weavers, Order in advance their goods.

References

1. Ahl, H. (2006). Why research on women entrepreneurs needs new directions. Entrepreneurship Theory and Practice, *30*(5), 595–621.
2. Barbaranelli, C., & Caprara, G. (2012). Gender differences in the Big Five personality development: A longitudinal investigation from late adolescence to emerging adulthood. *Personality and individual differences, 53*(6), 740-746.
3. Brush, C. G., De Bruin, A., & Welter, F. (2009). A gender-aware framework for women's entrepreneurship. *International Journal of Gender and entrepreneurship, 1*(1), 8-24. https://doi.org/10.1108/17566 260910942318
4. Dhaliwal, S. (2000). Entrepreneurship–a learning process: the experiences of Asian female entrepreneurs and women in business. *Education+ Training,* 42(8), 445-453.

5. Dimitriadis, E., Anastasiades, T., Karagiannidou, D., & Lagaki, M. (2018). Creativity and entrepreneurship: The role of gender and personality. International Journal of Business and Economic Sciences Applied Research, *11*(1), 7–12. https://ssrn.com/abstr act=3155088.
6. Hisrich, R. D., & Ozturk, S. A. (1999). Women entrepreneurs in a developing economy. *Journal of Management Development, 18*(2), 114–120.
7. Holland, J. L. (1997). *Making vocational choices: A theory of vocational personalities and work environments*. Psychological Assessment Resources.
8. https://freethoughtblogs.com/iris/2016/07/11/not-funny-not-a-compliment/
9. https://www.businesstoday.in/latest/trends/story/these-engineer-sisters-turned-rs-6-lakh-investment-into-rs-50-crore-biz-347499-2022-09-17
10. https://yourstory.com/herstory/2019/02/incredible-story-behind-suta-handwoven-sarees-69nhln5fzn.
11. Ida Ketut, K., & Partiwi Dwi, A. (2021). Mediating role of entrepreneurial competencies: Influence of personality traits on entrepreneurial intention. *Problems and Perspectives in Management, 19*(3), 211-220.
12. Jiatong, W., Li, C., Murad, M., Shahzad, F., & Ashraf, S. F. (2021). Impact of social entrepreneurial factors on sustainable enterprise development: mediating role of social network and moderating effect of government regulations. SAGE Open 11, 215824402110306–215824402110315. doi: 10.1177/21582440211030636.
13. Kephart, P., & Schumacher, L. (2005). Has the 'glass ceiling' cracked? An exploration of women entrepreneurship. *Journal of Leadership & Organizational Studies, 12*(1), 2-15.
14. Kumar, Y. (2016). Women participation in Indian Msmes in globalized era. *International Journal of Information, Business and Management, 8*(2), 277.
15. Leyton-Roman, M., de la Vega, R., & Jimenez-Castuera, R. (2021). Motivation and commitment to sports practice during the lockdown caused by Covid-19. *Frontiers in psychology, 11*, 3846.
16. Li, S. B., Wang, C. B., Zhou, D. Q., Liu, H. X., Li, L., Shen, Q., & Zhang, L. M. (2018). Preparation of dense La0. 67Ca0. 33MnO3 ceramics by plasma activated sintering and hot-pressing. *Ceramics International, 44*(1), 550-555.
17. Mangenda Tshiaba, S., Wang, N., Ashraf, S. F., Nazir, M., & Syed, N. (2021). Measuring the sustainable entrepreneurial performance of textile-based small–medium enterprises: A mediation–moderation model. *Sustainability, 13*(19), 11050.
18. Memon, S. A. (2012). A study of women entrepreneurship development in Kolhapur city. *Zenith International Journal of Business Economics & Management Research, 2*(5), 12-22.
19. Saikia, P. (2017). Motivational factors and empowerment of women entrepreneurs in Assam: An exploratory study. *Indian Research Journal of Extension Education, 17*(4), 87-92.
20. Sarri, K., & Trihopoulou, A. (2005). Female entrepreneurs' personal characteristics and motivation: a review of the Greek situation. *Women in management review, 20*(1), 24-36.
21. Sarwoko, E., & Nurfarida, I. N. (2021). Entrepreneurial marketing: Between entrepreneurial personality traits and business performance. *Entrepreneurial Business and Economics Review, 9*(2), 105-118.
22. Schmitt, D. P., Realo, A., Voracek, M., & Allik, J. (2008). Why can't a man be more like a woman? Sex differences in Big Five personality traits across 55 cultures. *Journal of personality and social psychology, 94*(1), 168.
23. Soto, C. J., John, O. P., Gosling, S. D., & Potter, J. (2011). Age differences in personality traits from 10 to 65: Big Five domains and facets in a large cross-sectional sample. *Journal of personality and social psychology, 100*(2), 330.

24. Thebaud, S. (2016). Passing up the job: The role of gendered organizations and families in the entrepreneurial career process. *Entrepreneurship Theory and Practice, 40*(2), 269-287.
25. Troise, C., & Tani, M. (2020). Exploring entrepreneurial characteristics, motivations and behaviours in equity crowdfunding: some evidence from Italy. *Management Decision, 59*(5), 995-1024.
26. Ushakiran, V., Rajeswari, M., & Karunasree, M. (2012). A study on business women in micro enterprises. *International Journal of Multidisciplinary Research,* 2(1), 211-219.
27. Vecchione, M., Alessandri, G., Barbaranelli, C., & Caprara, G. (2012). Gender differences in the Big Five personality development: A longitudinal investigation from late adolescence to emerging adulthood. *Personality and individual differences,* 53(6), 740-746.
28. Voda, A. I., & Florea, N. (2019). Impact of personality traits and entrepreneurship education on entrepreneurial intentions of business and engineering students. *Sustainability, 11*(4), 1192.
29. Wang, C., Walker, E. A., & Redmond, J. (2006). Ownership motivation and strategic planning in small business. *Journal of Asia Entrepreneurship and sustainability,* 2(4), 50.
30. Weisberg, Y. J., DeYoung, C. G., & Hirsh, J. B. (2011). Gender differences in personality across the ten aspects of the Big Five. *Frontiers in psychology,* 2, 178.
31. World Bank (2020). Total Early-Stage Entrepreneurial Activity. Available at https://tcdata360.worldbank.org/indicators/aps.ea.total?country=FRA&indicator=3116&countries=CHN,LVA,GBR,USA,HRV,SVN,ESP,RUS,ITA,JPN&viz=line_chart&years= 2001,2017&indicators= .
32. Zhao, H., & Seibert, S. E. (2006). The big five personality dimensions and entrepreneurial status: a meta-analytical review. *Journal of applied psychology, 91*(2), 259.

*****